D0897695

THE PUBLIC PAPERS

Louis Sullivan at about age 44, c. 1900. Courtesy of The Louis
H. Sullivan Collection, The Art Institute of Chicago.

LOUIS SULLIVAN
The Public Papers

EDITED BY
ROBERT TWOMBLY

THE UNIVERSITY OF CHICAGO PRESS
Chicago and London

ROBERT TWOMBLY is professor of history at the City College of New York. His *Louis Sullivan: His Life and Work* is published in paperback by The University of Chicago Press.

The University of Chicago Press, Chicago 60637
The University of Chicago Press, Ltd., London
© 1988 by The University of Chicago
All rights reserved. Published 1988
Printed in the United States of America

97 96 95 94 93 92 91 90 89 88 54321

Library of Congress Cataloging-in-Publication Data

Sullivan, Louis H., 1856–1924.
    Louis Sullivan: the public papers / edited by Robert Twombly.
        p.   cm.
    Bibliography: p.
    Includes index.
    1. Sullivan, Louis H., 1856–1924—Archives   I. Twombly,
    Robert C.   II. Title.
    NA737.S9A35   1988
    720'.92'4—dc19   87-27865
    ISBN 0-226-77996-3   CIP

CONTENTS

ACKNOWLEDGMENTS

The motivation for compiling this volume came from two sources. Students in my City College course, "Organic Architecture: Louis Sullivan and Frank Lloyd Wright," complained about the difficulty they had in finding more than a handful of Louis Sullivan's essays. Excited by his books, *Kindergarten Chats* and *The Autobiography of an Idea*, and eager to read further (several students told me that they had finally encountered an architect who seemed to care about people), they discovered they could not get access to the ancient volumes in which many of his writings were buried. Their need was underscored by my own amazement (source of the second motivation) that these important documents by one of the giants of American cultural history had never been gathered together. Amazement turned to annoyance when I wrote a biography of Sullivan and found some of these essential sources difficult to obtain. There seemed to be a real need to make this material readily available. Given the growing interest in architecture coupled with the superficiality of much work that is taken seriously, that need may be greater than I initially imagined.

Motivation led to execution, and execution ultimately to the production of a book. My head- and heartfelt thanks go to the exceptional staff of The University of Chicago Press, whose humanity and professionalism ought to be a model, and to the two anonymous readers who saved me from my errors while adding their own good ideas. If this collection has shortcomings, they are mine alone.

My loved ones will understand why this volume is not dedicated to them. They know I am always grateful nevertheless. If dedication be needed, it is to the memory of Louis Sullivan, who stood most of all for personal integrity. By the standards of our culture he was a loser, but by other, more important criteria, he exemplified the examined life.

INTRODUCTION:
THE FORM AND
FUNCTION OF
LOUIS SULLIVAN'S
WRITING

During his lifetime, Louis Sullivan's architecture brought him international acclaim. His innovations with two building types, the urban skyscraper and the rural bank, have in some cases been landmarked and carefully restored. Some that are in the history books have been published over and over again. People who know architecture know his Wainwright and Guaranty buildings, the Chicago Stock Exchange, the Schlesinger & Mayer Store, his banks in Owatonna, Minnesota, and Grinnell, Iowa, and a few famous edifices of other genres: the Chicago Auditorium and the Transportation Building for the World Columbian Exposition in particular. His impact on American architecture and its history is profound, second only to that of his pupil and employee, Frank Lloyd Wright. In the 1980s major exhibitions and new books continue to enhance his reputation.

All this is rather remarkable, considering that Sullivan erected only seven steel frame high-rises and a like number of banks. A majority of his pioneering skyscraper designs, furthermore, were neither constructed nor widely published. An extraordinarily high percentage of his work has been destroyed, much of it long before its importance was appreciated. During forty-three years of designing buildings (from 1879 to 1922, and with his partner Dankmar Adler to 1895), Sullivan secured almost 240 commissions. Of these over 190 were realized: eighty percent of the total. But in 1987 only fifty were standing, barely one-quarter of his entire built oeuvre, including several that have been altered beyond recognition. Other buildings have lapsed into obscurity, known only to specialists, many of whom are themselves unaware of how much work he actually produced. This is partially because over one-third were unremarkable dwellings and warehouses now mostly demolished. Yet Louis Sullivan looms larger than all but one other American architect.

His olympian standing is also due to a lifetime of writing that produced the fifty-one papers in this volume, comprising all his known work for public audiences excepting books and assembled here for the first time. As determined to write as he was to build, Sullivan saw the two as parts of the same effort, each as necessary as the other. Not content to let his structures stand as his only voice, he wrote (and spoke) as often as he could about his mission: to redirect American architecture as a way of reforming American life. Underlying his strenuous activity was Louis Sullivan's fundamental goal: to uplift the society in which he lived.

Just as only a few of his buildings are known, so only a handful of his writings are familiar. But that handful made an enormous impact during his lifetime (from 1856 to 1924), and continues to do so, especially "The Tall Office Building Artistically Considered" (document 23), his most influential essay. "The Tall Office Building" has been reproduced continuously since it first appeared in 1896, proclaiming Sullivan's world-famous principle, "Form follows Function." Several more of these pieces have surfaced from time to time in literary and architectural anthologies, but with few exceptions they are elsewhere available only in dusty volumes of the (mostly out of print) professional journals in which they were originally published. The fifty-one public papers are of five types: essays, speeches and talks, committee reports, letters to editors, and interviews. All but three (documents 24, 27, 46) appeared in their entirety while he lived.

The largest collection of Sullivan's writings heretofore was compiled in 1947 by Isabella Athey, who included documents 2, 17, 20, 22, 23, 30, (part of) 31, 33, 36, and 41 in her George Wittenborn edition of Sullivan's *Kindergarten Chats*. Since his books are not excerpted in this collection, a word about them is appropriate.

Kindergarten Chats is a series of fifty-two essays in the form of an extended dialogue between an architectural master and his student, first published weekly from February 16, 1901 through February 8, 1902 by *The Interstate Architect and Builder* in Cleveland. Sullivan revised the manuscript in 1918 either by editing or, in the case of six chapters, by completely rewriting. For a time, four of the six were thought to be lost. The other two were substituted for the *Interstate* originals when architect Claude Bragdon published the texts in book form for the Scarab Fraternity Press in Lawrence, Kansas, in 1934. But as it happened, editor Charles H. Whitaker of the *Journal of the American Institute of Architects* had kept a copy of the 1918 revision including the six rewritten chapters, and it was this version (reduced by Sullivan to approximately one hundred thousand words from *Interstate's* one hundred thirty thousand) that Athey published in 1947. Dover Press has since reprinted this edition.

Sullivan's memoirs, *The Autobiography of an Idea,* first appeared in sixteen monthly issues of the *Journal of the American Institute of Architects* from June 1922 through September 1923. Sullivan had contracted for fifteen installments, but when the final chapter proved too lengthy for a single issue it was split in two. The Press of the American Institute of Architects published the memoir as a book in 1924 with an unnumbered section called "Retrospect" appended to chapter 15 of the same name. This was the format followed in subsequent editions by W. W. Norton & Sons in its "White Oak Series" ten years later, by Peter Smith in 1949, and by Dover Press in 1956 and 1980, all of which remained faithful to the original text.

A System of Architectural Ornament, According with a Philosophy of Man's Powers grew out of a 1922 commission from the Burnham Library at the Art Institute of Chicago for a folio of plates illustrating Sullivan's methods. Twelve of the nineteen drawings were exhibited at the library that year (see document 48) before the Press of the American Institute of Architects bound them as a book in 1924, with Sullivan's philosophical exegesis. In this format, *A System of Architectural Ornament* continued a tradition of handbooks and treatises on ornament stemming from the Renaissance. The Prairie School Press in Park Forest, Illinois reprinted it in 1962. In 1967 Eakins of New York put out a new edition supplemented by ten Sullivan drawings for his 1919 Farmers' and Merchants' Bank in Columbus, Wisconsin, and an afterword by *New York Times* architecture critic Ada Louise Huxtable.

Sullivan's last published book was originally called "Natural

Thinking, A Study in Democracy." It was begun around 1905 when, with some forty thousand words on paper, he told Harriet Monroe that he intended to change the title to "The People," for whom it had been written. But on completion in 1908 it bore its final name, "Democracy, A Man-Search"—a study, he wrote in chapter 5, of "the physical, the mental, the emotional and the spiritual facts of our civilization." At his death in 1924, Sullivan left an original manuscript, two signed copies dated April 18, 1908, and two unsigned carbons. One of the signature copies is slightly different from the original, suggesting a later revision, at least according to Elaine Hedges, who collated the texts for its 1961 publication by Wayne State University Press. Most of group 5, chapter 4 had been published by Harriet Monroe as "Wherefore the Poet?" in *Poetry* magazine of March 1916; about twenty pages from the manuscript's opening sections had appeared in *Twice a Year* between 1940 and 1941. As of this writing *Democracy* is not in print.

One reason is the discursive, esoteric, somewhat impenetrable prose reminiscent of "Inspiration" (document 4), though on a much grander scale. Sullivan frequently wrote and spoke in this manner, occasionally to the consternation of his audience. On the other hand, he was entirely capable of producing a tight, economical style, directly to the point (see, for example, document 47), and, as the material in this volume demonstrates, of employing different literary tactics within the same piece. It appears that Sullivan tailored his style to the occasion. In impromptu remarks or for committee reports, when paying tribute to others or trying to attract new clients—for more mundane matters, less important to him than philosophical issues—he used a plain, linear style, moving from point to point in a way that a later age, conditioned by the time and space constraints of mass media, has come to expect. But his mode of expression was different for philosophical discussions. The *strategy* here was often to argue by analogy and indirection in what seems today to be a teasingly didactic manner. If his subject was architectural creativity he might talk about poets, or if it was ornament about nature's forms, leaving it to the audience to close the circle, to make the final connection. He asked his readers and listeners, in other words, to work along with him, much like the master instructing his apprentice in *Kindergarten Chats*. His literary *tac-tic*—his prose style—in philosophical entreaties was almost painterly, not unlike contemporary Impressionism, piling up sentences or ideas nearly but not quite repetitively, moving from implication to nuance until he had exhausted the possibilities. His method was also characteristic of an era in which elaborate oratory and prose were highly regarded.

Sullivan has been condemned lately for vague words and con-tradictory ideas. There is some truth in the former assertion; but none at all in the latter. His words may indeed be vague when meanings have been changed or removed from context. But sometimes Sullivan was intentionally ambiguous, because words for him were *symbols* of ideas based on instinct, not the ideas themselves. Like others before and since, Sullivan believed that creativity began with the emotions, that it was primarily spiritual and instinctive. Only later, after an insight "came" to the recep-tive agent, could intellect and reason fashion it into a work of art. Sullivan's "vague" words were signposts of creativity in ac-tion: it was from the final patterns of words gathered together to form a speech or an essay that ultimate meaning came, not from particular phrases or ideas standing alone. And over the years Sullivan's patterns were remarkably consistent. At some moments he gave certain themes greater emphasis—the role of the architectural educator, for example, at the turn of the cen-tury—but overall, throughout his mature life, his message re-mained essentially intact.

It began with his contention that human evolution had moved from one distinct stage into another: from feudalism to democracy. His reading of John William Draper's *History of the Intellectual Development of Europe* (1876), filtered through the views of his friend John Edelmann and their colleagues in the Lotus Club, a Chicago literary/athletic group to which they be-longed in the 1870s, was never forgotten, nor was Edelmann's tutelage in German idealist metaphysics. To Sullivan, feudalism was less an economic system than the accumulation of power and freedom by a privileged elite. Feudalism made creativity im-possible except for the few because arbitrary authoritarianism re-pressed the human spirit. Democracy, on the other hand, had thrown off the shackles, offering power, freedom, and creativity to all, at least potentially. Sullivan's mission in his building and writing was to make this known, because as he observed America, especially after 1900 or so, he concluded that feudalism was anything but dead. What he saw, on the one hand, was a powerful elite in business and in architecture monopolizing possibility and controlling ideas and, on the other hand, a passive population content to let that happen.

Sullivan therefore preached the gospel of individualism, but not to the same purpose as Social Darwinists or apologists for untrammeled capitalism. He argued that democracy's removal of political constraints on spiritual and intellectual opportunity obligated people to act for their own, and therefore for the social, good. Only in a democratic system could people discover universal truths about their own potential, truths that could be found in nature, which was, to Sullivan, the ultimate democracy. In the natural world, species developed freely from inchoate entities, like seeds or shoots, into fully matured forms conditioned only by their function and environment. If left alone under congenial circumstances, nature always fulfilled its potential. And so should it be with democracy. Nature was democratic not because it was egalitarian—Sullivan knew it wasn't—but because it allowed for universal individual growth. If the strong sometimes overwhelmed the weak, it was not because the strong made it so, but because of natural law, natural competition— also a democratic trait—over which neither strong nor weak had control. By internalizing nature's laws, however, democracy's citizens could develop themselves to the point at which competition yielded social peace, not antisocial tension, the point at which careful self-pruning would turn the jungle into a garden.

Sullivan agreed with his contemporaries that in a democracy there would be different levels of individual achievement resulting in greater and lesser economic reward, and therefore higher and lower social rank. Where he demurred was in the brutality of it all. Most late nineteenth/early twentieth century Americans of Sullivan's class believed that democracy had been achieved and that vast differences in wealth and power were the inevitable result of free competition. But Sullivan contended that democracy existed in name only, leaving most people mental and physical serfs without opportunity for material or spiritual gain. Unrestrained inequality was a sign of lingering feudalism, and not in the nature of true freedom.

By stating these ideas publicly, indeed by making a social analysis at all, Sullivan assumed the function of the poet who was, by his lights, the guardian, interpreter, and bellwether of society's highest aspirations. His job as a poet was to immerse himself in the life of his times, determine the spiritual wants and needs of the people, and help them achieve their goals. If the people misunderstood or were unaware of their own best interests, the poet would become the teacher. Herein lay Sullivan's own brand of elitism: he knew better than they what the people should have. Certainly he was not the only architect to adopt this attitude; as artists became more socially peripheral during the industrial revolution, their role as "outsider" critics became a widespread form of self-justification. Sullivan simply accepted the fact that as a poet he was a reformer and that his architecture was a social art: a vehicle for cultural improvement beyond the needs of the client. In his field he may have been the first American to maintain that position.

Perhaps it was inevitable, given Sullivan's self-image, that he chose an actual poet as a hero, and given his beliefs, that the troubadour of democracy, Walt Whitman, was the particular poet he chose. It was not just Whitman's calling that so attracted Sullivan; it was also the common artistic struggle the two men seemed to share. Equally compelling as Whitman's ideas, or his sensibilities, however, was his literary style. Sullivan studied it, copied it, and entered into it so deeply that at times he compromised his own voice. In his 1882 edition of *Leaves of Grass*, for example, Sullivan rewrote "As I Ebb'd with the Ocean of Life," a section of "Sea-Drift," not trying to improve it, presumably, but as an attempt to absorb its power. He so identified with the poet, whom he never met, that in 1887, while making change after laborious change on designs for the Chicago Auditorium because his clients could not decide what they wanted, Sullivan sent Whitman a soul-searching letter. "I, too, 'have sweated through fog with linguists and contenders,'" he lamented, quoting the poet. "I, too, 'have pried through the strata, analyzed to a hair,' reaching for the basis of a virile and indigenous art." Whitman did not reply, but is said to have cherished the letter.

Although Sullivan took Whitman's writing as a model for his own, he never matched its lyrical prowess, try as he might. What he did match in intensity was Whitman's commitment to the belief that democracy could create a new kind of person.

Among other nineteenth-century authors from whom Sullivan drew, sculptor Horatio Greenough stands out. In his essays, particularly the 1843 "American Architecture," Greenough argued that the most admirable, beautiful buildings derived form from structure and function, citing plants, animals, and ocean vessels as other examples of appearance suited to purpose; he wrote that outward expression was best developed from an inward "nucleus," that detail should be subordinate to, but indicative of, mass—ideas that Louis Sullivan would later offer as his own. And when Greenough declared that buildings achieved monumental character by making reference to "the external expression of the inward functions," he very nearly anticipated the architect's famous dictum. Critic Harold A. Small has noted that in *English Traits* (1856) Ralph Waldo Emerson wrote of "American Architecture" that Greenough "announced in advance the leading thoughts of Mr. [John] Ruskin on the *morality* in architecture." In *The Seven Lamps of Architecture* (1849) Ruskin argued that architecture (as opposed to building) was infused with moral purpose and spiritual content. Sullivan learned from all these authorities—Greenough, Ruskin, Emerson, and the Transcendentalists generally—that art and architecture had the power to uplift and transform democratic life.

Many other theorists, philosophers, and designers influenced Sullivan as he assembled a point of view: Hippolyte Taine, whom he read and whose lectures he may have attended as a student at the Ecole des Beaux-Arts in Paris, and Owen Jones, the Welsh ornamentalist, whom he probably discovered while working in Frank Furness's Philadelphia office in the 1870s. Sullivan read Nietzsche, Darwin, and Herbert Spencer, was attracted to Swedenborgian theology, and was so staggered by the Sistene Chapel that he once vowed to emulate Michelangelo. Among architects, he admired Henry Hobson Richardson most of all. It is not the intention here to reconstruct the intellectual strands leading into Sullivan's mature philosophy. Readers are directed to the excellent books by Sherman Paul, *Louis Sullivan:*

An Architect in American Thought (1962), and Narciso Menocal, *Architecture as Nature: The Transcendentalist Idea of Louis Sullivan* (1981) for comprehensive treatments. Suffice it to say that Sullivan was like a sponge, absorbing ideas from his wide range of reading. He then distilled it all, making it his own. And the more he absorbed, the more he needed to write.

His sense of urgency led him to write with passion, offering opinions with a missionary's zeal, much like Frank Lloyd Wright, who once lamented the fruitlessness of his own pedagogical efforts: "Here I am at it again, trying, trying, trying, but what is the use?" A telling turn of phrase, "what is the use?" chosen by Sullivan as the title for chapter 1 of *Democracy* to indicate his existential frustration—the poet's frustration—at struggling against an uncaring, uncomprehending universe, not to mention uninterested contemporaries. But, like Wright, he kept on. If the poet was society's interpreter, and if, as Sullivan believed, architecture was society's fundamental language, then he, the poet/architect, was uniquely placed to create a vocabulary appropriate to its time and location, a new architecture he knew was desperately needed.

A measure of how much it was needed was the debate over the issue of style at the end of the nineteenth century. How was style defined? Architects wanted to know. What were its sources? What roles could history and technology play in its formation? What styles were appropriate for what occasions? Should there be an American style and what would it be like? Sullivan replied that style was a product of social conditions. It was the result of an interaction between the architect's experiences and his environment, between his history, personality, and the milieu—spiritual and material—in which he lived. This meant that every building reflected the designer's own emotional and intellectual past as well as his social context. Only in this sense ought architecture to be historical.

The profession as a whole did not agree. Many architects tried to apply a style or styles from the past to contemporary design problems. But Sullivan contended that while the gothic or the classical, indeed, all historic styles could convey important meaning to later generations, they should never be copied or even directly quoted for modern use because they had grown

out of their own social circumstances. He insisted that democratic, industrial America, like any society at any time, was obligated to develop its own language, its own forms of cultural
expression. These forms—whether literary, musical, entrepreneurial, or architectural—would react to but also shape contemporary life. It was therefore the purpose of American architects
to create the new, not by adapting architectural tradition, but by
consciously expressing democratic values with modern tech-
niques. To do otherwise was, as far as Sullivan was concerned,
nearly criminal. Of course, like any alert architect, Sullivan incorporated historical references into his work, but he never reproduced history for its own sake.

Because Sullivan pioneered the view that architectural evolution was preferable to historical reproduction, he is remembered
as the first important American in his field consistently to advocate "Progress before Precedent" (see document 28), a slogan
adopted by some of his younger colleagues. "Form follows
Function" spoke directly to this issue. Sullivan taught that once
the functions of a building were accurately determined, its forms
were obliged to be their outward manifestation. Greek temples
were therefore inappropriate for banking, nor would gothic ca-
thedrals suffice as models for tall business structures. By function, Sullivan did not mean the practical program only, because
architecture was also a social fact. A skyscraper should be an
efficient container for the transaction of business, to be sure, but
it should also address the larger social phenomena that had made
its very existence possible. Sullivan is known for emphasizing by
various means the steel frame and the quality of tallness on such
buildings as the Wainwright, the Guaranty, and the Schlesinger
& Mayer Store. Steel was a primal symbol of the new industrial
era, almost a metaphor for the era itself; height was the consequence of urban development and its impact on land values, an
emblem of economic achievement. Both steel and height stood
for power, success, and efficiency—hallmarks of a new business
culture reflected in Sullivan's buildings. As social commentary,
his skyscrapers conveyed a good deal more than technical information about structure and function, for Sullivan found large
meaning in even the tiniest architectural object, like the brick
(see document 44).

As metaphors for a range of social and spiritual matters, his ornament was also multifunctional. Sometimes it worked metaphysically to symbolize nature's processes. He used it to remind urbanites of their place in nature's order by occasionally etching the cycle of birth-growth-decay-death-rebirth on his building facades, or by suggesting that the unfolding of organic forms was analogous to the process of human creativity. Its spiritual purposes were to make large buildings more humane, softening hard lines as it relieved potentially overwhelming bulk and mass. It enhanced the street for pedestrians, welcomed visitors, and enriched interiors for tenants. Ornament had the practical value of signalling entrances, indicating structural systems, hiding mechanical devices, and crowning buildings as urban landmarks. Other architects applied ornament for some of these reasons, but Sullivan's was set apart by its systematic philosophical content. In the broadest sense his ornament was intended to bring physical beauty to ugly buildings, to insert spirituality into an amoral marketplace, and to make the industrial city a humanely nourishing place to live. Its very existence was a critique of the way things were.

The spiritual content of Sullivan's designs, like the objectives of his writings, was reformist: to uplift—to save—an all too grubby commercial civilization before it smothered its own democratic instincts. But since he perceived that business's buildings were the prototypical structures of the new America, he also believed that to erect them properly would be the most direct, appropriate way to create the long-anticipated American style. Sullivan specialized in commercial architecture, therefore, for the noblest of reasons.

His tragedy lies precisely in the resulting paradox: his attempt to inject spirituality into the artifacts of entrepreneurialism. In one sense he chose the proper vehicle for his mission, in that office buildings and banks were the most prominent billboards on which to display his message. In this regard he superficially resembled Richard Morris Hunt, whose intention was to elevate public taste through design. Had Sullivan left it there he might have prevailed. But since he aimed higher than that, his choice of commercial buildings as vehicles of reform was disastrous in another sense. Unlike Hunt, Sullivan worried, especially near the end of his life, that American business might be too corrupt—too avaricious—to save. He feared that the power of the very entrepreneurial class upon which his livelihood depended had gotten out of control. Whereas Hunt accepted his clients' values as his own, Sullivan could not. And for their part, businessmen and bankers—the barons of Sullivan's modern-day feudalism—were unlikely to accept critiques of the system they had created. It was only a matter of time until they went elsewhere, rejecting Sullivan for his opinions no matter how obliquely they may have been worded. That time came after 1895, when he had parted company with his social buffer, Dankmar Adler. Within a few years, Sullivan's standing in business circles spiraled downward until he had none at all.

These fifty-one papers represent Sullivan's attempt to save America from itself. They chronicle his struggle and illuminate his failure. But they also represent his very real success because his message is as cogent today as ever. As long as people believe that what architects do can be poetic and uplifting, that their work should aim at social improvement, not just private gain, and that creative thinking is better than historicism, Louis Sullivan's writings will remain required reading.

Robert Twombly
Paris and Amsterdam
November 1987

I
From Hooley's New Theater (1882)

Louis H. Sullivan was a twenty-five year old junior partner
at the firm of Dankmar Adler & Company when he gave
this interview, his first published statement. Perceiving
himself as an architectural innovator struggling to educate
an uninformed public, he refused to apply conventional
stylistic labels to his designs. Hooley's was the second of
seventeen theater and concert hall collaborations by Adler
& Sullivan (the firm name was changed on May 1, 1883),
the first commission on which Sullivan's work was discussed independently of his partner's.

The work of renewal has been accomplished in a very short time,
but it is substantial. Of course the effect in the theater nowadays
is about the stage, in the proscenium, in the boxes, that has been
the aim at Hooley's. Newness with uniqueness is the alliance and
the prevalence. There is about it all a something of indescribable
tone or story that the accomplished architect might be satisfied
to describe as an architectural syncrisis. Mr. L. H. Sullivan, of
the firm of D. Adler & Co., was the master spirit directing and
shaping the creation. Mr. Sullivan is a pleasant gentleman, but
somewhat troubled with large ideas tending to metaphysics, and
a deprecation of the non-development of the art protoplasm dormant in this city. It is therefore difficult to learn from Mr. Sullivan just what he has done. He refers to that work you will see
about the stage opening as the differentiation of an absolute
truth having something to do with Spencer's first principles and
Darwin's doctrine of evolution, with the predicate of a flower
and an ordinary staircase for an hypothesis. "I have no words to
characterize what you see," said Mr. Sullivan, gazing upon the
iron and plaster outgrowth of a primate of beauty. "I have not
given study to the nomenclature of the peculiar art forms developed in these boxes or carried out in that proscenium

crown. These are unclassified forms, and stock terms will convey
no adequate idea of the successful treatment under a formula
that is a new phase in the art view of architecture."

"But above that brace marking the superior lines of the opening I see light columns with peculiar arch and spaced with some
pretty effects in plaster. Byzantine in general effect. How do you
define that in words?" [the interviewer asked]

"That is an exceedingly difficult question to answer. I cannot
give it in words. I prefer that you speak of it as the successful
solution of a problem. The vaguer you are in such matters the
better I shall be pleased. It would be fatal to attempt anything
like a discursive consideration of art in architecture in Chicago
just now. People are not prepared for it. I very much regret we
have no appreciative art criticism here."

The Daily Inter-Ocean (August 12, 1882), 13.

2
Characteristics and Tendencies of American Architecture (1885)

Sullivan gave his first speech in October 1885, at the second annual convention of the Western Association of Architects in St. Louis, a meeting he had helped to organize.
Arguing that a national style could emerge only when the
ideals and cultural priorities of the people were expressed,
he anticipated his later contention that architects must first
of all be poets, interpreting society's finest aspirations. At
the age of twenty-nine, Sullivan was already highly regarded as a theater decorator, but this speech indicated the
breadth of his interests as well as the crucial social role he
envisioned for the profession.

Many who have commented upon the practice of architecture in
this country have regarded the absence of a style, distinctively
American, as both strange and deplorable; and with a view to
betterment they have advanced theories as to the nature, and

immediate realization, of such a style that evidence a lack of insight equally strange and deplorable. These theories have been for the greater part suggested by the feelings awakened in contemplating the matured beauty of Old World art, and imply a grafting or transplanting process. They have been proved empirical by the sufficient logic of time; their advocates have ignored the complex fact, that, like a new species of any class, a national style must be a growth, that slow and gradual assimilation of nutriment and a struggle against obstacles are necessary adjuncts to the purblind processes of growth, and that the resultant structure can bear only a chemical or metaphysical resemblance to the materials on which it has been nurtured.

We will, therefore, for the purposes of this paper disregard these dreams of a Minerva-like architectural splendor springing full-formed into being, and look rather for the early signs of a spontaneous architectural feeling arising in sympathy with the emotions latent or conspicuous in our people.

It is reasonable to believe that an unconquered country, peopled by colonization and natural increase, may bear in its younger and its coming generations a race whose birthright, implying freedom to receive and assimilate impressions, shall nurture emotions of rare quality and of a fruitfulness commensurate with the energy in an unexhausted soil.

It would be erroneous to assume that there will be no evidence of the activity of such emotions until as a large accumulation they break all bonds asunder. The individual is from day to day seeking expedients by means of which to shape his immediate surroundings into a realization of his desires, and we may assume it to be quite probable that the initial impelling force, operating through the individual, has already in many cases produced significant and valuable results. These results, if not thoroughly typical, must have in them much that is eminently characteristic, and that bears the stamp of internal origin.

To test this hypothesis we have therefore but to look into the daily life of our architecture, and, in the complexion of its many fleeting phases, seek here and there for instances, some perhaps almost trivial, in which the existence of spontaneous and characteristic emotional feeling may be detected. Sometimes we shall find this impulse appearing as an element of warmth tingeing scholastic formalism; sometimes as a seemingly paradoxical inspiration in the works of the uncultivated. We may certainly expect to meet with it in the efforts of those upon whose imagination the chromatic eloquence of words and of music have taken strong hold; and above all, we are to look for it in the creations of the gifted ones whose souls are finely attuned to the touching beauty of nature and of humanity. To an apprehension of this subtle element, we may be happily guided by the suggestions of analogy. Our recent American literature comes aptly to this use. Glancing through its focusing substance, as through the lens of a camera, we may perceive an image of the abstraction we seek, and, by an extension of the process, we may fix an impression of its form and texture, to be developed at will.

Our literature is the only phase of our national art that has been accorded serious recognition, at home and abroad. The noticeable qualities of its present phases seem to be: excessive regard for minute detail, painful self-consciousness of finish, timidity and embarrassment in the delineation of all but the well-behaved and docile emotions, and a tacit fiction as to the passions: all beautifully executed with much patient, earnest labor, and diplomatically tempered to the understanding.

Exquisite, but not virile, our latter-day literature illustrates quite emphatically the quality of our tentative and provisional culture, which must ere long throw off these seedling leaves, when a higher temperature shall infuse glowing vitality into root and stem, and exuberant foliation give more certain assurance of the coming flower of our soil. Our literature, and in fact all that which we Americans complacently call our art, is too much a matter of heart and fingers, and too little an offspring of brain and soul. One must indeed have faith in the processes of nature to prophesy order eventuating upon so strange a chaos of luxuries. But to this end, transmitted knowledge must gradually be supplemented by the fresh impressions of the senses and the sensibilities, the fund so accumulated yielding richly of its own increase. This supplemental acquisition must of necessity be of slow growth, for we have all been educated to a dependence upon our artistic inheritance.

Our art is for the day, is suited to the day, and will also change as the day changes. The law of variation is an ever present force, and coordination is its goal. The first step toward a new order of things is accomplished when there appear minds receiving and assimilating fresh impressions, reaching new conclusions, and acting upon them. By this sign, we may know that such a movement is already upon us, and by the aid of the indicated literary analogy we may follow its erratic tendencies, and note its increase in strength and individuality: we may see the germ of poetry which each man has within him, slowly awakening into life, and may feel the presence of an American romanticism.

This romanticism is, in the main, also exquisite but not virile. It seeks to touch all things with softened hand. Under the influence of its warmth of feeling, hard lines flow into graceful curves, angularities disappear in a mystical blending of surfaces.

One by one the completed styles of foreign climes are passing under this hand, each in turn being quietly divested of its local charm, and clothed in a sentiment and mannerism unmistakably our own. Power laments, meanwhile, at the feet of a modern Omphale, his voice attuned to the domestic hum of the times.

Appreciation of the beauties of this romanticism is to some extent dependent upon the verbal explanation and comment of its exponents. A knowledge of their vocabulary is often of assistance in disclosing softness and refinement in many primitive expedients, and revealing beauty in barren places. Familiarity with the current phraseology of the allied arts is also useful in assisting the student to a comprehension of many things apparently incomprehensible. Metaphor and simile are rampant in this connection, a well-chosen word often serving to justify an architectural absurdity.

But overloaded as is this fabric of impulse with florid and complicated intertwinings of affection, when we examine the material thereof, we find it excellent and valuable.

Searching critically among the works executed in this feeling, we note in the varying examples, and indeed in parts of the same structure, a curious *mélange* of super-sentimentalisms. Conspicuous at first glance, in some an offensive simplicity, in others a highly wrought charlatanism; further, we perceive ingenuity in device, or superb flow of spirits—all more or less leavened with stubborn common sense. After such an investigation, we may gladly become convinced that behind a somewhat uncertain vision resides a marvelous instinct.

National sensitiveness and pride, conjoined with fertility of resource, will aid as active stimuli in the development of this instinct toward a more rational and organic mode of expression, leading through many reactions to a higher sphere of artistic development.

We are now in the primary department, vaguely endeavoring to form a plastic alphabet by means of which to identify our beliefs. Progress in this respect has been very slow and results meagre: for our beliefs have still within them too much of uncertainty and diffidence to take rank as convictions. Without these latter a sufficient creating power is lacking. The formation of an alphabet, and the simplest combinations of its terms, are matters of much importance; and easy progress in this respect is seriously impeded by complications of thought. To look at things simply and clearly is quite easy, until counter influences are set at work; then comes a struggle for survival, which now and then is successful—the result being an addition, however small, to our stock of elementary forms.

The ability to develop elementary ideas organically is not conspicuous in our profession. In this respect, the architect is inferior to the business man and financier, whose capacity to expand a simple congenial idea, once fixed, into subtle, manifold and consistent ramifications is admirable, and a shining example which we have often ignored, creating thereby an undesirable impression.

This view leads us on to a consideration of the element of power. Until this element is widely introduced into our work, giving it the impress of brilliancy, intuition and great depth of feeling, that work, exhaustively considered, will remain but little more than a temporary expedient.

The presence of power, as a mental characteristic in one class of our people, augurs well for the belief that it may pervade our ranks. The beginnings of power are usually so crude and harsh as to be revolting to a refined taste, and hence it is instinctively shunned; but once subtilized, flushed with emotion and guided by clear insight, it is a worker of miracles; responsive to its ardent wooings, nature yields up her poetic secrets.

We surely have in us the germ of artistic greatness—no people on earth possessing more of innate poetic feeling, more of ideality, greater capacity to adore the beautiful, than our own people; but architects as a professional class have held it more expedient to maintain the traditions of their culture than to promulgate vitalizing thought. Here then we are weak, and should sentiment gain a pronounced ascendency, we may remain weak.

On us rests partially the responsibility, and partially on the public. We have at times individually sought to lead the public, when we more wisely should have followed it; and have, as a body, often followed, when, with beneficent results, we could have led. While we may compromise for a time, through a process of local adaptation, no architectural style can become a finality, that runs counter to popular feeling. The desire at once to follow and to lead the public should be the initial attitude of our profession toward the formation of a national style. For while we conduct the technical operations, the shaping and controlling process is mainly in the hands of the public who are constantly keeping us within bounds. We cannot wholly escape this control, while we are without a national architecture fully representing the wishes of the public, and ministering to its conceptions of the beautiful and the useful. This can evidently not come to pass forthwith, for the public itself can only partially and imperfectly state its wants. Responding readily, however, to the intuition of those who anticipate its desires, it accepts provisionally year by year all the satisfaction it can get; so that while one recognized style after another shall pass through our hands to be tried and finally rejected in the search for permanent satisfaction, a modified residuum from each will doubtless be added to a fund representing our growth in emotional and spiritual wealth. The progress of this growth toward consummation in a national style involves the lives of many generations, and need be of but little practical concern to us of today. We work at short range and for immediate results. Perhaps, however, there would be infused into our profession an abiding *esprit de corps,* should consideration of this subject and its associated themes lead to a substantial agreement upon our status, our tendencies and our policy.

If the conclusions set forth in this paper be accepted as correct, it becomes clearly evident, however, that the formative beginnings of this national style, now in progress, are of the utmost immediate interest to us, in part through feelings of patriotism, in part because of a surmise that those who approach most nearly in the substance of their work and administration to the qualities inherent to our race and potential to a national style, will come nearest to the hearts of our people.

Harassed though the architect may be by the cares and responsibilities of his daily life, there exists nevertheless within him, in the midst of this turmoil, an insuppressible yearning toward ideals. These delicate promptings should be both protected and nourished, that, like the flowering plants springing by the sun's gentle persuasion from little seeds buried in the coarser elements of the soil, they also, because of the warmth of human feeling, may bloom at times by the wayside, yielding refreshing odors and the joy of color to the plodding wayfarer.

The soft beams of the full-orbed moon fall with pathetic caress upon the slumbering life of the world; paling with the dawn, her tender vigil ended, she melts into the infinite depths when the ruddy herald of day proudly summons the workers. So does the soul watch over its greater ideals until the thrilling radiance of power shall awaken them to action.

Ideal thought and effective action should so compose the vital substance of our works that they may live, with us and after us, as a record of our fitness, and a memorial of the good we may have done. Then, in the affluence of time, when a rich burden of aspiring verdure may flourish in the undulating fields of thought, wrought into fertility through the bounty of nature and the energy of the race, the mellowed spontaneity of a national style reaching its full and perfect fruition shall have come from out the very treasury of nature.

The Inland Architect and Builder 6 (November 1885): 58–59.

3
We Are All Jolly Good Fellows (1885)

Louis Sullivan was articulate in interviews and an excellent public speaker. He was at his best on formal occasions, for which he prepared laboriously, and in one-on-one or small group encounters when he controlled the situation or knew exactly what to expect. "Wherever he sat," architect George Elmslie remembered, "was the head of the table." But if caught off-guard, especially in his younger days, he was not so self-assured. When asked to respond to a toast at the Western Association of Architects' second annual convention banquet, for example, he hardly knew what to say. Attempts at "jollity" fell flat. As this document makes clear, Sullivan tried to avoid such embarrassing situations.

I kept away from the banquet until about five minutes ago, when I opened the door about two inches or three-eighths of an inch, I think possibly it was five-eighths, and I heard a voice in the corner there. The voice attracted me and I came in and very modestly sat down at the end of the table, where I thought I was perfectly safe. I never made a speech in my life, and I think I don't know how to do it; I don't know what I am going to do. I have not the ease of diction of my predecessor.* I wish I had. I wish I had the faculty of weaving the ideas as gracefully and beautifully as he has. I cannot even get any inspiration from my theme. There are times when I might have got some inspiration from my theme; but unfortunately we have among us one whose presence inspires one rather with a sense of seriousness than jollity, and the general impression made upon me by the gathering as I came in was a pleasing one, a pleasing sense of unanimity. For jollity, I think, that is found rather in private and smaller gatherings. I will not attempt to report some of the little choice bouquets which I have accumulated during my stay here. I think, however, the future is full of promise in the matter of jollity. I think there is more jollity here than there was a year ago. I think another year will bring about still further increase. I think if certain results of our labor in this convention prove successful in bringing about the fruits which we expect, we will

---

*Sullivan's predecessor was Henry C. Meyer, described by *Inland Architect* as the "genial" editor of *Sanitary Engineer*. Meyer apparently amused the gathering with his witty response to the toast, "Sanitation and Ventilation."

then have occasion for being manifestly jolly. [Applause ended the banquet.]

The Inland Architect and Builder 6 (November 1885): 86–87.

4
Essay on Inspiration (1886)

When Sullivan read "Inspiration" to the third annual convention of the Western Association of Architects in Chicago in November 1886, his audience was stunned. Expecting a discourse on architectural matters, it was completely unprepared for this lengthy prose-poem on nature's—and by extension, humanity's—creative life-cycle. The essay marked the first public declaration of Sullivan's metaphysical concerns and the first public revelation of the importance of nature in his work. Rewritten and expanded several times, included as the first part of a group of poems he called "Nature and the Poet" (1899 and after), and published a second time posthumously by Ralph Fletcher Seymour in 1964, this is the original version of Sullivan's ambitious but ambiguous work. Although he "commanded close attention," according to one observer in 1886, impressing his listeners with his virtuosity, Sullivan was never again invited to address the Western Association.

PART I.

Growth. —A Spring Song.

When birds are caroling, and breezes swiftly fly, when large abundant nature greets the eye, clothed in fresh filigree of tender green, when all is animation and endeavor, when days are lengthening, and storm clouds smiling weep, when fresh from every nook springs forth new life,—then does the heart awake in springtime gladness, breezy and melodious as the air, to join the swelling anthem of rejuvenated life, to mate with birds and flowers and breezes, spontaneous and jubilant as the flow of dawn, to pulsate ardently with hope, rich in desire so tremulously keen,—then wondrous joy to simply live,—and question not, to walk into the ample air, to open wide the portals of the winter-bounded soul and eagerly to hail the new-born world with voice like mountain torrent quick melted from the heart's accumulated snows,—even so eagerly and so voluminously does the song gush forth and wildly leap, tumultuous as nature's self,—to fall in gentle spray upon the misty valley far below, and there, to live bound up within the very life it sung.

O wondrous joy that this should be the springtime, and this the heart to greet it and to sing a song more wondrous still of joy within the sun-touched soul.

For such a song doth rise within me like a boundless symphony, rich chorded, and intense with lambent melodies which come unbidden from the general glow of life; a symphony whose theme is interwoven with this eager springtime life, a theme whereof the measure, caught up by the senses quick from every growing thing, doth seem to move, as all in nature here now seems to move in rhythmic cadence toward some subtle and tremendous consummation.

In tender light of dawning spring that song's incentive filters through the mists when the ardent sun, flushed and impatient pulsates hotly toward the summit of the heavens; in urgent need the equal mounting soul too pulsates toward the crown of inspiration, while pensive nature wakening with the morn makes manifest the latent measure of her sweet and procreant rhythm. The lark floats up to vocalize the limpid atmosphere,—the shadows shorten with her tense refrain. Abounding joy starts nimbly forth from hidden sources; vibrant, the heart, filled to the quick, o'erflows, the tongue unloosens, and the inhaled breezes sing thus, respirant, anew:—

O, soft, melodious springtime! First-born of life and love! How endearingly the thrilling voice of destiny hath called thee, and with what devotion thou hast come! And thou thyself hast taken up that call, made doubly potent by thy sweet embrace, and thou hast wrought the self-same magic on my slumbering soul.

Joy of the radiant day, joy of the sun-kissed verdure, joy of the radiant soul! The instant power of sympathy girdles and binds them together with bands sufficient as the ethereal sympathy of the planets coursing around the central virtue of the sun. So, orbital and responsive, colored to its rise, high noon and twilight, revolves the planetary spread of nature round the attracting and illuminating soul. By that soul's effulgent light look I out again upon thee, wondrous springtime, casting on thee brilliant high lights, and beyond thee changing shadows.

Now do I know thee as thou art, look on thee, through thee, and beyond thee toward a far off source whence thy joy has come.

Surge and surge through thee to me, the hugely undulating waves from distant raging joy within the vast expanse, that now break on our shores in foaming and majestic surf of springtime life.

Abysmal spring! The myriad nebulae were surf upon your cosmic shores. Stupendous winter passed away, the dawn mists parted in primeval splendor, and through your vistas floating rose the lark, the world, uttering as a morning song of promise the melodious succession of the races.

Of such are we; and high above our struggling, joyous verdure, our parting mists, our urgent and propulsive dawn, posed serenely, soaring ever toward the azure heights rises the immortal spirit of man, showering tones exalted, prophetic, volatile, spontaneous—a spring song to the waiting soul, a hymm of praise to nature's bounty, a sweet and unnamed outburst of itself.

Of such melodious origin are all our hopes, our sympathies, our desires; whence here, among us, coming daily, hourly into being, are great and lesser springtimes—each with its dawn, its urgent ruddy sun, its trailing mists, its aromatic sprouting verdure—its trilling songster in the sky.

Of such come likewise protean thought and action; roused and sustained in eagerness by the touch and impulse of desire. Far transmitted yet ever present the creative call of nature sounds inspiring, jubilant and sweet. Responsive, imagination rising quickly to the heights makes thoughtful action magically vocal and complete.

———

Through lesser springtime expanding, merging, completing, courses mysterious life, unfolding toward greater, ever greater, ever broadening springtimes, successively through these, and through each intermediary winter sleep, at each renewed adjustment both farther removed yet more intrinsically here than before, ever jocund and agile, ever onward impelled by the rapidly surging and inflowing currents, comprehending and so transmitting the past, fulfilling the present, gestating the future—ever fecund and joyous.

And all this while the dawn-bird singing! On the wings of spring he ever rises, looking down on the lesser springtime growth; looking down on the meadows, the forests deep, ever rising, unfolding and blending in long looks down on the wide spreading plains, on the curving sea, on the shifting clouds that brood over all; alone, from the greater heights looks down on the distant enveloping haze of the swiftly receding world; and transmuted on high, now faintly heard, serenely attuning aloft it floats as the mellow companion the moon chanting softly.

In the stillness intent it now looks down on the balancing swing of the deep brooding world,—ever dawning; singing a hymn to its greater springtime, as I hear, floating high, sing a hymn to the perfect and spherical soul renascent of many a heaving springtime;—consorted still by a voicing spirit, the spirit of unending spring;—the desire, the appeasement, the joy of the world.

––––––

Effusing from such wonders interblended all around, has come to me thus, in soft pulsations, the elemental voice of Nature yearning. Whereby deeply do I know, thou generous and kindly Springtime, why I was touched, O, Prodigal! and captivated by thy presence. Now, nevermore to cease in its crescendo, has the lark's refrain returned in part to thee, a rhapsody of echoes from my soul.

Interlude.

And now the day is done. The trailing splendor in the west fills me with peace. The beckoning twilight leads me toward the cool and placid night. Shadows and the dusk surround me, while here, companioned by a cherished memory, soothed and lulled by the mystic moonlight, I meditate in swiftly deepening strain,—touched by a hint or weird suggestion, a premonition and uncertainty: whence comes it, I must know: wherefore, abiding here in gloom, residuary, musing, ineffably sequestered, do I follow hence the rich suggestive indirections of thy theme, thou softly dimming shade of springtime; undulating with it through the swell of ample summer, gliding detached and phantom-like athwart its mellowing term, to pass away in transcendental twilight, and coalesce with star-lit thoughts beyond.

PART II.

Decadence.—Autumn Reverie.

In pathless wilds, in gray subsiding autumn, where brown leaves settle through the air, descending one by one to join the dead, while winds, adagio, breathe shrill funeral lamentations, tired Nature, there, her task performed, divested of her lovely many-colored garment, withdraws, behind a falling veil, and sinks to sleep.

Like sentinels standing, like spectres, bare and fantastic the trees rattle their dry hard branches.

The migratory birds have gone.

The faded hills squatting grimly together, commune with wind and sky, echoing their miserere.

The sap has sunk into the ground. There is no life but in root, and precarious broadcast seed.

A summer has departed:—never that summer to return; a great life has passed into the tomb, and there, awaits the requiem of winter's snows.

And we, the living, in sympathy, view, ponder and speculate; take up the melancholy theme within our hearts, and through the sad attuning of the mind look out again upon the endless spread of life and dissolution—the fatal chance and certainty of change:—nor think to contravene the destined action and reaction.

The coupled opposites which we call light and darkness, good and evil, fortune and failure, growth and decay, sound and silence, harmony and discord, love and indifference, hope and dis-

appointment, life and death, law and chaos, and their quick en-
gendered brood pass in crowded processional through the deepening twilight of our inclination.

Sombre through the gloom come to the impassioned ear the
diminished strains of promise unfulfilled, melting the soul to
overflowing languorous compassion.

Now darkness holds full sway: the heart, in anguish, sinks
upon the bosom of the deep. The haggard winds moan to the
faint-appearing stars; the answering voice of Night, sitting in the
heavens, the crescent moon a gem upon her finger, her velvet
gown spread about the unhappy spirit, speaks rest to the discon-
solate. A hoar frost gathers, glimmering in the mild light; the
wanderer, chilled to resignation, moves into the deep valley of
negation, to garner up the lineaments of phantom souls.

Slowly the tenebrae unfolds its content; the darkness sepa-
rates, taking visible shapes—shadows within the soul, that are
revealed as blighted lilies, and the trampled violet, the shattered
oak, disintegrated rock, the parched air, the storm's destruction,
the jetsam of the sea; the ashes of a city; the fallen bridge;
impeded traffic; broken fortunes.

The shadows multiply,—a host of wraiths:—day dying in the
twilight, the waning moon, the fading of yesterday within the
sense. Their still, subjective voices spectrally recall our fleeting
states:—the departed joyousness of childhood, vanished youth,
faded illusions; bespeak the mind's indulgence toward the slow
decay of once fresh spontaneity; plead with the heart to feel in
sympathy and comprehend the sorrow of unrequited love:
golden-warp-dimming shuttle, and so, in turn, to know the language of the silent cot, the footfall heard no more, the touching
voice of reminiscence.

Then flock about erroneous judgments, aborted projects, fail-
ures of all kinds; as a multitude of seeds fallen upon barren soil,
a multitude of seedlings nipped by the frost, a multitude of sap-
lings stricken by adversity, a multitude of bearers shriveled by
drouth or worm, a multitude of the gnarled and moss-grown
vigorously dying, a multitude of rotting stumps,—a multitude
of vanished lives.

In extremity of woe, the hapless wanderer seeks to turn, but there is no turning, and but one result: a lonely, yearning thing of sorrow, with whose last sigh the departing spirit wafted, settles slowly, as a leaf, into the Nirvana.

A great soul is thus swallowed up by deepest gloom within this sepulchre, and can nevermore, the same soul, unregenerate, return. Without alternative it yielded up its life, through overwhelming sympathy with death.

So he who with compassionate solicitude looks on the actual face of dissolution, must surely die in sympathy forthwith. Yet is this not the end; for when in its predestined course the world of hope moves past another vernal equinox, in springtime ecstasy, mid the soft, persuasive rays of fixed serenity of purpose he will emerge from this abode of gloom, and greeting the warm air, will rise again into a nobler, greater life, to bear as rich fruition, a more complex sympathy, a metamorphosed insight, a profoundly changed belief.

And so, as wild flowers spring from manifold remains, do sympathies arise from regions of the dead, sending upward wondrous longings. As the plant grows, so thought grows, by what it feeds upon, its delicate chemistry changing poison into vital sap, to nourish growing sympathy, to the end that leaves and branches spread out in the generous, vivifying air, take on color, and firm visible growth heralding the bud that shall unfold with time its choicest worth:—the lovely flower at once of life and death, which here, hanging in fragrant equilibrium within the present joyous certainty of life and the imminent surrounding nearness, though remoter certainty of coming death, must need exhale its soul in rapture till such moment when the latter force shall prove ascendant; then does it softly yield its trusted heritage of vital wealth, and sink again into the realms of night.

And so the living present, firm-rooted in the past, grows within its atmosphere, takes on local coloring of identity, fulfills its ordained rhythm of growth, condenses its results, and, waning hour by hour in all that marks its physical, mesmeric presence, fading in the inevitable twilight, it too becomes in turn a stratum of the fertile past.

And so does the individual enterprise, the individual far-reaching purpose, the individual transitory emotion, the individual triviality and incidental, fulfill each its rhythmical allotted part, and pass away.

By how much and in what way the penetrating roots spread through the soil, grasp and absorb from it, by so much, and in correspondence, will the topmost branches tower, move with individual peculiar sway in the storm, rustle likewise in the breezes, or stand superbly, calmly silent.

By such virtue of limitation the lily nods in aromatic luxury, a proud weed overtops the timid violet.

How grand and self-sufficient seems the forest monarch, how fair the lily; how ardent is living personal desire, how lily-sweet true sympathy; yet the subsidence and withdrawal of vital sustaining elements comes not more surely to one of these than to the others; unto each in normal time comes the ineffable serenity of dissolution, whose outward sign and garment is decadence.

———

When brewing tempests sound a knell, who shall survive? The destroyer comes! Fearful its fury!

Afar at sea the angry waves engulf a bunch of pallid mortal specks. They are gone! with all their tiny hopes and fears. What are hopes and fears amid the raging elements, more than fantastic and circuitous sparks blown by the night storm from the chimney's throat to glow a troubled instant and vanish into black oblivion?

And in the surging forest, the tortured giants roar in such frenzied chorus that the exalted soul quakes at their awful music. In the intermittent glare the eye gloats on their huge resistance. A blinding flash! The instant deafening rattle and malodorous sizzling air. A hush! a frantic shattering roar, a prostrate growth of centuries, a mighty one laid low. Yet what is the forest, the labored and accumulated growth of years, but the plaything of the storm? And what is the total life of the forest more than the life of the human speck, or the spark, or the race, or the flitting smile? Each and all playthings of fate, momentary justifications, transitory trifles, great and wondrous only to the great and wondrous heart of man whose sympathetic soul envelopes them and draws them nigh, and interweaves them with its own catastrophe and bliss.

And when that heart, that soul, shall sing in duo, shall find a full, eventual expression, bursting into full-blown ecstasy of metaphor their rich and varied language shall tell a thousand thousand tales wherein the blended themes of life and death shall intermingle with our smiles and tears, wherein the limitless reality of nature and the limitless illusion of the heart shall coalesce, wherein the soul of man shall tell of Nature's soul in hymns of life, and yet wherein shall sound, responsive, murmuring in a gentle undertone, the constant, solvent song of death.

To death then, hear a hymn:—

Now crafty and concealed, now open jawed and furious, now bland and sophistical, void of form yet multitudinous in seeming aspect, patient of opportunity, certain of the final outcome, present everywhere, pressing against each individual life—testing it always and everywhere, gaining a little, losing a little, utilizing every means, missing no opportunity, pressing the whole surface and interior of all life, thy active resistance continually meets that ceaseless, aspiring force, while in tranquil depth thou dost simulate the soft, preliminary sleep of every germ.

Of many moods, all-devouring, insatiable, enormous and sinister, sublime, vast and terrible, to Thee, alike the vanished morning mist, the holocaust, the gurgling rale, and endless series of forgotten years, unnumbered longings, individual twinklings—Thou, Great Denier, hast gathered them in—and they are not!

Before the soul, comes pleading, self-justified in innocence, soft voiced and heartful, a beauteous bewitching form claiming, open-armed, expostulate, its individual dower of life. The soul, attentive, entranced, ecstatic, would overflow in plentitude of instant, ardent love, but thy inexorable form arises, and with unspeakable gesture thou dost spread an answering darkness that envelopes all.

And thou dost ride upon the agitating storm, thou sett'st a brake upon the coursing planets, thou art with the glorious meteors erratic through interstellar space, thou hast touched the burning suns and they are cooling; thou art with the microscopic crawling mite—following inseparably its earnest quest, looking through its minute eyes; thou speak'st with every mortal breath, and art resident in brightest smiles; thou art within thyself, thou fearful shade, and hast thine own great death.

More tenuous than air, more steadfast than the stars, harder than granite rocks, more mobile than running waters, variable and elusive as the winds, thou art beyond our touch, imponderable, yet definite and real as shadows.

Thou art the reactionary cause of every change, without thee there can be no palpable or seeming growth, no sentient being; thou art the everlasting and sublime companion of all life; thou art the eternal shadow cast from things mortal by the eternal light.

In catastrophe, O power sublime, we know thee dread, yet in solitude of meditation I view its fury as thy comedy and by-play; but in decadence, in peaceful subsidence and dissolution thou art so tragic that the soul spontaneously believes thee friendly, adorns thee with a name, and holds thee precious in its sight.

Interlude.

When from well-springs bubbling to the light in mystic dell, there flows a crystal rivulet gladsome and free, cradled by fresh mossy banks so lovingly tender, lulled by the twitter of birdlings and murmurous balsamic breezes, the sunbeams curiously peer through the leaves at its smiling, innocent face, and wish it joy.

Soon joined by rippling little ones who sweetly give it their all, it welcomes their tribute, and wantonly runs to the open meadows and alternate wooded reach.

Here sequestered' mid high grass and shrubs, it gurgles, and crows, and fattens; then turns hither and there with sinuous curve, sings soft cadenzas to the intercepting stones, and hastens on to leap in burnished cascade from the ledge.

Anon it grows in dignity with each succeeding token from the confluent streams which, mingling with its genial flow, add their qualifying mites of tender power, abstracted from perhaps desolate or, it may be, verdure-laden hills, the porous strata, overhanging rocks;—and wrought on by the alternating influence of storm and sunshine.

With mingled persiflage and serious undertone, growing ever in earnestness it flows through rich diversity of landscape,

spreading out at times to rest, in quiet sombre pool or solitary
lake.

Thus grown and quieted it now moves between yon tacit
banks which slowly individualize at each encountered bend and
seem to hold their counsel.

One by one the larger tributaries in turn converge upon this
widening stream and pour their inflow of rich abundant waters—slow-moving messages from many lands.

The banks widen apart, become serious and broad of aspect,
assuming each unto itself a separated and less kindly mien:—
sandy bluffs rising to beetling cliffs, severely wooded hills, the
austere forest coming to the water's edge:—whence all cast images of their restraining will and purpose on the receptive
breadth of the current moving now in affluence and majestic
ease.

The river-bed diversifies, shoals, snags, islands, soon irritate
the current which sullenly yields to corrode the opposing shore.

The channel deepens, is fugitive, tortuous, lurking with en-
gendered passions, and ever less friendly to the less friendly and
receding shores.

Grown avaricious of power, tributaries large and small are
swallowed up. Jealously the banks multiply their strength, each
one for itself, grim, determined, serious. Alike to all are storm
and sunshine, the slow succession of the seasons, moon and
stars, the grand each day arrival and departure of the sun; they
but take on a fleeting color from these things, and remain, themselves, preoccupied of their own destiny.

Increase and sombre intensity, culmination close by the limit;
deep, broad, and still; high, firm and still; divided, inimical, one
and inseparable, great river, great banks—(Behold here the
delta!) disdainful, fierce, haughty, descend to the sea, and with
measureless pride are lost in the depths.

PART III.

The Infinite.—A Song of the Depths.

Many a thought lies dormant in the sea;—exchanging secrets
with fortuitous winds, free with the driftwood and the birds, yet

sealing close its thoughts to thought-proud man, the vast sea broods and effuses ever, yet as I know, unspeakably, imparts with freedom only to the native one who equals it in elemental turbulence and serenity.

Deep-throated sea! sing to me now in occult murmurs, in rushing tumultuous plunging cadenzas, a song, an entrancing song of the Great Spirit; for here I sit impressionable, super-intent, and wholly given up to thee, to listen and to ponder.

The morning sun, young and blushing, o'erhangs thee, glanc-ing ardently. I see his image pictured broken and glittering on the waves. So do I o'erhang thee, mighty one, yet where may I find the image of my ardent soul, where may I hear the arcanum unfolded:—the song of the depths, the song that shall attune harmonious and amplifying to the song within,—the question-ing song, the unsatisfied song of the twilight.

The salt breeze, quickening, moves swiftly as the passing sea-gulls. Harshly they scream. Yet shall my thoughts ever circle and swiftly wheel in hunger over thee when the sea-gulls are fed?

In vain I sang with the jubilant springtime, inhaling balsam with the flower-laden air. It departed in sweetness, leaving me perplexed.

In vain I shuddered through the rustling depths of autumn's slow decay. That which I sought eluded me as before!

Here, then, in the simple air and by the simple water lies my refuge and my hope. Deny me not, for I am come as one nearing his journey's end; as a traveler at eventide, here must I seek final nourishment and rest.

For there must somewhere lie beyond this complex phantasm, beneath this eagerness of growth, this upheaval and fatuous en-deavor, beneath this sorrow-laden, inextricable fatality of subsid-ence and decay, that which stands to them as water to the waves: deep, fluid, comprehending all:—bearing quiescent and passion-less this endless agitation, this fascinating to-and-fro. Else why, as I tarry here expectant, am I so persuaded by the heavy rolling roar and subsequent gurgling thin-spreading swash and laconic return of the green transparent waves? How exultingly they rear and curve, how they plunge impulsively upon the slop-ing sands! Yet in a moment they return—inevitably and swiftly they return.

Clear blue and crystalline the firm sky arches overhead. My buoyant craving darts vividly upward, in instant search: to instantly return: resolved to learn all from the friendly sea, so tangible, so near at hand.

Sing jubilate, turbulent sea! Of all things that the crowded universe contains thou art nearest like the human soul. For in thy very self, thy liquid depths and shallows, thy lightless and unfathomable depths, thy restless surface waves and currents, impressionable, incontinently shifting and changing, in thy very self unquestionably I see, with wonder and amazement I see near by and luminous my soul's inspiring image which I sought.

And as my soul with joyous ardor gazes on that image pictured softly in thy depths, so thou seem'st to rest, in secret stillness, brooding o'er a wonderously reflected image—image mobile and serene beyond compare.

Yet, alas! though fervently I conjure thee, still remains inscrutable that rare reflection, hiding which, thou smilest calmly toward me, evanescent smiles of billowy waves.

———

My backward turning thoughts recall the sorrow and illusion of my days:—How, earnestly, Inscrutable, I struggled through entanglements unending, searching deviously amid perplexities to find thy abode; prying with sharp-pointed thoughts, testing with the delicate touch of the heart, yet heeding not sufficiently, trusting not at all the simple promptings of the soul which spoke to me often as the sea now murmurs; but it spoke not in a language that I knew, therefore I heeded not its tender voice, which died away 'mid the rising clamor of random words, to lie, overridden and hushed—dormant for many a year.

Patiently I sought thee, yet preoccupied I passed thee by in my haste, believing I would find thee yonder, where the alluring rainbow of my thoughts so gracefully ascended.

Where I saw power I looked beyond for greater power; where there was storm and stress, I peered out anxiously toward turbulence sublime; when in dismay I gazed on death in many forms I questioned closely if beyond this lay an answer:—yet all these disconnectedly, with manifold obliquities of view.

Once, after hot pursuit along a sinuous trail, I called thee long and loud by many names: thou didst answer, but I, alas, mistook the murmur of the winds for commonplace, I heeded not the drifting odor of the woods, nor marveled at the nearness of the mossy bank whereon I lay me down to rest:—prostrate that my labor should remain without reward:—drawing over me as I sank in fitful sleep, a coverlet ingeniously contrived of self-spun gossamer, subtly shuttled through and through by dexterous guesses, consummately resplendent with the dazzling embroidery of long transmitted thoughts.

In pride of thought I sought to seize thee deftly, as one seizes with an instrument; I sought to snare thee with a loop of words; to trap thee in arctic zones, as a trapper setting his falls on the bleak and lonely winter wilds. Yet all in vain.

Furious, I went by night, malignant, to glean an answer from the storm o'ershadowed sea. Foreboding winds were shrill with angry warnings. The ancient bowlders, heavy with odorous wet weeds, gloomily offered their support. Athwart the overcast and threatening sky the moon pushed rapidly from cloud to cloud, fitfully pouring her clear fresh light between, flooding the mysteriously approaching waves with shifting throes of shine and dark:—whence equal light and gloom within, sullenly revealing and obscuring dim far off undulating hints of unison, mysteriously approaching harmonies, modulating weirdly through the swell and subsidence toward tangible identity of sea and soul:—identity trembling here, now, in the awful hush before the storm, trembling in suppressed and vaguely lurking throes of consummation.

Lurking and trembling the lurid distant lightnings waver on the edge of the sea. In vain! In vain! The soft light disappears in murky night. No moon, no peaceful star. Hoarsely the wind-driven sea plunges furiously on the rocks. Enraged, and flashing through the sky, deliriously sweeps the fearful hurricane, swirling the rain-sheets, unloosening the thunder.

Elohim! Elohim! In utter darkness I! In vain, Inscrutable! Thou wert more near than my unhappy soul's desire was to itself, yet art Thou far off and unreachable as Thyself alone.

———

So fares the sea in rocking storm. So, tempest-tossed, I too abate, and balance with the measured swell, while storm clouds drift away, and heartsease, storm-abandoned, rests beneath the glory of the breaking day.

———

Clear morning light, refreshing air made vocal by the dashing spray, the neighboring beach low-spreading and withdrawn, compose my thoughts in strains akin to theirs which issue from the surf as jetsam from the wreckage of my hopes.

———

Deny me not, O sea, for I indeed am come to thee as one aweary with long journeying returns at last, expectant, to his native land.

Deny me not that I should garner now among the drifted jetsam on this storm-washed shore, a fragmentary token of serenity divine. For I have been, long-wistful, sitting here beside thee, my one desire floating afar on meditation deep, as the helpless driftwood floats, and is slowly borne by thee to the land.

Deny me not that now, awakening, as the spring awakes from mystic fleeting winter sleep, that I too may sing in tones rejuvenant yet softened by autumnal memories, in tones that shall have deep within them the thrill and intent of thine own native song, that I too may sing, as thou singest ever, a song of the depths, a wordless song of the near at hand, a song of the ardent present, a song of the vanished past, an inspiring song of the future:—the gladsome song of the soul at one with Inscrutable Serenity.

———

All hail, sublime serenity! Thou answerest the questioning heart, thou sendest peace and guidance to the striving soul. Thou art the voice of the morning lark, thou art the power whereof it sings, whereof we also sing and dream.

Wondrous thou wearest springtime-life and ecstasy upon thy brow, while watching, tranquil, by the grave.

Thou art the lark, thou art the falling leaf; thy breath is the breath of flowers, thy voice is sweeter than the zephyr, deep, below the rumbling storm.

Thou floatest with the swallow at evening skimming the surface of quiet waters:—over the placid soul thou likewise comest as a delicately fleeting thought at the hush of day.

Raging catastrophe is now as a silence wherein the hungry voice of fate is heard as wolves are heard at night in the depths of the forest.

Whence the wail of decadence is to me as the silence of caves, wherein thy voice is heard resembling the dripping of water-drops in the stillness.

Thou speedest thy rays to the sun, thou art dawn and twilight to the universe.

Life and death are as dreams of thy slumber; thou breathest and the seasons come and go.

Yet thou art near as the flowers of the field. To their lovely companions within the heart thou comest as storm and sunshine interblended with the melodies of spring.

I am sure that thou art very far and very near and round and about me, yet all that I may know of thee comes of the fragmentary token which I gathered on the sands by the sea.

But I know, best of all, that this token, once found, takes root in the soul as a seed that is dropped into virgin soil.

Through lesser springtime expanding its course doth lie to unfold 'mid the greater unfolding growths, to become in turn of nature's chosen, bearing joyous flowers and labored fruits in its onward course, impelled by the steadily inflowing currents of rotating seasons:—And I know 'tis by these fruits alone that the token is transmitted.

From this summit and consummation hence to decline as the sun declines in splendor from the zenith, merging with the roseate and gathering clouds, sinking tranquil through their midst, I know indeed that to thus depart in splendor as the sun departs is the final announcement of this token of serenity:—announcement echoed in the twilight by soft evening chimes from remaining hearts, denoting peace in the realms of night.

Over all, as a beautiful memory following deeds, arises 'mid soft refulgence the mellow companion, the moon, chanting softly a song of endearment, a token-song to the great departed, a song of the depths, a song near at hand, harmonious and amplifying to the song gone hence, a song of inspiration.

———

And thus my song, declining, now sinks to its rest through the peaceful sky. Whereafter prolonging thought arises, following close, as a harvest moon, shining with milder, reflected light.

The thought that dawn, noon and twilight are ever linked with the coursing sun; that invisible tomorrow is even now its gliding companion, and will appear with it anon, dawning our day in urgency.

Whence I believe that action thus ever attends on flushed and procreant purpose, continually mounting with it toward the shifting summit of desire.

Without the sun, no dawn; without sustained desire, no fruitful or efficient action.

The thought that from such desire emerges art as action.

The thought that tallying such desire, (native, widespread, and unawares), appears the art of a nation: dispelling the gloom in its dawn:—whence works awaken imperceptibly, like a tinge of green upon the land, rejoicing in their lesser springtime gladness.

Through speedy decadence the weak are denied; surely the autumn nipping winds dispose of the loose and tremulous, leaving the hardy sound.

How quickly the lesser seasons change! How, manifold and numerous, they ever turn involved in the greater and broadening rotation of growth and decay. Yet how tranquilly beneath the tumult and silence persists a hidden power, mysterious, inscrutable and serene, qualifying imperceptibly both growth and decadence, leading both, sustaining both, denying none, while through the lesser and greater unfolding springtimes, the tide of destiny ebbs and flows with mysterious undulations, working freely, through marvelous rhythms, toward subtle and tremendous consummations—consummations balanced in the end by a noble decay, and the sweet oblivion of death. Whence comes the strangely complex thought of rhythm—for all is rhythm.

The thought of attuning the rhythmic song of art harmonious and amplifying to the rhythms of nature as these are interpreted by the sympathetic soul: that herein lies a vital purpose and significance of art.

That to arrest and typify in materials the harmoniously interblended rhythms of nature and humanity, sustained and permeated by an essence wholly inscrutable, yet manifest as wondrously elusive mobility and abiding serenity, indicates the deepest inspiration and the most exalted reach of art.

The thought, that to perceive the material workings of this mysterious essence as the power underlying all growth and decadence, requires that the senses be highly spiritualized by the mobile, serene and sustaining influence of the soul.

That to attempt in cynical pride to seize this essence deftly with the mind as with a delicate instrument or by conscious strategic methods whatsoever, is illusory and utterly in vain.

That a reverent attitude of the mind is equally in vain.

That it is not at all an essence for the mind to deal with, but for the soul to deal with; and this alone with the help of exquisitely vital sympathy.

That the mind speaks in terms of logic, which is vital, yet conscious and secondary; but that the soul speaks in terms of inscrutable intuition which is involuntary, vital and primary.

Whence the thought that the greatest art is at once the most and the least thoughtful—that logic and intuition are therein marvelously interblended.

That moments when the soul loses the identity of conscious mind and merges with the infinite, are moments of inspiration.

In tranquillity of meditation the soul unites with nature as raindrops unite with the sea; whence are exhaled vapors, under the hot and splendid sun of inspired imagination, vapors rising through the atmosphere of high endeavor to drift away in beauteous clouds borne upon the imponderable winds of purpose, to condense and descend at last as tangible realities—sometimes in gentleness, sometimes in sombre fury, as the rotating seasons call. Here they nourish and refresh, and amid untold vicissitudes and metamorphoses, return at last to the great sea of Nature.

Whence the dominant, all-pervading thought that a spontaneous and vital art must come fresh from nature, and can only thus come.

That the specters of departed and once spontaneous art growths, which arise from their natural graves and walk abroad clad in tenuous garbs, like other phantoms and mock realities, must vanish with the dawn of artistic vitality.

That such a dawning is close upon this land there can no longer be any doubt. In the paling gloom the phantoms flit about, uneasy and restless, losing identity. The heavens are faint with the flow of a new desire; and with overflowing heart I rise through the mists, aloft, to catch a glimpse of the coming sun, and carol this prophetic song of spring.

The Inland Architect and Builder 8 (December 1886): 61–64.

5
Remarks on the Subject, "What are the Present Tendencies of Architectural Design in America?" (1887)

In January 1885 Sullivan helped to organize the Illinois State Association of Architects in Chicago as a chapter of the Western Association. Activities at its regular monthly meetings included symposia and informal discussions, sometimes on meaty philosophical issues that did not ordinarily arise during the day-to-day course of architectural business. On March 5, 1887, Sullivan disagreed with engineer Frederick Baumann and architect John Root, arguing that style developed from within living people, not ~~~~~~ ~~~~~~ ~daptation of historical precedents to contempo~~~~ ~ns.

I think we are starting at the wrong end entirely. We are taking the results of what has already passed, examining on the surface, and from that are searching for the source of impulse. I do not believe the origin of style is outside, but within ourselves, and the man who has not the impulse within him will not have the style. But the more he thinks, the more he reflects, observes and assimilates, the more style he will have. So, therefore, it seems to me that the eventual outcome of our American architecture will be the emanation of what is going on inside of us at present, the character and quality of our thoughts and our observations, and above all, our reflections. If I were to forecast the outcome of American architecture I should search for it by the study of my own generation; not by studying the architecture of the past. We are in a vast ferment at present, and like most of them, the top of the liquor is covered with scum, but the real process is down below; and it is from this gradual clarifying of the fermentation of thought that the style will result, but the impulse must come first. Therefore, I think that to arrive at the style it is a great deal more important that we should be good observers and good reflectors rather than good draughtsmen.

[John Root argued that modern architecture could find inspiration in historical sources.]

With reference to Mr. Root's point, from such use there will gradually result a clinging to certain forms. It must come to everyone who has closely thought of the subject, that the use of historical motive, which once had a special significance, now seems rather thin and hollow when used in our designs.

The Inland Architect and News Record 9 (March 1887): 26. (Note: *The Inland Architect and News Record* was *The Inland Architect and Builder,* vols. 1–8.)

6
What is the Just Subordination, in Architectural Design, of Details to Mass? (1887)

Sullivan participated in and summarized the April 1887 symposium at the Illinois State Association of Architects' regular monthly meeting. Often abstract when he spoke, approaching a subject by analogy, he nevertheless outlined on this occasion some specific considerations for integrating the details with the massing of buildings. In his impromptu summary, on the other hand, he moved to a more philosophical plane, asserting that design inspiration could only come from the "contemplation of nature and humanity."

It is frequently difficult to understand that there may be two sides to a subject. It is proportionately difficult to imagine that

there may be more than two, the number, indeed, mounting
into the thousands. Therefore, while still in that placid and yielding state of mind, superinduced by distant and general considerations, I admit, once for all, that facets, without number, may
be cut upon the rough gem which is presented as the subject of
this symposium; and I further admit that each facet will reflect
its share of light. I still further admit that the gem, as a whole,
may be cut to suit the cutter; and taking advantage of this
concession, broadly accorded to all, I shall proceed to fashion
the stone after my own predilections, even as though it were the
very jewel after which I longed. To approach a step nearer: If
the question is a categorical one, demanding a similar reply, I
can only answer, I do not know. For who shall say what is possible and what is impossible? Who shall fathom the infinite
depths of creative art? Who drink up the sea, and say "all is now
dry land?" I cannot do these things; I do not believe anyone can,
or will ever be able. Therefore, I believe that in this regard the
question is an open one, and will forever remain an open one.
Assuming next that the question is not categorical, but rather
general and optimistic, I may consider its scope limited within
the confines of what has been done, what is for the moment
uppermost in recollection, with also an underlying curiosity with
regard to what may be done. This naturally makes prominent
considerations of climate, locality and temperament: climate,
which is the arbiter of material things; locality, with its accidental variations, superadded to those of the seasons, and both cre-
ators of temperament, which is in turn the creator and the arbiter of art. All of which makes possible as a general and qualified
answer: "That depends." Storms and frost would tend to influence a softening away of detail into the general mass; localities,
more or less favorable, would intensify or relax this influence,
while temperament would exert its just or morbid all-controlling
sway of sentiment. Similarly, countries of sunshine and flowers,
or the valleys, the mountains, the seacoast, the far-reaching
plains, the preponderance of heat or cold, the lakes, rivers, bleak
and fertile regions, regions of snow and ice, or sultry south
winds, would each according to its rhythmic nature, simple or
qualified, awaken corresponding sympathies within the heart,
which, if left untrammeled by ill-fitting theories, would sponta-

neously evolve a coordination of mass and detail, so normal, so indigenous, that it would instinctively be recognized as literally and poetically just.

Hence, this section may be closed with the broad sentiment that all is free and open, provided the general trend is in the direction of indigenous and sincere results; that when we become justly sympathetic, ward off extraneous and irrelevant influences, and make an earnest effort to reach real and intense results, we shall probably some day find a local answer to the question—an answer which none can gainsay. As for me, I do not yet know what that answer is to be, though I believe I share with others a premonition of its nature.

Finally, assuming that the question is local, and specific in its import, and calls for merely an individual expression of opinion as to what is today and here in Chicago the just subordination of details to mass, I willingly make such an explanation as I may.

Candidly, I do not especially believe in subordination of detail in so far as the word "subordination" conveys an idea of caste or rank, with the involved suggestion of a greater force suppressing a lesser; but I do believe in the differentiation of detail from mass (the idea of subordination occurring incidentally and as of no controlling import), because this word symbolizes to my mind an idea which is very congenial to it, namely, that of an expansive and rhythmic growth, in a building, of a single, germinal impulse or idea, which shall permeate the mass and its every detail with the same spirit, to such an extent, indeed, that it would be as difficult to determine (not matter of arithmetical ratio, but rather as a factor complex impression on the beholder) which is the tant, which in fact subordinates, detail or mass, as difficult to say of a tree, in its general impression upon us, "which is more to us, the leaves or the tree?"—a question which I believe has never arisen. For I do not know that it has occurred to anyone to ask what is the just subordination of leaves to mass in a tree? What are the just ratios of leaves, branches and trunk? Should the leaves be large, and hide the branches, as in the horse chestnut, or should they be frivolous and dainty things, coquettishly exposing the branches? Should the trunk prevail, as in the proud and mournful southern pine, or should the trunk be short and sturdy, as the oak, with powerful gnarled and spreading branches, bared and grim before the tempest? It would be interesting if someone would kindly invent a precise formula for the growth of trees, so that we might forthwith declare any tree which grew at variance with the dictum to be altogether vulgar and devoid of savoir faire. For my part, I find their thousand ways all charming, and fruitful in suggestion. I graciously permit them to grow as they will, and look on with boundless admiration. For I know that they are simply trees; that they have no occasion to be ill at ease, or covert, or dyspeptic with introspection; therefore I trust them and regard them abidingly with love and veneration.

It may be said that I am at fault in comparing animate with inanimate things; but this is the very heart of a mysterious subject; for I insist strenuously, that a building should live with intense, if quiescent, life, because it is sprung from the life of its architect. On no other basis are results of permanent value to be attained.

The more I ponder the title-question, the more I am at a loss for a precise answer; the possibilities, even within the limitations of climate, are so manifold, and so native. But for the moment it suits me to favor a very simple outline, particularly at the roof, which is the part most vulnerable to the elements.

Within this simple outline, then, I prefer such subdivision of the masses into detail as is strictly called for by the utilitarian requirements of the building; and that they should comport with its size, location and purpose. That the materials of construction should largely determine the special form of details, and above all, that there shall effuse from the completed structure a single sentiment which shall be the spiritual result of a prior and perfect understanding and assimilation of all the data.

In summing up the results of this symposium, I am at once impressed with the independence and the courtesy of my co-laborers, as well as with the fact that their comments bear out my preliminary statement that each facet cut upon this gem would reflect its share of meaning and suggestion.

Mr. Pierce's statement, that a building with a soul is a work of architecture, and Mr. Cleveland's* emphasis of the fact that a building tells a wordless story, are peculiarly agreeable to me, for they are statements which carry sincerity of purpose within the words.

I substantially agree with all that these gentlemen have said; though I gather that Mr. Pierce attaches prime importance to mechanical and abstract explanations such as are implied by the words, radiation, repetition, unity in variety, etc. His right to this point of view I do not question, yet I cannot accept it, for myself, as a finality. His "masculine" and "feminine" simile, however, seems to me far-reaching in its implied analogies; recalling even the exquisite "correspondences" of Swedenborg.**

Mr. Cleveland is upon catholic and humane ground when he calls for a recognition of the claims to poetic richness of the solemn and fateful work of the Druids—as indeed of the charms of story hid within the silent stones of many ages. With him I turn back thoughtfully to read the mystic and impressive volume of the past; leaving it as he does, with the heartfelt wish that we in turn may tell our story as they of old told theirs, in a language of simple and majestic fervor.

The subject of our symposium seems all bound up with general and special considerations of style—its causes and manifestations—involving naturally enough a sentiment of solicitude regarding our future development in architectural art.

It is for this reason that I wish to add a work of my own, by way of conclusion, to forcibly emphasize that which I believe seems to us three to be the inherent suggestiveness of the theme.

This conclusion I shall mold under much heavier pressure of intensity than was given to the introduction, to wit:

I value spiritual results only. I say spiritual results precede all

*Sullivan refers here to two symposium participants: architects L. D. Cleveland and O. J. Pierce.

**This is the first public indication that Sullivan knew the work of Emanuel Swedenborg, the eighteenth-century Swedish mystic, philosopher, and scientist, who theorized that the "correspondences" of wisdom and love, reason and emotion, and masculine and feminine helped bridge the gap between the universe's physical and spiritual spheres, which were part of a transcendent whole. See Narciso Menocal, *Architecture as Nature: The Transcendentalist Idea of Louis Sullivan* (Madison: University of Wisconsin Press, 1981), 24–34.

other results, and indicate them. I can see no efficient way of handling this subject on any other than a spiritual or psychic basis.

I say present theories of art are vanity. I say all past and future theories of art were and will be vanity. That the only substantial facts which remain after all the rubbish, dust and scientific-analytic-aesthetic cobwebs are brushed away are these facts, which each man may take to himself, namely: That I am; that I am immersed in nature here with my fellow men; that we are all striving after something which we do not now possess; that there is an inscrutable power permeating all, and the cause of all.

And I say that all we see and feel and know, without and within us, is one mighty poem of striving, one vast and subtle tragedy. That to remain unperturbed and serene within this turbulent and drifting flow of hope and sorrow, light and darkness, is the uttermost position and fact attainable to the soul, the only permanent link between the finite and infinite.

On this rock I would stand. And it is because I would stand here, that I say I value spiritual results only. It is for this reason that I say all mechanical theories of art are vanity, and that the best of rules are but as flowers planted over the graves of prodigious impulses which splendidly lived their lives, and passed away with the individual men who possessed these impulses. This is why I say that it is within the souls of individual men that art reaches culminations. This is why I say that each man is a law unto himself; and that he is a great or a little law in so far as he is a great or a little soul.

This is why I say that desire is the deepest of human emotions, and that prudence is its correlative; that it is the precursor, the creator, the arbiter of all the others. That great desire and great prudence must precede great results.

This is why I say that contemplation of nature and humanity is the only source of inspiration; this is why I say that without inspiration there can be no such thing as a just coordination of mass and details. That, as there may be countless inspirations profoundly vital, so, also, there may be countless coordinations of mass and details unspeakably just. That material results are to be measured by their contained inspiration; that these results will phase as the inspiration phases.

I say that the whole inquiry as to the just subordination of details to mass, in so far as it contains the implication of a fixed rule, is simply a pedagogic scarecrow.

Nor does this signify a plea for lawlessness. On the contrary, inspiration, such as I have indicated, has too much of pathos within it, too much of the calm of nature's mysterious decadence, to permit the forgetfulness, for more than a passing moment, of this deep-down conviction, that an idea lives according solely as by its power and prudence it compromises with death.

If cultivated mediocrity is what is wanted, the title-question can be answered readily and specifically for each historic style. If the culture of action is demanded, then indeed we have a task before us to find an answer, which shall at best be painfully and laboriously worked out. For every problem is for us, as yet, unsolved; we are merely as pioneers in a primeval forest. Yet while our results can be but relative, they may be the fruit of great desires, and hence, may speak of greatness.

Therefore I say that each one must perforce answer the question for himself, and that his answer will be profound or superficial according to the reach of his inspiration, and the gentleness and power of his sympathy; and that this answer can be found, in tangible form, only in his works; for it is here that he records his life, and it is by his works, and not his words, that he shall be judged; for here he can hide nothing—standing to the spiritual as one naked.

Therefore, again I say, I value spiritual results only, and regard all else as vanity.

It is needless, I trust, for me to say my feet are upon the ground; though Mr. Pierce seems to hold the placing [*sic*] this discussion upon a psychic basis as a species of ballooning. Here I differ with him radically, for I regard spiritual or psychic facts as the only permanent and reliable facts—the only solid ground. And I believe that until we shall walk securely upon this ground we can have but little force or directness or purpose, but little insight, but little fervor, but little faith in material results.

The Inland Architect and News Record 9 (April 1887): 52–54.

An Architects' Code of Ethics

At the November 1887 annual convention of the Western
Association of Architects, chairman Louis Sullivan read the
report of the Committee on a Standard of Professional Requirement (document 7), which had been charged to prepare guidelines for admission to the organization. The
committee's deliberations during the previous year led it to
propose that a second or replacement committee be
formed to write a code of ethics, feeling that the Association must set ethical standards for itself before attempting
to judge the qualifications of applicants. As chairman of
the new Committee on a Code of Ethics, Sullivan gave his
informal report (document 8) at the fifth annual convention in November 1888.

7
Report of the Committee on a Standard of
Professional Requirement (1887)

Gentlemen,—The difficulties which arise in connection with this
subject are manifold and perplexing. If the standard of admission
to membership be fixed with sole regard to what is supposedly
an ideal, the numerical growth of the Association would be seriously checked, and its usefulness in many ways impaired. For
it is evident that such a policy would preclude the admission of
those of average capacity, and of the many bright ones who are
contending against the difficulties which beset a beginner.

On the other hand, if the standard be fixed so low as to make
possible the admission of all, it is evident that the standard of
the Association would degenerate, and through the prevalence
of a low tone its influence for good would cease, and its career
be short-lived.

It is assumed by your Committee that the policy of the Association in this regard should be broad and democratic. That it
should not set up factitious barriers against those who ask for
admission; that the Association wishes to count among its mem-

bers every thoughtful, earnest, ambitious man in the profession; that it desires its strength and stability to be derived from the standing and capacity of the average man; that it welcomes the fervor of youth; that it cherishes the honorable record of old age; that, above all, it shall not place its standard for admission higher than it is itself prepared to exemplify.

It is assumed as a paramount consideration that the applicant's record, be it short or long, should prove honorable; second, that he evidence fair artistic, constructive, or executive skill; third, that his admission shall necessitate an expressed pledge upon his part to sustain by individual effort a sound standard of professional bearing

We believe, moreover, that this Association, prior to raising in any way the standard for admission to membership, should itself declare the standard which it is willing should govern its own course; that in short, we believe the time is now ripe for the promulgation of a code of ethics which shall define a desirable and practicable relationship of the members of this Association to each other, and to the incorporate body: a code which, in a word, shall indicate the degree and nature of the self-respect and good faith of this Association.

Each year we meet in conference for three days; but it is during all the days of the year that we each, individually, should labor to raise, a little at a time, the standard of attainment in our profession. During the three days of the convention we compare notes, we reach joint conclusions, we formulate them—we crystallize the experience of the year past. Therefore the Association would seem to stand, and should stand before the world, as a symbol and index of the architectural profession in the West—a sign by which it may be known and judged.

Although we do not understand this consideration distinctly to lie within the province of your Committee, yet it seems so close upon the border, that we feel justified in earnestly recommending to the Association that a committee be appointed to prepare such a code, and that its report be considered at the Convention of 1888. That such a committee consist of three members from each State who shall constitute sub-committees each with its own chairman; that the sub-committees shall report to the chairman of the general committee on the 1st of April,

1888; that the general chairman shall forthwith collate these reports, and report the results to the sub-committees on the 1st of August; and that the consensus of their revisions, as formulated by the chairman of the general committee, shall constitute the report of the Committee to this Association.

By such means, after a year of careful investigation and deliberate thought, the full sense of this Association may be obtained—and expressed in a code of ethics.

To resume the prime consideration—this Committee recommends the following form, for application-blanks, to be addressed through the Secretary to the Board of Directors.

——, 188——

To the Board of Directors, W. A. A.: —

My full name is ——

My business address is ——

The name of my firm is ——

I have practised the profession of architecture for —— years.

The accompanying photographs (unmounted), numbered, respectively, 1, 2, and 3, show completed buildings erected from my plans and under my supervision.

No. 1 is a [here give general description of building, giving also name and address of owner and contractors.]

No. 2, do.

No. 3, do.

The accompanying letters, numbered 1, 2, and 3, are from the respective owners of the above buildings, and endorse my character and proficiency.

We, members of the W. A. A. hereby endorse Mr. ——
——'s application for membership. We know him personally; we believe him to be worthy of membership.

These applications are to be considered confidential by the Board of Directors, who shall meet on the first Monday in August of each year for the purpose of considering applications, after which date no application will be received.

The Board of Directors shall pass upon the application, rejecting such as seem to them unfit, and as soon thereafter as practicable, but not later than the 1st of September, shall cause to be printed and mailed to each member of the Association a list, containing the names and addresses of the provisionally-accepted applicants, together with the names and addresses of their lay and professional endorsers.

Opposite the names of each applicant shall be printed the words "yes" and "no," and each member shall vote by striking out the word alternative to his decision.

This list shall then be signed by the voter and shall be mailed to the chairman of the Board of Directors through the Secretary of the Association, who, at the ensuing Convention, shall announce the election of all such who shall not have received more than five negatives.

Should vigorous protest be made by any member at the time of voting, it shall be the duty of the Board of Directors to make thorough investigation, and their decision shall be final as to the protest. The Board of Directors shall advise methods for maintaining the privacy of such letter-ballot.

The following blank form is recommended as embodying the above:

Office of Secretary W. A. A., ———— ———, 1887.

Dear Sir,—Please vote by striking out the alternative word under the heading "vote," and return this sheet to me at your earliest convenience.

....

Vote.   Applicant.   Lay Endorsers.   Endorsing Members.

....

Name. Address. Name. Occu. Address. Name. Address.

....

No.   Yes.

....

No.   Yes.

....

———, *Secretary W. A. A.*

By order Board of Directors.

———, *Chairman.*

[The report was accepted.]

The American Architect and Building News 22 (November 26, 1887): 252–53.

8
Remarks on an Architects' Code of Ethics (1888)

Mr. President, of this committee of which I am the general chairman, there are forty-eight members, fourteen members of this state. The scheme laid out was that the members from the different states, of which it was composed, would form sub-committees, each with a chairman, and these were to report to the general chairman for revision, who was to return it to them for their further consideration. I have allowed things to take their natural course, and have heard nothing from them, and the sub-committees have also allowed things to take their natural course and have heard but little from me. When I perceived how matters were drifting, I thought personally to take matters in hand, but on further consideration I thought best not to do it. I still think the scheme a good one, and I certainly believe a code of ethics should be adopted. I have thought of what it should be in a general way, that it should cover the several specialties of professional practice. In the first place, it should relate to the artistic side of the practice, and, in the next place, it should point out the architect's place as a business man. It should state when one architect is having business relations with a client, that that shall be a sufficient warning that interference on the part of an-other architect is non-professional and not allowable. Such a code, I think, should be reported as would prevent one member to war against another, and stimulate all to honorable profes-sional action. Fourth, and the most important of all, it should distinctly point out the relation of the architect to the public. I think it should very distinctly outline the architect's course of action toward his client. The great difficulty, and the complica-tion of the whole matter in getting at some action by this com-mittee, has been, in my opinion, the cumbersomness of the com-mittee. I think it should be cut down in numbers. By experience I have found that the larger the committee, the smaller the amount of work done. "What is everybody's business is no-body's business." A few men naturally feel a pride in what they are selected to do, and work for the best results, realizing that something is expected of them. This question also comes up in view of the proposed consolidation of the American Institute of Architects and the Western Association of Architects, and should we by advocating the adoption and promulgation of such a code by [*sic*] taking the initiative in a step which will meet the approval of all reputable architects—an initiative we can, as an association, take pride in—a good deal will be done in that direction, and certainly no harm can be done. I think more and more of the worth of such a code—more than I did one year ago, and I am in favor of it, and hope to see its realization in a year from now.

The Inland Architect and News Record 12 (November 1888): 64.

9
The Decoration of McVicker's Theatre,
Chicago (1888)

Although signed by both partners, this letter to the editor of the *American Architect* dated February 1, 1888, was written by Sullivan, who was responsible for the ornamental and decorative features of the McVicker Theatre remodeling in 1885. Joseph Twyman, a well-known lecturer and interior decorator, had worked on the job, later claiming in print a much larger share of responsibility than Adler and Sullivan felt was warranted. In addition to rebutting Twyman, this letter provides important insights into Sullivan's design method and objectives. It is, in fact, one of his clearest pronouncements on the subject of architectural ornament.

We are led to reply to Mr. Twyman's note in your issue of January 28, solely for these reasons: First, to relieve Mr. Blackall from the embarrassment of an apparently false position; second, to protect ourselves and our profession. For we feel that such irresponsible statements, allowed to go unanswered, cannot be otherwise than detrimental generally to those of us with whom architecture is a loved and cherished art.*

We beg, therefore, to say, that Mr. Blackall is thoroughly right in his statement that the decorative work in McVicker's Theatre, Chicago, was executed from our designs; and Mr. Twyman is thoroughly in error when he claims credit for the same. In Mr. Twyman's statement, however, there is a faint suggestion of truth which will be clearly understood, we think, when it is made known how Mr. Twyman, who, at the time of the remodelling of McVicker's Theatre, was a salesman in charge of the retail wall-paper and interior-decorations department of the extensive wall-paper house of John J. McGrath, Chicago, plays upon the meaning of the word decoration.

The architectural treatment of the interior of McVicker's Theatre is based upon a single consistent scheme or plan which is differentiated into form, color and illumination. The transitions and interblendings are subtle; and we deem it evident to the critical observer that the conception is identical throughout form, color and illumination.

The decorations, as we understand the term, take their origin in certain changes of form initiated in the constructive subdivisions of the design. This tendency toward change gathers in-

---

*A prolonged imbroglio began when Boston architect Clarence H. Blackall concluded his review of McVicker's Theatre in "Notes of Travel," *The American Architect and Building News* 22 (December 24, 1887): 299–300, by saying that "all the work, including the decoration, was designed by Adler & Sullivan." Joseph Twyman objected in a letter to the editor of the journal (23 [January 28, 1888]: 47): "the decoration of McVicker's theatre . . . was executed under my charge and dictation and was my own conception without control of architect or owner." Adler & Sullivan's February 1 response, as printed here and in the *American Architect's* issue of the 11th, prompted an elaborate rejoinder from Twyman on the 25th. When it was published in part on March 10, the editors added: "Our correspondent's letter, if all put in type, would fill nearly three pages of this journal, but we hope he will not accuse us of unfair use of the editorial pencil, since we allow him the same number of lines occupied by the statements he refutes. As we believe this matter is of vastly more interest to the disputants than to the rest of our readers and as the statements are clearly irreconcilable, we must ask them to leave the matter an open question (*The American Architect and Building News* 23 [March 10, 1888]: 118). Apparently the disputants did just that.

creased definiteness as it passes through certain geometrical ramifications, and, taking on swiftly but without abruptness an organic semblance, culminates finally in intricate and involved fol-
liation and efflorescence. Within this work, and incidental
thereto, are placed the bulbs of the incandescent system of illumination. This method of treatment applies to the proscenium
with its large sounding-board and twelve boxes: the whole con-
verging toward the stage-opening and elaborately framing the
same. It applies also to the main entrance vestibules. For this
part of the work we not only made the designs, but we furnished
carefully worked-out full-size details, even for the foliated work,
which were most faithfully and without the slightest deviation
carried into execution by James Legge, the carver, with whom
the contract for the same was placed. Inasmuch as this work,
executed in plaster, was completed, stored and covered by an
insurance policy prior to our entertaining the idea of asking
sketches and bids for color decoration from decorative concerns,
it is manifest that neither Mr. Twyman's conception nor handi-
work nor supervision entered into this part of our operations.

Considerations of economy necessitated that the remainder of
the auditorium and its appendages should be treated very simply, we, therefore, at the time the general contracts were let, did
no more as regards appearances, in addition to the purely utilitarian and acoustic handling, than to definitely determine the
number and approximately the location of the electric-light
bulbs and the inlets for the supply of fresh air for the fans.

When the time approached that the contract for color decoration should be considered, we began anxiously and carefully to
think of the coloration, for it became distressingly evident that
the delicate rhythms and modulations of the plaster ornamentation, now in place, would be deprived of their sequence, significance and context by an inadequate or bizarre scheme of applied
color. Gradually then arose the conviction that the structural, the
geometrical and the foliated parts could not be given relative
color values which should differ essentially from their relative
solid values, lest, through false accentuation the equilibrium and
repose of the single simple idea or impulse underlying the conception be disturbed, and thwarted of its full expression. From
this sense of balance followed logically the belief that these parts

should be in close and delicate self-tones; and, finally, the determination that the principle of gradual and smooth change carried out in the design should also be the dominant idea in coloring. Upon reaching this decision, or rather, as it would seem, reverting to the original conception of the whole, we made known our idea and wishes to Mr. Twyman and to other decorators, and asked them for sketches covering the unfinished parts above referred to, and for schemes and prices for the color-work of the whole. Mr. Twyman was the only one of these who submitted a proposal in accordance with our suggestion (the choice of color as between many desirable and befitting ones was left open). His choice of color and treatment was in the main sympathetic with our architectural treatment, and to him, or, rather to his principal, John J. McGrath, the contract was awarded. Here, then, we begin to discern the first awaking of Mr. Twyman's conception. Let us progress a step nearer to it.

Mr. Twyman proposed to use for the wall-covering a wall-paper which we had designed, full-size, for Mr. McGrath some two years previously. The pattern of this paper required six or seven blocks twenty inches square for its development, and as it had the characteristic movement we were glad to use it in this house. Mr. Twyman proposed to heavily flock the pattern, and to add a raised rosette to the centre of the flower. This suggestion was accepted. To use this paper was Mr. Twyman's own thought: we had utterly forgotten its existence.

There now remains for examination only the flat part of the main ceiling, the ceiling under the gallery and under the balcony, and the *foyers* and retiring-rooms, which are small. For these were required flat treatment in paper, bits of *papier-maché* foliated work at the electric-bulbs, and the limited amount of stencilling called for by Mr. Twyman's sketches. In actual execution, these forms seem to us, as they must to any skillful and discerning eye, to possess that peculiar suggestion of caricature that the ear notes in the speech of a foreigner uttering our native language neither grammatically, musically, nor with deft and rhythmic enunciation. The plastic forms here are Mr. Legge's execution of an already beheaded conception, which, in that condition, is assuredly the exclusive property of Mr. Twyman. The stencil patterns were carried out full-size by the foreman on the work. The great pressure and rush of the whole undertaking toward completion, unfortunately made it impossible for us to give the time to a revision of these designs.

As to Mr. Twyman's statement, "The work was executed under my charge and dictation, and was my own conception without control of architect or owner," this is manifestly absurd; for the work was done under our regular form of contract. This contract was between John J. McGrath and J. H. McVicker as principals, and contained the customary stringent clauses regarding the supervision and rejection of work by the architects, payment upon acceptance and certificate, etc. These powers were used. Mr Twyman represented his principal at the building in the capacity of overseer or superintendent, or what-not, or as what is known in the trade parlance of these houses as their "artist."

This is a correct statement of the case. How, then, shall we understand the full scope and content of Mr. Twyman's connection with this work otherwise than by applying to the language of his note his evident "conception" of the meanings of English words.

The American Architect and Building News 23 (February 11, 1888): 70–71.

IO
Style (1888)

Sullivan delivered this paper on April 9, 1888 to the Chicago Architectural Sketch Club, an organization of mostly younger practitioners. The Club's exhibitions, competitions, and lecture programs made it a substantial force for nonhistoricist thinking in the decades flanking the turn of the twentieth century. Sullivan was never a member, but he served regularly during the 1880s on juries and as a speaker, becoming something of a philosophical guiding light as his reputation grew. In this talk, which he revised for publication, he declared style to be the "response of the organism" to its environment, "the explicit reality of your

own inner life and your own outward surroundings." At a
time when most architects solved design problems by
adapting a style or a series of historic expressions to contemporary situations, Sullivan insisted that style was the
essence of an individual person or thing, conditioned by
the physical and social milieu. By proclaiming the architect
a mediator between the particular and the general (between the individual and society), Sullivan was perhaps the
first American in his field to interpret design as a social
force and cultural expression.

It would appear to be a law of artistic growth, that the mind, in
its effort toward expression, concentrates first upon matters of
technical detail, next upon certain abstractions or theories—for
the greater part mechanical, and quite plausible as far as they
go—and at last upon a gradual relinquishment of these, involving a slow and beautiful blending of all the faculties with the
more subtile manifestations of emotion. In other words, such
growth evidences at the beginning of its rhythm the objective,
and toward maturity, the subjective view.

This order of development, all things considered, is probably
the one the most nearly consistent with the tendency of normal
faculties. By normal faculties I mean those of average strength
and keenness, free from any serious hereditary warp, or morbid
bias, and subjected to the ordinary conditions of education.

I shall not in this connection directly consider the law of
growth as manifested in the works of the few great masters, and
which differs profoundly from the above; for their art in all its
potentiality is born with them, and prophesies in earliest childhood the destiny of its great consummation.

But rather, I shall proceed from this basis: that the larger
number of the art works of all ages are products of a cultivated
mediocrity—mediocrity of the sort that therein technical dexterity aspires to compensate us in a measure for the absence of a
motive impulse; cleverness and an oblique mentality usurp the
place of an absent psychic life; wherein words are accepted in
the stead of things, and things in the stead of meanings—in
brief, that phase of culture which may be called the comedy of
art.

To the master mind indeed, imbued with the elemental significance of nature's moods, humbled before the future and the past, keenly aware of the present, art and its outworkings are largely tragic.

Between these extremes there lies a quasi-transitional zone, wherein the concomitant elements that constitute the artistic nature are so varied in their relative energy and fruitfulness, wherein the growth of the faculties proceeds, not as a slow consistent and definite expansion of a pronounced individuality, but rather by a succession and gathering together of substitutious [*sic*] amendments and accidentals, that, to the earnest student uncertain as yet of his status, and unwilling to make the larger sacrifices, there lies within this field the greatest harvest of attainment that can come to his hand.

And such considerations shape this fundamental difference between the great and the little master—that the latter acquires by means of painstaking and industrious re-hypothecation, while the former is driven on to his destination by forces superior to his yea or nay.

While it is true that the little master can never become the great one, yet is his domain large, and it includes all that ingenuity, talent, fine sensibilities and a considerable genius can accomplish.

To the domain of the little master let us therefore direct our attention. As to the great master, no hand may lighten his burden, no power shall make for him the crooked straight, and the rough places plane.

That which we call style, or rather, the word style itself, is as dubious in meaning as is any word in common use. The fact that a word is, and has been for generations, in common use, signifies that it has gathered to itself the multiple experiences of the race, and has become thereby thoroughly vitalized. Now note that the greater number of such experiences are largely independent of words, and the more subtile ones almost absolutely so, and this will suffice to indicate how true it is that one's capacity to interpret the meaning of a word, to perceive its obscure but real significance, is dependent upon the richness of his life experience within the domain of feeling that the word has come to symbolize.

If this is true of a word, how peculiarly true is it of a work of art. How much more essential is it, in turning from the word, style, to contemplate the thing, style, that our experiences be real, our judgment sober, our sympathy humane. And, most of all, how urgent is it, when we seek the meaning, style, in art, in nature, and in the soul, that every faculty be keyed to most delicate and exquisite tension, and our concentration be absolute as in a dream.

Style, in its essence, and amid all its spontaneous manifestations, is as unsearchable as is any other attribute of life. Analysis, however keen, can at best but discourse of its grosser material envelopings, or formulate abstractions concerning its rhythms. Where reasoning fails, however, intuition goes blithely on, and finds the living quality in things common and near to the hand.

Have you thought much on common and simple things? Has it occurred to you how complex, how beautiful and mysterious they really are? Take, as an instance, a cow eating the grass of the field. Where other than in these natural doings may you behold perfectly spontaneous and unequivocal adjustment of means to end? At first glance how commonplace: to the thoughtful view how impressive and awakening an exampler [*sic*] of unattainable style! Who shall portray that simple scene and infuse his work with the poetry which the soul sweetly and perfectly attuned to nature's life perceives therein? Who shall apprehend the soul of the cow and of the grass, who shall, with *naïve* sincerity, express the explicit circumstance that the cow eats the grass?

We are prone to heed too little those things that are near us; we strain our eyes with looking afar off; we are meanwhile unaware that the grass, the rocks, the trees and running waters— that nature's palpitating self, indeed, is at our very feet. Through vanity of intellect we ignore that which is common; and by the same token we are lost to the sense that a poetic infinity resides in these, the commonest of things. No pathos can exceed their pathos, no inspiration can surpass their inspiration; there is not tenderness, not power, not alluring and impelling greatness which is not in them.

Therefore, I counsel you, if you would seek to acquire a style that shall be individual to you, banish from your thought the word style; note closely and keenly the thing style, wherever found; and open your hearts to the essence style at all times and in all places. This is the germ.

The formative process is tedious and burdensome, clear and obscure, joyful and desponding, discouraging and bewildering to the last degree.

To be patient, observing, reflective, industrious and sincere; to possess that fortitude which constrains one to perseverance in spite of adversity, wounded pride, revulsion and disgust, and the secret consciousness that each successive endeavor is but a little less fatuous than its predecessor; to carefully train and nurture the eye, the ear, the hand, the heart, the soul; to work and watch and wait for a long time; these are part of the price which one must pay for a sound style, and the price mounts ever with the aspiration.

Thus do the faculties unfold with time, and the most precious one, that of self-criticism, comes in due season. Lastly comes the saddest of all—the power clearly to discern one's own limitations; for this inevitable warning surely indicates the end of growth, and fixes the permanent status.

The word soul is a symbol or arbitrary sign which stands for the inscrutable impelling force that determinates an organism and its life; it is that mysterious essence which we call our identity; it is that in us which is the most simple though seemingly the most complex; it is that which is born with us and which can undergo no fundamental change. Disregarding the perplexities and dogmas which, by natural inference, may be associated with this symbol, we must not fail or fear, in our search for an intimate understanding of the essence of style, to note that this elemental and abiding quality of identity or soul is inherent in all things whatsoever. Thus: we see the pine-tree—we notice its general shape, we examine its tapering trunk, its mode of branching, its hold upon the soil or the rocks, its branches, branchlets, bark, leaves, flowers, cones, seeds, inner bark, fiber of wood, sap; we reflect that these have all of them something quite in common, and this something impresses us as quality segregating this tree from other trees and other things. To communicate the sum and resultant of these impressions in speech we invent or make use of the word pine, which word expresses

a tacit recognition of the peculiar nature or identity of this kind
of tree, and, in a general way, as single words go, sums up its
style. Pushing our investigation further, we discern that there are
several kinds of pine-trees, each with a peculiar and well-defined
nature; and it is this collateral definition which establishes for us
a clearer perception of the identity of each. Ever unsatisfied, we
become aware that one pine-tree is not precisely like another of
the same kind; we conceive that it possesses a subtile and permanent charm of personality. Our sentiment is touched; we are
drawing near to nature's heart. We love this tree. We watch by
it through all its experiences. We are with it by night and by
day. We see it respond to the warm caresses of the spring-time
sun, and observe with a thrill how it sparkles and drips amid the
glories of an April shower. It sways so gently in the passing
breeze; it tosses and protests in the grasp of the furious storm.
Among its brethren, in the summer forest, it stands so calm, so
content; it freely gives its odor to the still air. Within the solitude of winter's sleep it also sleeps, and we too sleep its sleep in
sympathy; erect and somber it stands, so motionless under its
mantle of snow, so unspeakably calm, so content, so wild. Some
day the storm snaps its life. The end is come. Slowly and surely
time works decay, and that which was a pine-tree, though vanished, has left its individual trace upon us, never to depart.
Through all these changes it was a pine-tree, ever a pine-tree;
they but evidenced its inner nature. Such was its identity, such
was its little history, of such was its exquisite style.

This is true of a pine-tree. Is it not also essentially true of an
oak-tree, of a willow, of a rainstorm, of a river, of a man?

If it is true, as it would appear, that the style of a pine-tree,
or any other tree, is the resultant of its identity and its surroundings, is it not equally and especially true that the style of an artist
is in its essence and form the resultant of his identity and his
experiences?

The style is ever thus the response of the organism to the
surroundings. How simple are the surroundings and experiences
of a tree. How multiple are the surroundings of a man. When
his eyes are opened to them, how complex become his experiences.

How does the man respond to the gentle procreant influence
of springtime? As the pine-tree, as the oak, as the lark? Which-

ever it be, of such is his style. Is he stirred by the gentle and impalpable breezes that come from nowhere and are gone? Surely the pine-tree greets with delicate tremor every slightest impulse of the air. How much more is the man than a tree? how much less?

In reality the first essential condition toward a style is to be born with a subtile identity, the rest goes of itself; for one should bear in mind, and take much comfort in the fact, that there exists, in addition to himself, a very considerable universe.

It is the function of intuition, the eye of identity, the soul, to discern the identity of truth inherent in all things. It is the function of sympathy, the soul of love, to cause one's own identity to blend for the time being with the identity or inner nature of other things. It would be well, therefore, if there were choice in these matters, to be born possessed of the germs of intuition and sympathy; many are.

Many have within them somewhat of the native simplicity of the forest tree. There are not very many, and their portion is not always very great. Yet to him who has this simplicity of soul I say take hope, for to him shall be given. From him who has not this tiny impulse of faith in himself and of confidence in nature, I say from such an one shall be taken even that which he has; for all else that he may acquire is as vanity. Herein lies the difference between the real and the spurious artist; and of such is the obscure origin of art and of style.

In examining a work, for purposes of analysis and criticism, bear ever [sic] mind that no amount of dexterity, of learning, of sophistication, of trickery, can successfully conceal the absence, in its author, of sincerity. Learn, also, not only to look at a work, but into it; especially learn not only to look at nature but into it; emphatically strive to look into men. When you have learned to do these things you will live; for it is then that you will see in an art work the identity and spiritual nature of the man who produced it. He cannot escape; nor can you in turn escape. Think not that you may for long conceal your littleness or your largeness behind ink and paper, behind pigments, behind brick and mortar, behind marble, behind anything; for to the relentless eye, searching out identities, the work melts away and the man stands forth; and so it should be.

Did you ever stop to consider that when one produces a work

he plainly stamps upon it the legend: This is the work of a fool—of a trickster—of a cynic—of a vacillating and unstable spirit—of a vain and frivolous presumption—of a good heart and weak head—of a conscientious and upright man—of one who loves his fellow men—of a tender and exquisite spirit—of a large and serious nature—of a poet born—of a soul that walks with God?

For if a tree speaks to the attentive ear, if a storm speaks, if the waters speak, so then do all things, animate and inanimate, speak, and their speech is the universal language of the soul.

Take heed, then, lest you trifle, for at best we may but trifle; and thus, if you would really seek a style, search for it not altogether in books, not altogether in history, but search for it rather in the explicit reality of your own inner life and your own outward surroundings.

The Inland Architect and News Record 11 (May 1888): 59–60.

An Architects' Protective League

A dramatic increase in the number and complexity of law suits brought against architects nationwide during the 1880s exposed the ambiguity of their legal rights. Sullivan argued (in document 11) at the June 1888 meeting of the Illinois State Association that a national organization was necessary for professional self-protection. At the request of the Illinois body, he immediately prepared a circular letter (document 12) describing the benefits his colleagues might expect from a Protective League. The executive committee sent this letter to every architect in America during the summer. Although work on the League was suspended pending the imminent merger of the Western Association of Architects (of which the Illinois State Association was a branch) with the American Institute of Architects (see document 13), Sullivan's leadership on this and the matter of a code of ethics illustrated his commitment to strengthening the integrity and the independence of his profession.

II
Remarks on the Subject of an Architects' Protective League (1888)

I wish to talk on the subject of a Protective League. When the idea of such an organization came up last fall, it was suggested that all the architects of the country should be united in one organization. It was argued by those favoring the movement, that such an organization should be a working organization, through, perhaps, a central committee, and it was assumed at the same time that the duty of this committee in a large sense, working in the interest of the entire profession, would be, in certain cases where equities were involved and not clear to have the matter transferred from the owner, that the organization should take the matter out of the hands of the individual architect, and carry it as far as may be through the courts, until a final decision was arrived at that would establish a settled principle. It was presumed that weaker members might tire of fighting for their rights, if not in the first courts, in the second, perhaps. It was claimed when the knowledge of such a strong organization became broadcast, when the country became thoroughly aware that the committee would not take up the petty quarrels between architects and owners, but would defend all equities of architects on principle to a finality, there would be less disposition for litigation with the unscrupulous. My own preference would be to see such an organization include the profession of all the associations in the country, rather than to have it confined to the efforts of a local association. Of course such an organization would require money to conduct its prosecutions and defenses, which would be subject to the call of the committee. I wished to introduce the subject, and should like to hear the views of the members upon it.

Mr. Patton*: Mr. President, I have an experience which, it seems to me, might develop into a case that would properly

---

*The other speakers in this exchange were Sullivan's partner Dankmar Adler, architects N. S. Patton, William W. Clay, and Samuel Treat, chair and president of the Illinois State Association.

come before such an organization. It is of a contract for certain work which was practically finished—only a small amount being incomplete. I had not personally examined the work for some little time, as it was done under the supervision of a superintendent. In making a certificate I happened to overlook one matter, and issued it for a larger amount than was due by the stipulations. A short time afterwards a defect in the work began to appear, and when the work was finally done it wasn't a first-class job. The owner thought the contractor should not be paid in full, and fell back on the architects. We assessed the contractor for damages as far as the amount still due him, and told him he should pay the owner a certain amount of money, and the owner that he had a good claim against the contractor. There the matter rests. The question comes up, how much damage has the architect to assess. It seems to me it should be governed by the money held back, and whatever else should be decided by a court of law between the owner and contractor. If it should be found after work has been accepted that unforeseen defects occur by fault of the contractor, and there is not money enough due the contractor to make the damage good, then comes up the question how far the architect can be held for issuing the certificate?

The Chair: It would seem as if in the first case the architect was to blame. Certainly he issued the over-certificate.

Mr. Patton: The point involved is that while some defects might have been discovered there are some that could not. It often happens that they appear afterwards through the fault of the contractor, and the architect ought not to be held responsible in such cases.

Mr. Sullivan: That would not be such a case as would come properly before such an organization. It is one, as I understand it, between the contractor and owner, which the committee would not be called to take cognizance of.

Mr. Adler: As long as an architect has the power to withhold money, he is to a reasonable extent responsible for its expenditure. I have two cases in my mind that happened within the last ten months. In both cases defective work appeared before settlement. In the one case, before the necessary work was done, it happened the contractor was taken sick, and it had to be done by other parties. When all was done, the bills were rendered for it to the contractor, and paid by him. There were two batches. The first was paid at once; the second, he didn't pay promptly, but paid it after a month or so. In the other case, the contractor quit business and had gone to Duluth, and could not be found, and the work was paid for by the architect, which I think was a much easier solution than to submit to a court of law.

Mr. Sullivan: Where the amount of money involved is small it is not so serious a matter, but when the amount gets up into the thousands of dollars the question of an architect's responsibility for defective work does become a very serious question. I have heard of some cases recently that are rather alarming: where the owners found the wall an inch out of line, ordered it taken down and put up again; and another case, where the owners came along and in the piers found bond stones cracked, and said they wouldn't have this, the architect was to give them a perfect building, and it was his business to see that cracks would not occur; that they should be taken out, and perfect stones put in at the expense of thousands of dollars; that they would withhold the money due on commission, and the architect could get it out of the contractor.

Mr. Clay: Had the architect passed upon the work? It seems to me that the contract is between the owner and the builder; but if the architect has passed upon the work there is a decided difference in that case and one where he has not passed upon it.

Mr. Adler: Just take the practical case cited by Mr. Sullivan, which is the experience of an architect well known in this country. Here the foundation was built and the stone covered with earth. There may be from five to a dozen stone cracked without imperiling the building. I do not think the architect will be responsible, after the building is completed and apparently sound, because the owners have gone and excavated around the building and found, say, three cracked dimension stone, and insist that is not the kind of work paid for, and be obliged to replace them because the owners insist upon it.

Mr. Sullivan: I know of three cases today where such a situation of affairs is likely to result. The bigger the building the larger the commission, hence the larger will be the risk to the architect. It is a matter in which the responsibility of the architect should be definitely fixed.

After quite a prolonged further discussion, participated in by Messrs. Clay, Beaumonth, Adler, Sullivan, Patton and others, in which it was held there was a growing tendency to a species of blackmail being levied on architects by a class of owners and, elsewise, in other grave matters pertaining to the equities of honorable architects, there existed a necessity for some such league for mutual protection, Mr. Adler presented the following resolution:

Resolved, That Mr. Sullivan be requested to prepare during the summer months a circular letter to be submitted to the Executive Committee of this association, to be distributed by the committee among the members of the profession throughout the country, and that this be done on or before the first day of August next, and that the discussion of the subject be made the special order of business of this association, which shall take place the last Saturday in September, at which meeting the architects of Chicago and elsewhere that take an interest in the matter shall be invited to participate; that the circular be issued to the architects of Chicago and throughout the country, with the request that such as may take an interest and cannot be present, may send in their written opinions regarding the best method of procedure to meet this exigency in professional practice.

On being put to vote the motion prevailed unanimously.

The Inland Architect and News Record 11 (June 1888): 76.

12
Proposal for an Architects' Protective League (1888)

Dear Sir:—In pursuance of a request from the Illinois State Association of Architects, Mr. L. H. Sullivan, of Chicago, has kindly put in form the substance of a recent discussion upon the advisability of "protective organization." The Executive Committee of the Association take pleasure in fully endorsing the views as herein given, and, in commending them to your consideration, earnestly request such co-operation as you may deem it expedient to give them in the matter as placed before you.

                         S. A. TREAT,
                         WILLIAM W. CLAY,
                         F. BAUMANN,
                         ALFRED SMITH,
                         J. L. SILSBEE,
Chicago, August 1, 1888.   Executive Committee I.S.A.A.

It is a fact, of daily increasing gravity, that the status of the architect, in its aspect of pecuniary responsibility, is vague to a degree which justifies and indeed necessities [sic] a large prudence and forethought of organization for our common defence.

The interests centering in the erection of buildings are now so complex that questions of very delicate nature not unfrequently arise, the adjustment of which is fraught with anxiety and hazard, because of the lack of that guidance which higher court decisions would supply.

It may therefore happen that the architect, through uncertainty, through fear of powerful opposition and the distress of long and expensive litigation, and, above all, shrinking from the thought of malignant and reckless cross-examination in the lower court, waives what he may believe his rights and suffers often an undue and burdensome taxation, which, it is easy to perceive, may in some cases amount practically to confiscation.

The cases here had [sic] in mind are chiefly those arising between client and architect. It may happen that the client believes his claim for damages or rebate to be entirely equitable, yet there is sometimes reason to infer that his belief is considerably strengthened by a feeling of possession and of superior financial strength. On the other hand, it may happen that the client has no such belief, and that his demands are arbitrary to the verge of sharp-practice.

The cases may therefore be grouped into two classes as regards the client, namely, those in which there is a manifest belief in the justice of the claim, and those in which the claim hinges on a perverse and farfetched insistence upon minute and abstract fulfillment of the duties of architectural service. Within this latter class the possibility of risk and evil result to the architect are appalling. Within the former class they are quite serious enough to merit our earnest attention.

It is presumably evident to casual observation that the annual losses to the profession, due to these varied causes, must be very considerable; and, in the absence of statistics, it would seem an entirely reasonable assumption that the aggregate of these losses should far exceed the sum necessary for a fund devoted to common protection, even though a percentage of the typical cases thus brought to the attention of the courts were to fail of success in the issue.

At present such desultory litigation as is carried on is devoted to the gain of a particular and immediate end; and for this reason, cases are rarely carried to the highest court of appeal.

On the other hand, we, as a particular professional class only recently come into active and responsible association with affairs, broadly regarding the interest of one as the interest of all, and holding the converse to be equally true; we looking to the future and desiring that our status as it advances and differentiates should come into harmony with all other associated interests at the least possible cost to ourselves, do or should take a more abiding interest rather in those cases which are comprehensive and typical in their nature, and which, once passed upon by the higher courts, would permanently establish a guiding principle.

It is true, there is much to concern us in the fact, that in connection with our growth in power and usefulness, we have gradually drifted into a tacit assumption of responsibilities so vague that the developments of a day may prove such assumption to have been reckless.

It is doubtful, moreover, under present conditions, if a contract between client and architect can be so worded as to satisfactorily cover the risks above mentioned.

It is these considerations, thus generally stated, that have suggested the organization of a protective league, which shall diminish litigation by handling only typical cases, and insure stability and protection by securing in such cases the decision of the highest court of appeal. Compromise would therefore seem foreign to the policy of such an organization which, it would seem, through the moral effect of its mere existent power and singleness of purpose, would largely restrain those who now suggest a lawsuit as alternative to compliance with their own arbitrary views of a settlement out of court.

It would, moreover, not only compel parties on either side of a dispute to more searchingly examine the grounds of the opposition, but would assure to each member of the league the backing of a power superior to his own.

It is suggested that such a league be formed in each State, and that it should enroll all of the members of the profession in good standing; that its affairs be conducted, absolutely, by a small executive committee made up of men known to be sagacious and conservative; that only counsel of high legal attainment be retained; and that the party seeking the aid of such executive committee transfer his interests to them by full power of attorney, and that they conduct all cases in the name and interest of the league.

It is obvious that the mere taking up of petty quarrels should form no part of the work of the executive committee, and that they should espouse the cause of a member only after examination has convinced them that it is a vital one, a decision in which would be of undoubted value to the profession as a whole. To prevent abuse, wise by-laws will suggest themselves; and all questions of league meetings, elections, assessments, records, etc., may well be left to the discretion of each organization.

All who feel an interest in this matter will please communicate with the executive committee of the Illinois State Association of Architects. It is their desire at once to form a Protective League for the State of Illinois, and to assist to the extent of their ability in the formation of leagues in all other States.

Address all communications to

R. C. BERLIN, *Secretary,*
61 Ashland Block, Chicago, Ill.

Building 9 (August 25, 1888): 64.

13
Remarks on the Merger of the Western Association of Architects with the American Institute of Architects (1888)

Sullivan had endorsed the proposed merger even before the fifth and final Western Association convention in 1888, believing it would enhance the national power and influence of the profession. But when it was suggested by some in AIA that all westerners be accorded the secondary status of "associates" rather than "fellows," he objected. There should be absolute democracy in architectural organizations, he believed; no individual should be elevated above another except for personal achievement, and certainly not because of arbitrary official action. Sullivan's position, which was also Dankmar Adler's and most westerners', ultimately prevailed. In November 1889 at the twenty-third AIA convention in Cincinnati, the Western Assocation disappeared as an autonomous body. Sullivan's active participation in AIA affairs continued into the late 1890s.

It is with exceeding regret that I feel myself constrained to differ with the American Institute of Architects in this matter when it comes to the consolidation of the two associations. I have given the subject considerable thought, and I am deeply impressed that it is a scheme that is fraught with danger. In the present condition of architectural growth there should be an absolute democratic condition. No man should be placed above his fellows any more than his own individuality will place him. I think instead of two classes we might better make it two bodies, which would increase the most in time I have no doubt in my own mind. I believe that a favored or special class is dangerous to any party, or government, or country. I think the members of the Western Association feel as deeply as I do in this matter of making fictitious classes or grades in the profession. For my own part, I do not believe it appeals to the sober convictions of this convention. I think a man can do better work when he feels that he is an equal with others who claim no higher standing by reason of

some official action. The promotion of two classes [*sic*]. I truly
desire the consolidation, but I feel that the proposition to effect
two grades of membership is insurmountable to the uniting of
the two bodies if it is to remain. It is in my mind whether it is
better for the Western Association to enter into such an alliance
or to remain a distinct organization, as now.

The Inland Architect and News Record 12 (November 1888): 68.

14
Blessed by Masons (1889)

In a ceremony on October 2, 1889, the Grand Lodge of
Free and Accepted Masons topped out the tower of the
Auditorium Building (1886–90), Adler & Sullivan's most
massive structure. After marching through Chicago's
streets followed by thousands of well-wishers, the Masons
assembled at the corner of Congress and Wabash in the
shadow of the nearly completed edifice. There it was revealed that when the final copestone was set in place on
the southwest corner of the tower, it would carry two copper plates inscribed with the date and with the names of
the Auditorium Association Board of Directors, of Masonic officials, and with those of the architects. One of the
architects was present that day. During the ceremony the
Masonic Grand Master introduced Louis Sullivan, who responded according to ritual:

Most worshipful Grand Master: Having been entrusted with the
duty of designing this edifice and of supervising and directing
the workmen in its erection, and having been enabled to witness
its completion, I now, with due respect present to you for inspection and approval the last stone that enters into its composition, and with it the implements of operative Masonry, there
being no further occasion for their use.

Mr. Sullivan delivered the tools, square, level, and plumb, and
the ceremony of testing the stone followed. The deputy grand

master, senior grand warden, and junior grand warden reported
that the stone was square, level, and plumb, and the grand master addressing the architect said:

Mr. Sullivan, from you, as the architect of this building, I
accept the work, assuring you of my hearty approval, and will
forthwith consecrate it according to ancient usage.

The Chicago Tribune (October 3, 1889), 1, 2.

15
The Artistic Use of the Imagination (1889)

Building on the themes of "Style" (document 10) introduced the year before, Sullivan insisted here that creativity
stemmed primarily from inspiration, not reason, and that
emotions were as important as intellect in the creative process. As artists and poets, architects must heed inner voices
and feelings, he implied, learning to distill practical applications from imaginative musings. Sullivan acknowledged
that he spoke metaphorically, that he left much unsaid, and
that he argued by indirection. But he also declared that his
abstractions were at the same time tangible because every
design was autobiographical; the work always revealed
something of the architect's personal search for truth and
meaning.

He is an artist, who, gifted with a capacity to receive impressions, and to transmit them in a more or less permanent form,
adds, to the body of his work, a certain quality or spirit characteristic of himself.

This individual quality is natural to him as is his walk, or his
gestures, or the inflections of his voice; and when the work of
his hands first begins to assume that definiteness of form an-
nouncing growth, he for the first time, and with a certain joyful
surprise, notes those peculiarities, incidental or deep-set, as the
case may be, which mark his work as a something existing more
or less independently of the work of his fellows.

These peculiarities he will note much as one might see his own features for the first time in a mirror; that is to say, as something which unmistakably exists, and which, though he did not and could not create it, he nevertheless feels to be his own.

He is quick to perceive these beginnings, to mark their tendency, and to foster their growth; for he instinctively knows them for true children of his own emotions, and he is pleased with the likeness. He knows that he has had within him certain thoughts, certain feelings, certain longings; that the people and the objects daily surrounding him produce on him certain attractions and repulsions from which his aptitudes and the drift of his ambition take their rise and shape their course. He knows that many sights and sounds are food for him, that some make a stifling, others a wholesome air to breathe.

It is not probable that he reasons much about these things, for the true artist is, as he should be, rather a creature of instinct than of reason. It is only when, to the qualities of artist are added those of poet, that reflection takes a powerful hand in shaping the results.

Yet the artist will naturally seek in thought to project the line of his tendencies towards its goal, much as the mariner outward bound, after many days looks anxiously for the land. But the voice of the top-man shouting "Land ho!" does not bring that land a little nearer, for the wind must blow, the sails be trimmed, the helm shifted, soundings made, the pilot Prudence taken aboard, and time elapse before a safe haven can be made and the cargo called secure. The artist is much such a ship—a creature of wind and current, rising and falling on an unstable and capricious sea. Yet has he a compass and determined rudder, and if storms be not too fierce he will arrive.

Or shall I say that the artist is more like a rounded year, ushering in with a clamorous and nimble springtime, bearing charming flowers in his heyday, sobering and quieting with the heavy growths of summer, bearing rich fruitage in the mellow autumn. For the lapse of time thus works these varied changes, and the lapse of time alone can cause the artist flower to ripen into fruit. This flower is his own sensitive nature, needing, perhaps, to be fertile in its bloom, the presence of the busy little bee of self-deception and complacence. Ere long one by one the pretty petals fall, and the serious business of growth and ripening proceeds. For a long time the fruit is green and unsavory, but it promises much, and in the end fulfills when maturity with color and sweetness come to it. Some natures, indeed, are like the persimmon, and need a sharp frost to bring out their flavor.

Or shall I say, with, perhaps, nearer approach to truth, that the artist is like an orange tree—bearing, continually, flowers and ripeness in every stage—pendant golden thoughts in the last; fruits all of that sap we call imagination.

Letting these comparisons go for what they are worth, the fact remains prominent that the growth of any faculty is very slow, that its normal course can not be hastened, that the element of time can not be eliminated from any natural process, that continued nourishment and the putting forth of endeavor are necessary to insure healthful growth.

To produce vigorous results in art the emotions must follow close upon the mind and give it sure support. Sometimes the mind, in its own perversity, travels on ahead and alone; there then comes about that disjointed condition, which Solomon characterized as the "Pride which goeth before destruction," and which, in more homely modern parlance, we call the "big head."

Slowly and patiently, therefor, must be accumulated and stored those small and frequently homely experiences upon which, in the aggregate, the imagination rests, as a tower upon its foundation. And these small experiences, to produce a real result, must be of two distinct kinds, namely: first, the prosaic and sometimes tiresome happenings and learnings of every day, and the patient coming into touch with many things through the senses and the observation, coupled with a willingness to do one thing at a time and give one's whole attention to it; for it is axiomatic that to know one must touch—from every touch there comes a sensation, and it is this sensation that we call an experience. Memory preserves these experiences for us intact, and the longer we live the greater does the accumulation become, the more elastic our feeling of strength, the more secure our equipoise in difficulty, because the more precise and ready our sense of reality.

Nothing is more interesting to me in examining a master-

piece, than to observe the vast wealth of small experiences that
is to be seen stored up in it. They do not give it its quality of
mastership; that were, indeed, a puny view to take of a large
thing; but just as surely it would not be a profound work without them, for the imagination is important without this basis of
common and matter-of-fact experience, and can no more make
its spring than can the lion without a firm footing.

These experiences we speak of as practical, and their sum we
call a knowledge of detail; if one yields wholly to their influence,
the results in the work are likely to be rather dry, methodic and
precise; correct as to mechanics, but devoid of a certain finer
truth, a more subtle accuracy, a still more delicate touch, a yet
more exact sense of reality; these latter qualities are the final attributes of true art, and to impart them to his work, the author
must have passed through and accumulated in connection with
the practical, a second and distinct set of experiences, which amplify the practical and give to it the keen intuitive incisiveness of
life; namely, the emotional.

The sensations of a true artist are always complex, for to susceptibility of the senses, he adds susceptibility of the heart. Every
object, therefor, that he regards, will give him a double sensation, specifically the sensual and the emotional. The two should,
in truth, come so interblended that they shall appear to be one
impression, and such an impression can be nothing less than an
artistic experience.

Emotion is a big and a high-sounding word, which appears
to fit something occurring only rarely, and to the few. Yet, when
we stop to consider that emotion is simply the attention that the
heart gives, and is as natural and easy as the attention that the
sense of sight or of hearing gives; when we think, at a glance of
the infinite variety of objects and actions that may be seized on
by the eyes, the ears or the hands, separately or collectively, it
becomes easy to see how immense may be the corresponding
variety of emotions, reaching from the simple, the calm, the se-
date, the joyous, through the serious and melancholy, to the
complex, the turbulent, the sublime.

Nor should it be forgotten that among the more important
of one's experiences are those derived from contact with his

fellows, with the works and thoughts and experiences and qualities of those who have gone before, and last, but not least, from the communion of the artist with his own spirit.

We see now, therefore, how, if he be simple and wholesome in his nature, the surroundings of an artist appeal to him, and in what manner he may answer the appeal. Into all that he sees he enters with sympathy; and in return, all that he sees enters into his being, and becomes and remains a part of him. Walt Whitman beautifully expresses this idea in one of his shorter poems.*

This poem contains in its form all that I have thus far said, and encloses by its suggestiveness and its indirect purport all that I am likely to say of the subject in hand. I may well, therefore, take it as a text, and a firm footing for the short imaginative spring that I shall make from here to the end of my address. For it is clear, or I conceive it to be so when I test the matter by my own judgment, with an eye on cause and effect, that the true meaning of this poem lies mostly in what is left unsaid; that the poet ceases when he has excited the sympathetic thoughts of the reader, and leaves to the imagination of the latter the work of extending the impulse as far as may be. It is this capacity to excite responsive imagination that characterizes a poet; 'tis a sign that he provides the active germs of thought; that he has compressed much into little. Much comes from him because much has come to him; what, then, shall come from the child who went forth every day? Is not the child the artist? If others were so much to him, and so influenced him, if all the objects that he looked upon and received with wonder, pity, love, or dread, so wrought upon him that in sympathy he became them, and that, absorbing them they become a part of him, will not they, when he, so enriched, seeks to voice himself, will not they, indeed, live again and show again in that work which he must perforce of his very nature regard with such warmth of love that it becomes himself and he it? And what is himself but the sum of his experiences and faculties? Therefore, if his work is himself, it, in turn, is the sum of his experiences and faculties. It needs, then, only

---

*At this point Sullivan read Whitman's "There Was a Child Went Forth" from the "Autumn Rivulets" section of *Leaves of Grass*. The poem was omitted by the editors of *Building*.

the saying to make clear the profound truth which underlies and encloses even this poem, "By your works shall ye be known."

Here I would wish substantially to end, leaving these few thoughts to stimulate your imaginations as the poem stimulates mine, as nature and his fellows stimulated the poet; leaving it to you to supply what has been left unsaid, to carry on such impulse as there may be as far as you may.

But, lest you should tend to consider this sort of writing too metaphysical, too fine-spun, too unpractical—ornamental rather than useful—I will not leave you till I have laid my finger at the side of my nose in a practical hint:

Let us suppose, then, that I have now before me on this table a collection of drawings containing an original work by each one of you. I tilt back in my chair and examine them leisurely one by one, meanwhile keeping my thoughts entirely to myself.

Being known by your works, it is, of course, the man that I hold in my hand in each case and look secretly into.

How, now, do you suppose I am sizing you up? What, now, do you suppose I am thinking, in each case? What do you think is my estimate of your experiences and your faculties?

Do I understand that my poetic web has caught your practical fly?

Building 11 (October 19, 1889): 129–30.

16
Sub-contracting—Shall the National Association Recommend That It be Encouraged? (1890)

At the annual meeting of the National Association of Builders in Chicago in February 1890, Sullivan tackled the thorny problem of subcontracting. He pointed out that under the prevailing system, in which architects hired general contractors to parcel out specialized tasks to subcontractors, master craftsman and skilled artisans were often unrecognized and underpaid. After praising the "practical workman," he offered a resolution encouraging the Na-

tional Association to endorse individual contracts between
architects and the several skilled tradesmen or firms on the
job, thereby eliminating the general contractor middleman.
Although often depicted as a lonely theoretician, Sullivan's
extensive labors on down-to-earth matters suggest his willingness to participate in collective efforts toward raising the
standards and regularizing the workings of his profession.

No question can probably be propounded which possesses a
more comprehensive and far reaching interest, not alone to
builders, but also to the general public, meaning thereby the
projectors of building enterprises of every description, than this
question which I shall endeavor to elucidate.

It is almost unnecessary to say that, in consequence of the
great development of building within the past decade, or for a
longer period, this problem of the just and equitable distribution
of the responsibilities, the emoluments, and the honorable recognition by the public of every master workman, every guiding
hand and directing mind engaged in the construction and em-
bellishment of a building, has called forth much diversity of
opinion, and no small amount of discontent on the part of those
to whom this question comes directly home, namely, the sub-
contractors, that large and by far most numerous class of mechanics or craftsmen—call them by what name you will—whose
life-long training must of necessity be intense, peculiar and all-
absorbing, and upon whose efforts, in the very nature of things,
the success of every building project, great or small, hinges and
depends, and it is on behalf of this class of sub-contractors that
I essay a few words of argument, or rather of explanation, with
respect to rights which are sometimes unjustly invaded, often
thoughtlessly overlooked, and, when so slighted, always to the
injury of the purchasing public.

The practice of awarding extensive building contracts, embodying many and peculiar branches of mechanical or decorative
industry, to an individual or a firm assuming the functions of a
general contractor, in other words, the general contract system,
as opposed to the separate or independent contract system,
which gives to the one, business man or mechanic as he may
be, the financial control—and any further control is mere pre-

tense—of the many specially trained and expert sub-contractors, while it may command the approbation of the few, appeals, in my humble judgment, mainly to one dominant feeling—avarice; the feeling which prompts the one to absorb the profits of the many, oblivious of, or indifferent to consequences respecting the just aims and aspirations which must ever guide and control the capable and accomplished artizan, and, deprived of which aims and incentives, he cannot arrive at the goal of acknowledged excellence, the master's rank, to which constructive and decorative effort must ever be directed, or fail of the highest achievement.

The specific questions implied in the preceding remarks seem to me plain and answerable only on the part of the sub-contractor. I shall state them briefly:

We expect of the master mechanic, the sub-contractor, that he shall be a practical workman, shall have worked at and learned his trade, and that in his line of mechanical industry he shall be esteemed an expert, a recognized master. Can such a man pursue his calling and obtain such recognition without a just pride in his work, and an equally just hope of ample regard for the mastery and skill he has acquired? Assuredly he cannot, else he would be more or less than human. Acquirements, competence, distinction, honor, these are and should be his impelling motives. Can these motives be subserved, his honest ambition gratified, his incentives to greater effort stimulated if he finds that his efforts, his distinctive personal aims, or personal consequence, are apt to be merged in those of another, or, as I have before intimated, entirely overlooked, and, not infrequently, his just profits partly or wholly absorbed by the spirit of greed which, under the guise of convenience or facility, prompts the system of general contracting?

Here it may be urged that I assume too much, as bearing against the subcontractor; that I am, so to speak, begging this question of his just and honorable recognition which I claim as the grand motive that should actuate every true artizan. I do not think the experience of the large majority of those to whom I address myself who have figured in the role of sub-contractors could be quoted adversely to my position, and it is a question only to be tested and settled by such experience.

How often have we received the attentive consideration, even of the owners, during the progress of their buildings, where the general contract system obtains? Do we not know that such cases are merely incidental, and that even then they are as frequently of a discouraging as of a cheering character?

Referring now to the pleas of convenience, facility, the capitalizing of building projects, and other kindred pretexts; the ostensible ones which might be and are urged in favor of building on the general contract system. Granting that at times these may be fairly advanced, are they not frequently over-estimated? To whom do these considerations become of most consequence? To the owner? Perhaps so, when financial management, credit, or some such underlying motive must influence him, but not always even then, and with a counterpoise in that lack of closer business relation, appreciation and confident esteem which, on every true principle of economy, should prevail between the owner, who is the actual buyer, and the artizan, the master mechanic, who is the actual producer, the actual seller.

Again, does the convenience or the facility of the general system come home to the architect? I answer, it would hardly be an argument in its favor if it did, because the architect's first and paramount care should be excellence of work, and my proud experience with members of that honorable profession is that excellence is the dominant idea, but, the fact is—and close examination will bear out the statement—that the general contract system relieves the careful and conscientious architect not at all, and too often, in the adjustment of differences between the general and sub-contractor, occupies many of his overtaxed hours.

Let me here state that many, *very* many times I have been brought into relation with principal contractors under the general system, and such experience satisfies me that there are and will always be found such men, of high character and personal skill; yet, here comes in another and I may say my final consideration, which is: That no matter what the character or experience of the general contractor; no matter what special training he may possess, let us not lose sight of the vital question, namely, the vast strides made in the art of building in this country, even within the past few years; the almost total revolution in the application of building materials and decorative inventions; the advance in masonry, stone, wood, and iron and steel construction, and the complex nature of the many items of sanitary work, convenience or adornment which go to complete the modern American edifice, and who will deny that these results, astounding in their magnitude and variety, and to the inventive genius displayed, are the fruitful outcome of the labor of the tireless mechanic, the artizan, the inventor, the master of his craft; surely not of the general contractor.

I say then, with all confidence in your judgment, let us not approve any system of contracting which, however remotely, could tend to relegate that individual merit, that heretofore triumphant energy of the artizan to obscurity. Let us not divert one ray of light, in all the turmoil of our daily lives, from the individual form of the master mechanic.

Rather let us say, with that giant in intellect, that noble friend, teacher and toiler for art and the artisan, John Ruskin: *"In all buying consider first, what condition of existence you cause in the producers of what you buy; secondly, whether the sum you have paid is just to the producer; thirdly, to how much clear use, for food, knowledge, or joy, this that you have bought can be put; and fourthly, to whom and in what way it can be most speedily and serviceably distributed; in all dealings, whatsoever, insisting on entire openness and stern fulfillment; and in all doings, in perfection and loveliness of accomplishment."*

No great nation without great artizans, great producers, great toilers! To them, as in this splendid passage, will the thoughts of great men ever be directed, and it is for them too, the master mechanics, the artizans, the toilers in this greatest of all human industries, to whose fertile brains and busy hands this great land already owes so much, that I would present my humble plea.

Mr. President and gentlemen, I will offer the following resolution, which I will read, in order to bring this matter up for discussion:

WHEREAS, The custom at present prevails, to a great extent, of awarding several items of building work to one contractor or firm, under which has become to be known as the "General Contract System"; and

WHEREAS, This general contract system seems to be on the increase and to be the occasion of much discontent among the numerous classes of mechanics who thus reluctantly find themselves compelled to occupy under such a system the position of sub-contractors; therefore, be it

Resolved, That it is the sense of the National Association of Builders, in convention assembled, that the system of sub-contracting should not be encouraged; that the said system is, on the whole, unjust to the master mechanic; that it is detrimental to the progress of mechanical skill and knowledge, inasmuch as its tendency is to obscure, if not altogether ignore, the trained and capable artizan, who is often debarred, by the very nature of his calling, from entering into competition as a general contractor, thereby decreasing the sense of individual consequence and responsibility which should attach to every man who aims at the direction and control of any branch of the building business, and without which incentives the results which attend continuous and ambitious efforts in his special department cannot be expected.

That the said general contract system also tends, in a marked degree, to do away with the just and reasonable profits of the sub-contractor; and, therefore, that under proper limitations we consider the time has come for stringent and well-defined regulations which shall check this growing evil and place the master mechanic on a fair footing as an independent contractor.

The Inland Architect and News Record 15 (February 15, 1890): 18–19.

17
From Church Spires Must Go (1890)

During construction of his Kehilath Anshe Ma'ariv Synagogue in Chicago, designed in 1889–90, Sullivan was interviewed about its style, which was considered somewhat unusual. Critics suggested Romanesque and Venetian in vain attempts to find familiar categories and to pin him down. But following the pattern he had established years before (see document 1), he refused to cooperate, saying that his work was ahistorical, that it belonged to no particular "school," and that adherence to ancient styles and "schools" impeded progress.

The most noted departure in church architecture in this city, or anywhere else, perhaps, is the new synagogue now building on the corner of Indiana Avenue and Thirty-third Street. It is the design of Adler and Sullivan, who furnished the plans of the Auditorium. The accompanying cut nor any other cut can give the reader anything like an idea of this structure. The lower portion is of Bedford stone. The upper portion is of copper with geometrical ornamentations. The roof is red slate. The size of the building is 91 × 116 feet. The height of the ceiling is 70 feet. The length of the auditorium is 98 feet, the breadth being 86 feet. The ceiling is arched, the seats of the auditorium will be arranged like those in a theater, and three galleries will add to the capacity and appearance.

Even this singular construction is not regarded as being what it ought to be in church architecture. The upper portion, which is of copper, according to competent architects ought to be of stone. But this is not the fault of the architect. The congregation, through the building committee, wouldn't have it.

"It is the nineteenth century school," said Mr. Sullivan. "That is all I can say for it. It has no historical style. It is the present. We have got to get away from schools in architecture. As long as we adhere to schools of anything there is no progress; nothing gained; no advancement. What school does that represent? None. The church spire in the city is a thing of the past. Now and then there is a fad, but that is not an advancement. A fad develops nothing permanent. Architecturally, I do not hesitate to say that there isn't a church spire in Chicago."

The Chicago Tribune (November 30, 1890), 36.

18
Plastic and Color Decoration of the Auditorium (1891)

The most massive and time-consuming commission of Louis Sullivan's career was the Chicago Auditorium Building (1886–90), a ten-story (plus tower) edifice of 63,350 square feet in plan, 8,737,000 cubic feet in volume, and weighing 110,000 tons—the heaviest building in the world at the time—containing a 4,200-seat theater, a 400-room hotel, 136 office units, and several other facilities. The decorations were the most extensive and among the most luxurious of his oeuvre. In this paper he offered a rationale for his ornamental work while devoting considerable attention to the theater murals of which he was particularly proud, in part because they depicted themes he had first discussed in his 1886 essay, "Inspiration" (document 4). This was one of Sullivan's first statements about his system of decorative color.

The plastic and color decorations are distinctly architectural in conception. They are everywhere kept subordinate to the general effect of the larger structural masses and subdivisions, while lending to them the enchantment of soft tones and of varied light and shade. A single idea or principle is taken as a basis of the color scheme, that is to say, use is made of but one color in each instance, and that color is associated with gold. The color selected varies with each room treated, but the plan of using one color with gold is in no case departed from. Thus the main Auditorium is in old ivory and gold, the recital hall in white and gold, the restaurant in brown and gold, the ladies' parlor in blue and gold. In some instances, the color is graded from a dark to a light tone, in others the color and gold effects are intermingled; in still others they are kept distinctly separate. The materials used are oil colors and pure gold leaf. A consistent use is made in all parts of the building of rich and varied forms in relief, yet such is the sobriety of their placing, and such the delicacy of coloring, that all is rich, quiet and harmonious, showing everywhere one purpose definitely and intelligently adhered to—a clear conception skillfully executed. Rich foreign marbles, onyx and fine woods are much used in the treatment of the main public rooms, and from the beautiful natural colorings of these materials the applied color decorations take their key note in each case, and produce with them a well-balanced unity of effect, either through the contrast or analogy of their respective tones. The stained glass, of which a moderate use is made, is carefully harmonized with the prevailing tone of color in the decoration.

The most notable of the decorations are, of course, to be seen in the main Auditorium. Here the color scheme is broad, simple and grand, consisting of gold and old ivory in graded tones. Three large mural paintings form the pièce de résistance. One of these is placed over the proscenium arch, and one on each of the side walls. Their purpose is to express, allegorically, the two great rhythms of nature, namely, growth and decadence. The central painting consists mainly of figures; the side paintings are outdoor scenes, containing each but a solitary figure, that of the poet communing with nature. The direct expression of these paintings tends toward the musical, for that "the utterance of life is a song, the symphony of nature," is the burden of the proscenium composition; in its "allegro" and "adagio" are expressed the influence of music. The side paintings are further expressive of the symphony of nature, for in them her tender voice sings joyously or sadly to the attentive soul of the poet, awakening those delicate, responsive harmonies, whose name is inspiration. On one side, corresponding with the allegro of the central painting, is the "spring song," a scene at dawn within a wooded meadow, by a gently running stream. The poet is abroad to greet the lark; the pale tints of sunrise suffuse the landscape; the early tinge of green is over all; the joy of this awakening life deeply touches the wandering poet, who sings in ecstasy, "O soft melodious springtime, first born of life and love!"

The scene then changes to the side corresponding with the adagio. Here is depicted the natural and calm decline of life. It is an autumn reverie, the twilight, the symbol of decadence. The scene is of pathless wilds, in gray, subsiding autumn, where brown leaves settle through the air, descending one by one to join the dead, while winds, adagio, breathe shrill funeral lamentations. Tired nature here, her task performed, divested of her lovely many-colored garment, withdraws a falling veil and sinks to sleep. Sadly musing, the poet turns to descend into the deep and somber valley, conscious that "a great life has passed into the tomb, and there awaits the requiem of winter's snows." Thus have all things their rise and decline, their dawn and twilight, their spring song and their autumn reverie, and thus by their symbolism do these mural poems suggest the compensating

phases of nature and of human life in all their varied manifestations. Naturally are suggested the light and the grave in music,
the joyous and the tragic in drama. The central painting, on its
more conventional background of gold, expresses in its many
minor figures the manifold influence of music on the human
mind—the dance, the serenade, the dirge; while a deeper meaning, conveying the rhythmic significance of life's song, is embodied in special groups and figures wholly symbolical in character.
At the right is an altar on which burns the lambent flame of life.
Before it poses an exultant figure typifying the dawn of life, the
springtime of the race, the early flight of imagination. At the left
another altar is seen on which a fire is burning and flickering
toward its end; near it the type of twilight, of memory, tenderness and compassion, stands with yearning, outstretched arms.
The central group signifies the present, the future, and the past.
The present, a lyre in her hand, sits enthroned, the embodiment
of song, of the utterance of life. Toward her all the elements of
the composition tend, and at this focal point is developed their
full significance and power, for the present is the magical moment of life; it is from the present that we take the bearings of
the future and of the past.

Industrial Chicago 1 (Chicago: Goodspeed Publishing Co., 1891): 490–91.

19
The High-Building Question (1891)

Adler and Sullivan designed two Chicago skyscrapers in
1891—the Schiller Building and the Odd Fellows Temple
project—that were pioneering in part because of their setbacks, which enabled light and air to penetrate more
rooms more deeply, including those at the interior of the
lot. The problems posed by tall buildings of providing adequate light and air for tenants and the streets, as well as
the matter of pedestrian congestion, led Sullivan to propose a formula of ratios between building heights and tho-
roughfare widths utilizing setbacks. This was a principle
later embodied in the pioneering New York City zoning

ordinance of 1916. Sullivan's article demonstrates his very real concern about negative social consequences of design, including his own.

To elaborate in all its details and ramifications, its varied selfish and unselfish interests, its phases of public and individual equity, its bearings present and future, its larger and narrower values, to attempt indeed but a sketch of its general outline would carry the discussion of the high-building question far beyond the limits of space that a journal such as this could afford. I desire, therefore, to pass by untouched the broad sociological aspects of this very elaborate discussion, and to confine myself to a phase of it which, so far as I am aware, has not yet been touched upon, but which may prove a factor in the final solution.

It must seem a hardship to the individual owner of land that he should be debarred from erecting upon it such building as he deems fit. It will seem, however, to the remaining stubborn majority of the community—non-owners of land—a distinct impudence that the individual should build otherwise than as they themselves see fit. It is between these extremes that my suggestion lies, for I believe it is possible to preserve in a building of high altitude the equities both of the individual and of the public.

Briefly, then, the individual owner seeks rentable space, the public wish light and air; it follows, then, that up to a certain limit of height the individual owner manifestly should be free to regulate his rentable space as he chooses, but beyond this limit a sense of public welfare should control him either with or without his consent. What more simple solution can there be than this—that the individual be allowed to continue the further erection of his building above the prescribed limit, provided that, in so continuing, the area of his building as it emerges from the limit shall occupy not more than, say, fifty per cent of the area of his land? Let him so continue until he has reached, say, twice the height of the original limit. If the area of his land is sufficient that he may profitably continue, let him be allowed to do so, provided, however, that in so doing he occupy, not to exceed, say, twenty-five per cent of the area of his ground; and so on indefinitely, restricting the area as he progresses upward.

This is, so far, a very pretty theory. But we well know, after a moment's reflection, that with his customary go-ahead proclivities, the average American citizen, desiring, as usual, to be right up in the front row, would translate this to mean a thirty-story building on the street line with a great big hole behind. We would, therefore, have to teach him the manners he does not possess, and would gently inform him that after the first limit is passed the fifty per cent restriction will apply not only to area but to frontage. He will scowl at this condition, but if there is "money in it" he will accept it just the same. When the second limit is reached we will push him back unceremoniously from the street line to the middle of his ground, and if he can see a dollar in it he will accept this condition also.

There is, no doubt, a somewhat amusing side to this controversy. For the spectacle of an otherwise intelligent individual being compelled to do that which enlightenment would lead him to do freely and of his own accord is not without its compensation to a student of human nature.

I have suggsted three limits to height. We are now to consider the very practical question of the actual number of feet in these limits, merely stopping to say in passing that if the area of the ground is sufficient, the number of successive limits may be continued indefinitely on the plan indicated, reducing the area fifty per cent successively at each limit, thus leaving the individual free to soar as high as it may please his lot, his purse, and his pride, and thus insuring to the community the benefit of a permanency in the supply of light and air. If we say that the angle of light to be effective shall be thirty degrees of vertical inclination, we say that which, while it may be true, is not very intelligible. If we say, however, that the frontage of a building shall not exceed in height twice the width of the street, we begin to talk ordinary, every-day English. But if, pushing our definition further, we say that on a 66 foot street a building 132 feet, or ten stories, may be erected, we realize how great is the temptation to increase this limit to 137 feet so that we can just get in eleven stories. Yet, under any arrangement, some must gain a little and some must lose a little. Particularly does this apply to him who owns a corner lot fronting on a wide as well as a narrow street. What is to be done with him? We know well enough that he cannot see the narrow street at all and will demonstrate, by traditions descending from the Pottowatamies, that his lot fronts on the broad street only. Suppose we say to him that the height of his building shall equal the sum of the street widths. Would we be unjust? I think not, and he will think so too, perhaps, after a little reflection. It might occur to him that, after all, his neighbors had rights, and that if they had rights he in turn had them as against other neighbors, especially corner neighbors. So it will follow that "to him that hath shall be given"; in other words, he who has the biggest lot can build the highest, and why shouldn't he? For he has to give up what his smaller neighbor has to give up; namely, fifty per cent for each limit. If he can afford it, so can the smaller neighbor.

It seems to me a subject not all debatable that here in Chicago the freedom of thought and action of the individual should be not only maintained, but held sacred. By this I surely do not mean the license of the individual to trample on his neighbor and disregard the public welfare, but I do just as surely mean that our city has acquired and maintained its greatness by virtue of its brainy men, who have made it what it is and who guarantee its future. These men may be selfish enough to need regulation, but it is monstrous to suppose that they must be suppressed, for they have in themselves qualities as noble, daring, and inspired as ever quickened knights of old to deeds of chivalry. As I said at the beginning, the subject is large, complex, and difficult. I have tried to point to the quick of it, and trust I have not wholly failed.

The Graphic 5 (December 19, 1891): 405.

20
Ornament in Architecture (1892)

By 1892 the Chicago Auditorium, the Getty Tomb, the theater in the Schiller Building, and several other commissions had established Louis Sullivan's national reputation as a premier architectural ornamentalist with a unique philosophy. In this essay Sullivan emphasized the importance of uniting ornament and mass, of making them one, arguing that the essential meaning of a structure could be distilled and made manifest in its decoration. The publication of an article on ornament in an engineering magazine—Sullivan's most direct confrontation with the subject before *A System of Architectural Ornament, According With a Philosophy of Man's Powers,* his 1924 treatise (see document 48)—indicates not only the respect his views commanded but also the cross-fertilization existing between two vastly different and sometimes antagonistic branches of the building profession.

I take it as self-evident that a building, quite devoid of ornament, may convey a noble and dignified sentiment by virtue of mass and proportion. It is not evident to me that ornament can intrinsically heighten these elemental qualities. Why, then, should we use ornament? Is not a noble and simple dignity sufficient? Why should we ask more?

If I answer the question in entire candor, I should say that it would be greatly for our aesthetic good if we should refrain entirely from the use of ornament for a period of years, in order that our thought might concentrate acutely upon the production of buildings well formed and comely in the nude. We should thus perforce eschew many undesirable things, and learn by contrast how effective it is to think in a natural, vigorous and wholesome way. This step taken, we might safely inquire to what extent a decorative application of ornament would enhance the beauty of our structures—what new charm it would give them.

If we have then become well grounded in pure and simple forms we will reverse them; we will refrain instinctively from vandalism; we will be loath to do aught that may make these forms less pure, less noble. We shall have learned, however, that ornament is mentally a luxury, not a necessary, for we shall have discerned the limitations as well as the great value of unadorned masses. We have in us romanticism, and feel a craving to express it. We feel intuitively that our strong, athletic and simple forms will carry with natural ease the raiment of which we dream, and that our buildings thus clad in a garment of poetic imagery, half hid as it were in choice products of loom and mine, will appeal with redoubled power, like a sonorous melody overlaid with harmonious voices.

I conceive that a true artist will reason substantially in this way; and that, at the culmination of his powers, he may realize this ideal. I believe that architectural ornament brought forth in this spirit is desirable, because beautiful and inspiring; that ornament brought forth in any other spirit is lacking in the higher possibilities.

That is to say, a building which is truly a work of art (and I consider none other) is in its nature, essence and physical being an emotional expression. This being so, and I feel deeply that it is so, it must have, almost literally, a life. It follows from this living principle that an ornamented structure should be characterized by this quality, namely, that the same emotional impulse shall flow throughout harmoniously into its varied forms of expression—of which, while the mass-composition is the more profound, the decorative ornamentation is the more intense. Yet must both spring from the same source of feeling.

I am aware that a decorated building, designed upon this principle, will require in its creator a high and sustained emotional tension, an organic singleness of idea and purpose maintained to the last. The completed work will tell of this; and if it be designed with sufficient depth of feeling and simplicity of mind, the more intense the heat in which it was conceived, the more serene and noble will it remain forever as a monument of man's eloquence. It is this quality that characterizes the great monuments of the past. It is this certainly that opens a vista toward the future.

To my thinking, however, the mass-composition and the decorative system of a structure such as I have hinted at should be separable from each other only in theory and for purposes of analytical study. I believe, as I have said, that an excellent and beautiful building may be designed that shall bear no ornament whatever; but I believe just as firmly that a decorated structure, harmoniously conceived, well considered, cannot be stripped of its system of ornament without destroying its individuality.

It has been hitherto somewhat the fashion to speak of ornament, without perhaps too much levity of thought, as a thing to

be put on or omitted, as the case might be. I hold to the contrary—that the presence or absence of ornament should, certainly in serious work, be determined at the very beginnings of
the design. This is perhaps strenuous insistence, yet I justify and
urge it on the ground that creative architecture is an art so fine
that its power is manifest in rhythms of great subtlety, as much
so indeed as those of musical art, its nearest relative.

If, therefore, our artistic rhythms—a result—are to be significant, our prior meditations—the cause—must be so. It matters
then greatly what is the prior inclination of the mind, as much
so indeed as it matters what is the inclination of a cannon when
the shot is fired.

If we assume that our contemplated building need not be a
work of living art, or at least a striving for it, that our civilization
does not yet demand such, my plea is useless. I can proceed only
on the supposition that our culture has progressed to the stage
wherein an imitative or reminiscential art does not wholly satisfy, and that there exists an actual desire for spontaneous expression. I assume, too, that we are to begin, not by shutting our
eyes and ears to the unspeakable past, but rather by opening our
hearts, in enlightened sympathy and filial regard, to the voice of
our times.

Nor do I consider this the place or the time to inquire if after
all there is really such a thing as creative art—whether a final
analysis does not reveal the great artist, not as creator, but rather
as interpreter and prophet. When the time does come that the
luxury of this inquiry becomes a momentous necessary, our architecture shall have neared its final development. It will suffice
then to say that I conceive a work of fine art to be really this: a
made thing, more or less attractive, regarding which the casual
observer may see a part, but no observer all, that is in it.

It must be manifest that an ornamental design will be more
beautiful if it seems a part of the surface or substance that re-
ceives it than if it looks "stuck on," so to speak. A little observation will lead one to see that in the former case there exists a
peculiar sympathy between the ornament and the structure,
which is absent in the latter. Both structure and ornament obviously benefit by this sympathy; each enhancing the value of

the other. And this, I take it, is the preparatory basis of what may be called an organic system of ornamentation.

The ornament, as a matter of fact, is applied in the sense of being cut in or cut on, or otherwise done: yet it should appear, when completed, as though by the outworking of some beneficent agency it had come forth from the very substance of the material and was there by the same right that a flower appears amid the leaves of its parent plant.

Here by this method we make a species of contact, and the spirit that animates the mass is free to flow into the ornament—they are no longer two things but one thing.

If now we bring ourselves to close and reflective observation, how evident it becomes that if we wish to insure an actual, a poetic unity, the ornament should appear, not as something receiving the spirit of the structure, but as a thing expressing that spirit by virtue of differential growth.

It follows then, by the logic of growth, that a certain kind of ornament should appear on a certain kind of structure, just as a certain kind of leaf must appear on a certain kind of tree. An elm leaf would not "look well" on a pine-tree—a pine-needle seems more "in keeping." So, an ornament or scheme of organic decoration befitting a structure composed on broad and massive lines would not be in sympathy with a delicate and dainty one. Nor should the ornamental systems of buildings of any various sorts be interchangeable as between these buildings. For buildings should possess an individuality as marked as t[ ]ists among men, making them distinctly separab[ ]other, however strong the racial or family resembla[ ]

Everyone knows and feels how strongly individual is each man's voice, but few pause to consider that a voice, though of another kind, speaks from every existing building. What is the character of these voices? Are they harsh or smooth, noble or ignoble? Is the speech they utter prose or poetry?

Mere difference in outward form does not constitute individuality. For this a harmonious inner character is necessary; and as we speak of human nature, we may by analogy apply a similar phrase to buildings.

A little study will enable one soon to discern and appreciate the more obvious individualities of buildings; further study, and comparison of impressions, will bring to view forms and qualities that were at first hidden; a deeper analysis will yield a host of new sensations, developed by the discovery of qualities hitherto unsuspected—we have found evidences of the gift of expression, and have felt the significance of it; the mental and emotional gratification caused by these discoveries leads on to deeper and deeper searching, until, in great works, we fully learn that what was obvious was least, and what was hidden, nearly all.

Few works can stand the test of close, business-like analysis—they are soon emptied. But no analysis, however sympathetic, persistent or profound, can exhaust a truly great work of art. For the qualities that make it thus great are not mental only, but psychic, and therefore signify the highest expression and embodiment of individuality.

Now, if this spiritual and emotional quality is a noble attribute when it resides in the mass of a building, it must, when applied to a virile and synthetic scheme of ornamentation, raise this at once from the level of triviality to the heights of dramatic expression.

The possibilities of ornamentation, so considered, are marvelous; and before us open, as a vista, conceptions so rich, so varied, so poetic, so inexhaustible, that the mind pauses in its flight and life indeed seems but a span.

Reflect now the light of this conception full and free upon joint considerations of mass-composition, and how serious, how eloquent, how inspiring is the imagery, how noble the dramatic force that shall make sublime our future architecture.

America is the only land in the whole earth wherein a dream like this may be realized; for here alone tradition is without nd the soul of man free to grow, to mature, to seek

this we must turn again to Nature, and hearkening to her melodious voice, learn, as children learn, the accent of its rhythmic cadences. We must view the sunrise with ambition, the twilight wistfully; then, when our eyes have learned to see, we shall know how great is the simplicity of nature, that it brings forth in serenity such endless variation. We shall learn from this to consider man and his ways, to the end that we behold the unfolding of the soul in all its beauty, and know that the fragrance of a living art shall float again in the garden of our world.

The Engineering Magazine 3 (August 1892): 633–34.

21
The Transportation Building (1893)

The Transportation Building (1891) for the 1893 World's Columbian Exposition or Chicago World's Fair was one of Sullivan's most famous and highly acclaimed designs. Attributed to the partnership but actually done by Sullivan alone, its most conspicuous feature was the so-called "Golden Doorway," a visual landmark at the Fair, for which the Union Centrale des Arts Decoratifs in Paris awarded him a medal in 1894. This description dated February 25, 1893 was signed by both partners but was written by the designer. It explains the building's overall concept, paying particular attention to its decorative color system.

The Transportation Building, designed by Messrs. Adler & Sullivan of Chicago, is one of the group forming the northern, or picturesque, quadrangle. It is situated at the southern end of the west flank and lies between the Horticultural and the Mines buildings. It is axial with the Manufactures Building on the east side of the quadrangle, the central feature of each of the two buildings being on the same east and west line. The Transportation Building is simple in architectural treatment, although it is intended to make it very rich and elaborate in detail. In style it is somewhat Romanesque, although to the initiated the manner in which it is designed on axial lines, and the solicitude shown for good proportions and subtle relation of parts to each other, will at once suggest the methods of composition followed at the *Ecole des Beaux Arts*. Viewed from the lagoon, the cupola of the Transportation Building will form an effective feature southwest of the quadrangle; while from the cupola itself, reached by eight elevators, the northern court, a beautiful effect of the entire Exposition, will be seen. The main entrance to the Transportation Building consists of an immense single arch enriched with carvings, bas-reliefs, and mural paintings; the entire feature forms a rich and beautiful yet quiet color climax, for it is treated entirely in gold-leaf and called the golden door. The remainder of the architectural composition falls into a just relation of contrast with the highly wrought entrance, and is duly quiet and modest, though very broad in treatment. It consists of a continuous arcade with subordinated colonnade and entablature. Numerous minor entrances are from time to time pierced in the walls, and with them are grouped terraces, seats, drinking-fountains, and statues.

The interior of the building is treated much after the manner of a Roman basilica, with broad nave and aisles. The roof is therefore in three divisions. The middle one rises much higher than the others, and its walls are pierced to form a beautiful arcaded clear-story. The cupola, placed exactly at the center of the building, and rising 165 feet above the ground, is reached by eight elevators. These elevators of themselves naturally form a part of the transportation exhibit, and as they also carry passengers to galleries at various stages of height, a fine view of the interior of the building may be easily obtained. The main galleries of this building, because of the abundant placing of passenger elevators, proves quite accessible to visitors. The cupola, with its broad balconies, and the wide terrace at the foot of the clear-story roof is used as a promenade for visitors. From these points a most beautiful view of the surrounding country can be obtained. The roof over the great main entrance is used as an outdoor restaurant.

The main building of the transportation exhibit measures 960 feet front by 256 feet deep; from this extends westward to Stony Island Avenue a triangular annex covering about nine acres, and consisting of one-story buildings sixty-four feet wide, set side by side. As there is a railway-track every sixteen feet, and as all these tracks run east and west, these annex buildings may be used to exhibit an entire freight or passenger train coupled up with its engine.

Not the least interesting feature of the Transportation Building is the beautiful scheme of polychrome decoration to be applied to its exterior. To treat the building externally in many colors was the original thought of the architects in the first conception of their design. The architecture of the building, therefore, has been carefully prepared throughout with reference to the ultimate application of color, and many large plain surfaces have been left to receive the final polychrome treatment. The ornamental designs for this work in color are of great and intricate delicacy; the patterns, interweaving with each other, produce an effect almost as fine as that of embroidery. As regards the colors themselves, they comprise nearly the whole galaxy, there being not less than thirty different shades of color employed. These, however, are so delicately and softly blended and so nicely balanced against each other that the final effect suggests not so much many colors as a single beautiful painting.

The general scheme of color treatment starts with a delicate light-red tone for the base of the building. This is kept entirely simple and free from ornament in order to serve as a base for the more elaborate work above. The culmination of high color effect will be found in the spandrels between the main arches. Here the work is carried to a high pitch of intensity of color, and reliance is placed on the main cornice of the building, which is very simply treated, to act as a balancing and quieting effect in the general composition. In the center of the spandrels is placed a beautiful winged figure representing the idea of transportation. This figure is painted in light colors, and will have a background of gold-leaf.

The color scheme of the building as a whole, of course, culminates in the great golden doorway. This entire entrance, 100 feet wide and 70 feet high, which is incrusted over its entire surface with delicate designs in relief, is covered throughout its entire extent with gold, and colors in small quantities are worked in between the designs and reliefs so as to give the whole a wonderfully effective aspect.

Handbook of the World's Columbian Exposition (Chicago: Rand, McNally & Co., 1893): 30–34.

22
Emotional Architecture as Compared with Intellectual: A Study in Subjective and Objective (1894)

When read to the annual convention of the American Institute of Architects in New York, October 1894, this essay was called "Emotional Architecture as Compared with Classical," the title proposed by AIA Secretary Alfred Stone and later changed by Sullivan. The essay ends by comparing the "almost exclusively intellectual" architecture of ancient Greece with the overly emotional Gothic. Sullivan admired both, but neither one, nor any other historical style, he said, was a suitable model for American design in the late nineteenth century. Yet both styles had a great deal to offer to the present. If Greek could be merged with Gothic, or to put it Sullivan's way, if architects could condition intellect with emotion, they might develop culturally appropriate ways to express themselves.

How strange it seems that education, in practice, so often means suppression: that instead of leading the mind outward to the light of day it crowds things in upon it that darken and weary it. Yet evidently the true object of education, now as ever, is to develop the capabilities of the head and of the heart. He, therefore, who possesses a sound head and a responsive heart is worthy of enlightened guidance, is amenable to educational influence.

Let us now imagine a simple youth so equipped, so gifted, I am almost forced to say, an inborn poet, untaught, unschooled, and living an out-door life. So familiarly has he fared with sunshine and air and the living things, that they seem, as indeed they are, every-day and common to him.

Yet the mere community of their lives, the similarity in the experiences of the boy, the plants and the animals in that native, simple, naïf, unsullied state that we who are perhaps unduly artificial call by contrast natural, this state has drawn him very near to them all.

Breathing the same air as they, maturing in the same glowing sunshine, sustained by the same satisfying moisture, he and they expand side by side, defining themselves intimately to each other; and the boy, growing always, after a while feels himself to be not only with them but of them. His is a brotherhood with the trees; a wistful eye he softens to the flowers; he has a comely friendship for them all.

He knows that the young leaves love the dew; that the tendril reaches quietly for the twig it may cling to. He has seen the fern unfolding its brown spiral to become anon green and regular. He has splashed knee-deep in the marsh; he knows the dank fragrance very well; he parts his friends the rushes to make a way for his eyes that seek what they may devour—his eyes with a keen and endless appetite. His hands touch the warmish water: sniffing the active air, he lives as only a boy can live—his lively sensibilities always in physical touch with his surroundings, in the full and irrepressible enjoyment of his five senses.

These five senses, and they only, stand between him and nature. It is they that interpret her affection; and the ready language that they deal in keeps him in such a natural sympathy, so well in touch, so intimately at ease, that he does not for a moment realize that he is then and there doing that which education, so called, once having made inoperative in him, he will in after years, poet though he be, reacquire only with the utmost difficulty the power to do.

This something that he is doing, and the physical and psychic state that it implies, we call *Touch:* meaning not the touch of the painter, not the touch of the sculptor, not the mechanical and technical touch of the fingers only, nor quite their negligent contact with things, but the exquisite touch of the sensibilities, the warm physical touch of the body, the touch of a sound head and a responsive heart, the touch of the native one, the poet, out of doors, in spontaneous communion with Nature.

So has our youngster started easily and naturally, all alone without premeditation or guidance, upon the road to knowledge, to leadership and power. For this sensibility, this healthfulness, this touch, this directness of apprehension, this natural clearness of eyesight that is his, is the first essential prerequisite in the early analytical strivings of the mind: it is that perfect concrete analysis by the senses and the sympathies which serves as a basis for the abstract analyses of the intellect.

Let us not forget our little man, for he is to companion me in spirit through this discourse. I believe he exists somewhere, has in his breast the true architectural afflatus, and will some day come forth the Messiah of our art. For he has that early and sure understanding by the eyes that will survive the future uncertainties of the brain. He has that exalted animal sense which alone can discern the pathway to hidden knowledge; that acute and instant scent in matters objective leading to matters subjective that we call *Intuition*.

This physical endowment, this sense of touch, is, decidedly, wherever found, a generous gift of nature, but it is potent for results in so far only as it is urged into sustained and decisive action by a certain appetite or desire.

This desire, this insistence, this urgency which will not be denied; this uncomfortable hunger, this uneasy searching, this profound discontent, oh! so deep; this cry for more; this appetite, this yearning, ever unsatisfied, is not of the body alone but of the soul, and, always and everywhere, in all times and in all places, high or low, wherever found, it is the dominant characteristic of man's eminence in nature—it is the justification of the eminence of a few men among their fellows.

For appetite, in a state of nature, implies not only a keen desire and a search for the food wanted, but, as well, a rejection of all else, thus insuring a wonderful singleness of purpose, a concentration of action, a definiteness of end in the selection of that nourishment of the faculties which, when assimilated, is to become in turn thought and expression through the agency of a second desire equally great, equally intense, equally insistent, namely, the desire to act. This desire to act we call *Imagination*.

These two great desires, which are in essence the desire to absorb and the desire to emit, the desire to know and the desire to test, the desire to hear and the desire to utter, are the basis not only of a true and effective education, not only are they the wholesome body and the enchanting voice of art, but they are greater than these, for they are the animating quality of that higher purpose and significance of art that we call poetry.

Now the desire to act that in due time follows upon nutrition can assert itself tangibly and fully only by means of three agencies, the which, by virtue of its lifegiving qualities, this nutritive power has called into being. All three of them must cooperate in turn in order to produce a fully rounded result. They are first, the *Imagination*, which is the very beginning of action because it is a sympathy that lives both in our senses and our intellect— the flash between the past and the future, the middle link in that living chain or sequence leading from nature unto art, and that lies deep down in the emotions and the will. It is this divine faculty which, in an illumined instant, in that supreme moment when ideas are born, reveals the end with the beginning, and liberates, as an offspring of man, that which before had rested, perhaps for untold centuries, dormant but potential in the inmost heart of nature. This is the supreme crisis. This is the summit of the soul, the fertile touch of the spirit, the smile of nature's bounty—the moment of *Inspiration!* All else is from this moment on a foregone conclusion, an absolute certainty to the mastermind: a task surely, but not a doubt.

Second in this trinity comes *Thought*, the faculty that doubts and inquires, that recognizes time and space and the material limitations, that slowly systemizes, that works by small increments and cumulation, that formulates, that concentrates, works, reworks and reviews, that goes slowly, deliberately, that makes very firm and sure, and that eventually arrives at a science of logical statement that shall shape and define the scheme and structure that is to underlie, penetrate and support the form of an art work. It is the hard, the bony structure, it is the tough, tendinous fibre; it may be at times perhaps as limber as the lips that move, yet it is never the need of smiling—never the smile.

Third, last, and the winsome one, exuberant in life and movement, copious in speech, comes *Expression,* open-armed and free, supple, active, dramatic, changeable, beautifully pensive, persuasive and wonderful. Hers it is to clothe the structure of art with a form of beauty; for she is the perfection of the physical, she is the physical itself, and the uttermost attainment of emotionality. Hers is an infinite tenderness, an adorable and sweet fascination. In her companionship, imaginative Thought, long searching, has found its own, and lives anew, immortal, filled with sensibility, graciousness and the warm blood of a fully rounded maturity.

Thus Art comes into Life! Thus Life comes into Art!

And thus by reason of a process of elaboration and growth,

through the natural storage and upbuilding of the products of nutrition lifting themselves higher and higher into organization, the physical and spiritual experiences of our lives, seeking reproduction, shall find imaginative utterance, in their own image, in a *harmonious system of thinking and an equally harmonious method of expressing the thought.*

And so it shall come that when our nourishment shall be natural, our imagination therefore fervid, intense and vision-like; when our thinking and our speech shall have become as processes of nature; when, in consequence, from its mysterious abode in visible things, the invisible and infinitely fluent spirit of the universe passing to us shall have made our tongues eloquent, our utterance serene, then, and not till then, shall we possess, individually and as a people, the necessary elements of a great *Style.*

For otherwise and without this unitary impulse our expression, though delicate as a flower, our thinking as abstract as the winds that blow, our imagination as luminous as the dawn, are useless and unavailing to create: they may set forth, they cannot create.

Man, by means of his physical power, his mechanical resources, his mental ingenuity, may set things side by side. A composition, literally so called, will result, but not a great art work, not at all an art work in fact, but merely a more or less refined exhibition of brute force exercised upon helpful materials. It may be as a noise in lessening degrees of offensiveness, it can never become a musical tone. Though it shall have ceased to be vulgar in becoming sophistical, it will remain to the end what it was in the beginning: impotent to inspire—dead, absolutely dead.

It cannot for a moment be doubted that an art work to be alive, to awaken us to its life, to inspire us sooner or later with its purpose, must indeed be animate with a soul, must have been breathed upon by the spirit and must breathe in turn that spirit. It must stand for the actual, vital first-hand experiences of the one who made it, and must represent his deep-down impression not only of physical nature but more especially and necessarily his understanding of the out-working of that *Great Spirit* which makes nature so intelligible to us that it ceases to be a phantasm and becomes a sweet, a superb, a convincing *Reality.*

It absolutely must be the determination and the capacity of the artist that his work shall be as real and convincing as is his own life: as suggestive as his own eyesight makes all things to him; and yet as unreal, as fugitive, as inscrutable, as subjective, as the why and wherefore of the simplest flower that blows.

It is the presence of this unreality that makes the art work real: it is by virtue of this silent subjectivity that the objective voice of an art song becomes sonorous and thrilling.

Unless, therefore, subjectivity permeate an art work that work cannot aspire to greatness; for whatever of imagination, of thought and of expression it may possess, these as such will remain three separate things—not three phases of one thing.

An artist must necessarily, therefore, remain a more or less educated hand worker, a more or less clever sophisticator, a more or less successful framer of compromises, unless, when he was born, there was born with him a hunger for the spiritual; for all other craving avails as naught. Unless, as a child, with that marvelous instinct given only to children, he has heard the voice of nature murmuring in the woodland or afield or seaward, no after hearing can avail to catch this revelation.

And thus it is that subjectivity and objectivity, not as two separate elements but as two complementary and harmonious phases of one impulse, have always constituted and will always constitute the embodied spirit of art.

No phase of human nature can contain greater interest for the student of psychology than the history, natural, political, religious and artistic, of the successive phases for good and for ill of Objectivity and Subjectivity. *They are the two controlling elements of human endeavor.* They have caused in their internecine warfare misery and perturbation. They are ordinarily known and spoken of as the intellectual and the emotional, but they lie deeper, much deeper, than these: they lie in the very heart of Nature. Coming into man's being, they have been antagonistic because of the fanaticism and one-sidedness of human nature, because of its immobility. Because from the beginning man has been beset by beautiful, by despicable, illusions. Because one set

of men have believed in what they could see and another set
have believed in what they could not see. Because it has too
often happened that the man who could see with the outer eye
could not see with the inner eye; because the other man, rhap-
sodizing with the clear insight of faith, had no thought for the
things of this world. Neither has believed in the virtue of the
other. Neither has inferred, from the presence of the other, the
necessary existence of a balancing but hidden power. Now and
then through the ages they have come twin-born in the bosom
of an individual man—upon whose brow the generations have
placed the wreath of immortality.

So vast, so overwhelming is the power of a great, a properly
balanced subjectivity, so enormously does it draw on the spiritual nutrition and stored-up vitality of the world, that, soon sap-
ping this up, and still craving, the man possessed of it, urged by
it, goes straight to the unfailing bounty of nature, and there, by
virtue of his passionate adoration, passing the portals of the objective, he enters that extraordinary communion that the sacred
writers called to "walk with God."

*There can be no doubt that the most profound desire that fills the
human soul, the most heartfelt hope, is the wish to be at peace with
Nature and the Inscrutable Spirit; nor can there be a doubt that the
greatest Art Work is that which most nearly typifies a realization of
this ardent, patient longing. All efforts, of the body, all undertakings
of the mind, tend, consciously or unconsciously, toward this consummation, tend toward this final peace: the peace of perfect equilibrium,
the repose of absolute unity, the serenity of a complete identification.*

When, therefore, turning from this our contemplation we
compare the outworking of the vital processes of nature with the
so-called creative activity of the average man of education and
culture, we wonder at the disparity, we seek its cause.

When, after having with joy observed the quality of identity
and singleness that Nature imparts to her offspring, when with
aroused expectancy, with a glowing sense of the richness, fullness and variety that might and should come from the man's
brain with the impulse of nature's fecundity flowing through it,

we seek—we are amazed to find in this man's work no such thing.

When we, in place of a fertile unity which we had hoped for, come suddenly upon miscellany and barrenness, we are deeply mortified, we are rudely shocked.

We are dismayed at this: that man, Nature's highest product, should alone have gone awry, that with remarkable perversity he should have strayed—that for the simple and obvious he should substitute the factitious, the artificial.

The cause needs not a long searching, it is near at hand. It lies precisely in that much glorified, much abused word "education."

To my view no word in the entire vocabulary of the English language contains so much of pathos, so much of tragedy as this one pitiful word "education," for it typifies a fundamental perversity of the human soul, a willful blindness of the mind, a poverty of the heart.

For one brain that education has stimulated and strengthened, it has malformed, stupefied and discouraged thousands. Only the strongest, only the masterful, can dominate it, and return to the ownership of their souls.

For it is education's crime that it has removed us from Nature. As tender children it took us harshly away with stern words, and the sweet face of our natural mother has faded in the unspeakable past, whence it regards us at times, dimly and flittingly, causing in us uneasy and disturbing emotion.

And thus it is through a brutish and mean system of guidance, through the density of atmosphere that we have breathed, that we are not what our successors may easily become, a race filled with spiritual riches in addition to the vast material wealth.

That in place of a happy people, open-eyed children of Nature teeming with beautiful impulses, we are a people lost in darkness, groping under a sooty and lurid sky sinister with clouds that shut out the sunshine and the clear blue heavens.

Yet the murky materialism—the fierce objectivity, the fanatical selfishness—of this dark age of ours, in this sense the darkest of all dark ages, is so prodigious, so grotesque, so monstrous, that in its very self it contains the elements of change: from its own intensity, its own excess, its complex striving, it predetermines the golden age of the world.

The human mind in all countries having gone to the uttermost limit of its own capacity, flushed with its conquests, haughty after its self-assertion upon emerging from the prior dark age, is now nearing a new phase, a phase inherent in the nature and destiny of things.

The human mind, like the silk-worm oppressed with the fullness of its own accumulation, has spun about itself gradually and slowly a cocoon that at last has shut out the light of the world from which it drew the substance of its thread. But this darkness has produced the chrysalis, and we within the darkness feel the beginning of our throes. The inevitable change, after centuries upon centuries of preparation, is about to begin.

Human development, through a series of vast attractions and perturbations, has now arrived at a materialism so profound, so exalted as to prove the fittest basis for a coming era of spiritual splendor.

To foresee this necessity, consider but a moment the richness of our heritage from the past, its orderly sequence, its uplifting wave of power, its conservation of force.

Think of the Hindu, with folded hands, soaring in contemplation, thousands of years ago—think of what he has left us. Think of the Hebrew man coming out of Ur of the Chaldees, to find for us the One Great Spirit. Think of the sombre Egyptians, those giants who struggled so courageously with fate—think of the stability they have given to us. Think of the stars of Israel, singing in the morning's dawn. Think of the lonely man of Nazareth breathing a spirit of gentleness of which the world had never heard before. Think of the delicately objective Greeks, lovers of the physical, accurate thinkers, the worshippers of beauty. Think that in them the Orient, sleeping, was born anew. Think of the Goth, and with him the birth of emotion as we know it. Think of modern Science which has taught us not to fear. Think of modern Music, arising in glory as the heart took wings—*a new thing under the sun*. Think deeply of the French Revolution and Democracy—the utterance of freedom, the beginning of the Individual Man. Think now of our own age with its machinery, its steam power, its means of communication, its annihilation of distance. Think of the humanitarianism of our day. Think, as we stand here, now, in a new land, a Promised Land that at last is ours, think how passionately latent, how marvelous to contemplate is America, our country. *Think that here destiny has decreed there shall be enacted the final part in the drama of man's emancipation—the redemption of his soul!*

Think of these things, think of what they signify, of what they promise for us, and think then that as architects it peculiarly behooves us to review our own special past, to forecast our future, to realize somewhat our present status.

Summoned to answer before an enlightened judgment seat, how shall we now give other, alas, than a wretched accounting of our stewardship! How shall we excuse our sterility? We surely need to inquire, for we must need explain the emaciation of our art in the midst of plenty, its weakness in the midst of strength, its beggarly poverty in the midst of abundance.

By what glamour or speciousness of words shall we persuade a wrathful judgment toward kindness? How can our vapid record be made to plead for us?

Shall we summon the clear-eyed, intellectual Greek or the emotional and introspective Goth to bear witness that we stand as ambassadors in their names—we would surely be repudiated.

Shall we call to the fateful Egyptian or the dashing, polished Assyrian—one would scorn us, the other would flout us.

Who are we then, and how shall we explain our sinister condition, our mere existence?

Shall we claim we are second cousins to Europe, or must we, before we can ourselves behold the truth, so far abase our heads in the ashes as to acknowledge that we of the great and glorious ending of the nineteenth century are the direct lineal descendants of the original bastards and indiscretions of architecture?

Or, still seeking excuses in our fin-de-siècle pocket, shall we plead in the language of myth that our art, like Brünnehilde, lies sleeping: that she awaits a son of nature, one without fear, to penetrate the wall of flame, to lift her helmet's visor?

Dreading the storm, shall we seek shelter under the spreading plea that poets are born, not made; that, if Nature for all these centuries has not brought forth a great master-spirit in the architectural art, it must be for very good reasons of her own—

for reasons definitely interwrought with the beneficence of her own rhythmical movements? That, with her endless fecundity, there must be a profoundly significant reason for this barrenness.

Or, perhaps, shall we simply say that men have now turned to other gods, that they have forgotten the ancient deities?

That there has arisen in our land a new king who knows not Joseph; that he has set o'er us taskmasters to afflict us with burdens.

All these pleadings may be true, yet after all they do not explain why we make easy things very difficult, why we employ artificial instead of natural processes, why we walk backwards instead of forwards, why we see cross-eyed instead of straight-eyed, why we turn our minds inside out instead of letting them alone; they do not explain why we are so vulgarly self-conscious, so pitifully bashful, so awkward in our art, so explanatory, so uncertain that we know anything at all or are anybody in particular, so characterless, so insipid, so utterly without savor. They do not explain why the intellectual and emotional phases of the architectural mind do precisely the wrong thing when the right thing is quite attainable.

No! I pretend to advocate the real, the true cause of my generation, of my art. I do not wish to abase them except in so far as he who loveth chasteneth. I know that the secret of our weakness lies not only in our plethoric dyspepsia, in our lack of desire, in our deficiency of gumption and moral courage, but that it lies primarily in the utterly purposeless education we have received.

I know that the architectural schools teach a certain art or method of study in which one is made partly familiar with the objective aspects and forms of architecture. I know that this, as far as it goes, is conscientiously and thoroughly done. But I also know that it is doubtful, in my mind, if one student in a thousand emerges from his school possessed of a fine conception of what architecture really is in form, in spirit and in truth: and I say this is not primarily the student's fault. I know that before entering his architectural school he has passed through other schools, and that they began the mischief: that they had told him grammar was a book, algebra was a book, geometry another book, geography, chemistry, physics, still others: they never told him, never permitted him, to guess for himself how these things were actually intense symbols, complex ratios, representing man's relation to Nature and his fellow man; they never told him that his mathematics, etc. etc., came into being in response to a *desire* in the human breast to come nearer to nature—that the full moon looked round to the human eye ages before the circle was dreamed of.

Our student knows, to be sure, as a result of his teaching that the Greeks built certain-shaped buildings, that the Goths built certain-shaped buildings, and that other peoples built other buildings of still other shapes. He knows, moreover, if he has been a conscientious hewer of wood and drawer of water, a thousand and one specific facts concerning the shapes and measurements and ratios of the whole and the parts of said buildings, and can neatly and deftly draw and color them to scale. He moreover has read in the philosophies or heard at lectures that the architecture of a given time gives one an excellent idea of the civilization of that time.

This, roughly speaking, is the sum total of his education, and he takes his architectural instruction literally, just as he has taken every other form of instruction literally from the time he was a child—because he has been told to do so, because he has been told that architecture is a fixed, a real, a specific, a definite thing, that it's all done, that it's all known, arranged, tabulated and put away neatly in handy packages called books. He is allowed to believe, though perhaps not distinctly so taught, that, to all intents and purposes, when his turn comes, if he wishes to make some architecture for Americans or for this generation at large, he can dip it out of his books with the same facility that dubs a grocer dipping beans out of a bin. He is taught by the logic of events that architecture in practice is a commercial article, like a patent medicine, unknown in its mixture and sold to the public exclusively on the brand.

He has seriously been told at the school, and has been encouraged in this belief by the endorsement of people of culture, that he can learn all about architecture if he but possess the attributes of scholarship and industry. That architecture is the name of a system of accredited, historical facts as useful, as available and as susceptible to inspection as the books of a mercantile house.

Everything literal, formal and smart in his nature has been encouraged—the early and plastic glow to emotion and sensibility has been ignored.

He has been taught many cold and dead things, but the one warm living thing that he has not been taught and apparently never will be taught is the stately and all-comprehending truth that architecture, wherever it has appeared and reached a spontaneous culmination, is not at all what we so stupidly call a reality, but, on the contrary, it is a most complex, a glowing and gloriously wrought metaphor, embodying as no other form of language under the sun can do, the pure, clean and deep inspiration of the race flowing as a stream of living water from its well-spring to the sea.

He has not been taught that an architect, to be a true exponent of his time, must possess first, last and always the sympathy, the intuition of a poet; that this is the one real, vital principle that survives through all places and all times.

This seeking for a natural expression of our lives, of our thoughts, our meditations, our feelings, is the architectural art as I understand it: and it is because I so understand it, that, ignoring the viciousness of the past, I gladly make an appeal to the good that is in human nature—that goodness of heart and soundness of head, that ready and natural response of the soul in which I have always trusted and shall always trust. It is to this sane and wholesome quality that I plead for the abiding sincerity and nobility of our art. It is to this *manliness* that I call to come before the judgment seat and make an answer for us.

I know very well that our country will in due time possess a most interesting, varied, characteristic and beautiful architecture; that the time will begin whenever we take as our point of the departure the few and simple elements of architecture and not its complex forms. That this time will come just as soon as the young are relieved of the depressing weight of a factitious education, the benumbing influence of an instruction that insulates them from the vitalizing currents of nature. Just so soon as those having them in charge, coming to the full sense of the fact, re-

alizing how truly dangerous a thing is a little knowledge, a partial knowledge, dreading to assume the responsibility for
stunted, for imperfectly developed natures, feeling how deeply
necessary it is that a technical or intellectual training be supplemented by a full, a rich, a chaste development of the emotions,
shall say to the young that they are free, that from the musty
school they may fly to the open air, to the sunshine, to the birds,
the flowers, and, wanton and joyous in their own fancies, face
to face with the integrity of nature, they shall substitute for the
arbitrary discipline of the school the natural, the easy self-control
of a dignified manhood, to the end that not books but personal
feeling, personal character and personal responsibility shall form
the true foundation of their art

It has, alas, for centuries been taught that the intellect and the
emotions were two separate and antagonistic things. This teaching has been firmly believed, cruelly lived up to.

How depressing it is to realize that it might have been taught
that they are two beautifully congenial and harmonious phases
of that single and integral essence that we call the soul. That no
nature in which the development of either is wanting can be
called a completely rounded nature.

That, therefore, classical architecture, so called (meaning the
Greek), was one-sided and incomplete because it was almost exclusively intellectual. That the emotional architecture (meaning
especially the Gothic) was likewise one-sided and incomplete,
however great and beautiful its development of feeling, because
of the almost total absence of mentality. That no complete architecture has yet appeared in the history of the world because
men, in this form of art alone, have obstinately sought to express
themselves solely in terms either of the head or of the heart.

I hold that architectural art, thus far, has failed to reach its
highest development, its fullest capability of imagination, of
thought and expression, because it has not yet found a way to
become truly plastic: it does not yet respond to the poet's touch.
That it is today the only art for which the multitudinous
rhythms of outward nature, the manifold fluctuations of man's
inner being have no significance, no place.

That the Greek Architecture, unerring as far as it went—and
it went very far indeed in one direction—was but one radius

within the field of a possible circle of expression. That, though perfect in its eyesight, definite in its desires, clear in its purpose, it was not resourceful in forms: that it lacked the flexibility and the humanity to respond to the varied and constantly shifting desires of the heart.

It was a pure, it was a noble art, wherefore we call it classic; but after all it was an apologetic art, for, while possessing serenity, it lacked the divinely human element of mobility: the Greek never caught the secret of the changing of the seasons, the orderly and complete sequences of their rhythm within the calmly moving year. Nor did this selfsame Greek know what we now know of Nature's bounty, for music in those days had not been born: this lovely friend, approaching man to man, had not yet begun to bloom as a rose, to exhale its wondrous perfume.

That the Gothic architecture, with sombre ecstatic eye, with its thought far above with Christ in the heavens, seeing but little here below, feverish and overwrought, taking comfort in gardening and plant life, sympathizing deeply with Nature's visible forms, evolved a copious and rich variety of incidental expressions but lacked the unitary comprehension, the absolute consciousness and mastery of pure form that can come alone of unclouded and serene contemplation, of perfect repose and peace of mind.

I believe, in other words, that the Greek knew the statics, the Goth the dynamics, of the art, but that neither of them suspected the mobile equilibrium of it: neither of them divined the movement and the stability of nature. Failing in this, both have forever fallen short, and must pass away when the true, the *Poetic Architecture* shall arise—that architecture which shall speak with clearness, with eloquence, and with warmth, of the fullness, the completeness of man's intercourse with Nature and with his fellow men.

Moreover, we know, or should by this time know, that human nature has now become too rich in possessions, too well equipped, too magnificently endowed, that any hitherto architecture can be said to have hinted at its resources, much less to have exhausted them by anticipation.

It is this consciousness, this pride, that shall be our motive, our friend, philosopher and guide in the beautiful country that stretches so invitingly before us.

In that land, the schools, having found the object of their long, blind searching, shall teach directness, simplicity, naturalness: they shall protect the young against palpable illusion. They shall teach that, while man once invented a process called composition, Nature has forever brought forth organisms. They shall encourage the love of Nature that wells up in every childish heart, and shall not suppress, shall not stifle, the teeming imagination of the young.

They shall teach, as the result of their own bitter experience, that conscious mental effort, that conscious emotionality, are poor mates to breed from, and that true parturition comes of a deep, instinctive, subconscious desire. That true art, springing fresh from Nature, must have in it, to live, much of the glance of an eye, much of the sound of a voice, much of the life of a life.

That Nature is strong, generous, comprehensive, fecund, subtile: that in growth and decadence she continually sets forth the drama of man's life.

That, thro' the rotating seasons, thro' the procession of the years, thro' the march of the centuries, permeating all, sustaining all, there murmurs the still, small voice of a power that holds us in the hollow of its hand.

The Inland Architect and News Record 24 (November 1894): 32–34.

23
The Tall Office Building Artistically Considered
(1896)

This is Louis Sullivan's most influential essay, continuously reprinted and anthologized since its first appearance. Early in 1896 he was nearly forty years old and working alone, his partnership with Dankmar Adler having dissolved in 1895. Sullivan had just completed the Guaranty Building

(1894-95) in Buffalo, considered by many to be his most beautiful and most nearly perfect skyscraper, the fifth one constructed from a total of thirteen high-rise projects he had designed, beginning in 1890. Collectively, they were perceived as an aesthetically fitting and philosophically unique approach to the genre. And since the genre was a historically new one, Sullivan's pioneering work gave his words special import. Synthesizing his mature thinking on the skyscraper after six years, this essay explains how he formulated his system of façade organization and his vertical aesthetic, but most significantly, how he derived from nature study his famous principle, "Form follows function."

The architects of this land and generation are now brought face to face with something new under the sun—namely, that evolution and integration of social conditions, that special grouping of them, that results in a demand for the erection of tall office buildings.

It is not my purpose to discuss the social conditions; I accept them as the fact, and say at once that the design of the tall office building must be recognized and confronted at the outset as a problem to be solved—a vital problem, pressing for a true solution.

Let us state the conditions in the plainest manner. Briefly, they are these: offices are necessary for the transaction of business; the invention and perfection of the high-speed elevators make vertical travel, that was once tedious and painful, now easy and comfortable; development of steel manufacture has shown the way to safe, rigid, economical constructions rising to a great height; continued growth of population in the great cities, consequent congestion of centers and rise in value of ground, stimulate an increase in number of stories; these successfully piled one upon another, react on ground values—and so on, by action and reaction, interaction and inter-reaction. Thus has come about that form of lofty construction called the "modern office building." It has come in answer to a call, for in it a new grouping of social conditions has found a habitation and a name.

Up to this point all in evidence is materialistic, an exhibition of force, of resolution, of brains in the keen sense of the word. It is the joint product of the speculator, the engineer, the builder.

Problem: How shall we impart to this sterile pile, this crude, harsh, brutal agglomeration, this stark, staring exclamation of eternal strife, the graciousness of those higher forms of sensibility and culture that rest on the lower and fiercer passions? How shall we proclaim from the dizzy height of this strange, weird, modern housetop the peaceful evangel of sentiment, of beauty, the cult of a higher life?

This is the problem; and we must seek the solution of it in a process analogous to its own evolution—indeed, a continuation of it—namely, by proceeding step by step from general to special aspects, from coarser to finer considerations.

It is my belief that it is of the very essence of every problem that it contains and suggests its own solution. This I believe to be natural law. Let us examine, then, carefully the elements, let us search out this contained suggestion, this essence of the problem.

The practical conditions are, broadly speaking, these:

Wanted—1st, a story below-ground, containing boilers, engines of various sorts, etc.—in short, the plant for power, heating, lighting, etc. 2nd, a ground floor, so called, devoted to stores, banks, or other establishments requiring large area, ample spacing, ample light, and great freedom of access. 3rd, a second story readily accessible by stairways—this space usually in large subdivisions, with corresponding liberality in structural spacing and expanse of glass and breadth of external openings. 4th, above this an indefinite number of stories of offices piled tier upon tier, one tier just like another tier, one office just like all the other offices—an office being similar to a cell in a honeycomb, merely a compartment, nothing more. 5th, and last, at the top of this pile is placed a space or story that, as related to the life and usefulness of the structure, is purely physiological in its nature—namely, the attic. In this the circulatory system completes itself and makes its grand turn, ascending and descending. The space is filled with tanks, pipes, valves, sheaves, and mechanical etcetera that supplement and complement the force-originating plant hidden below-ground in the cellar. Finally, or at the beginning rather, there must be on the ground floor a main aperture or entrance common to all the occupants or patrons of the building.

This tabulation is, in the main, characteristic of every tall office building in the country. As to the necessary arrangements for light courts, these are not germane to the problem, and as will become soon evident, I trust need not be considered here. These things, and such others as the arrangement of elevators, for example, have to do strictly with the economics of the building, and I assume them to have been fully considered and disposed of to the satisfaction of purely utilitarian and pecuniary demands. Only in rare instances does the plan or floor arrangement of the tall office building take on an aesthetic value, and this usually when the lighting court is external or becomes an internal feature of great importance.

As I am here seeking not for an individual or special solution, but for a true normal type, the attention must be confined to those conditions that, in the main, are constant in all tall office buildings, and every mere incidental and accidental variation eliminated from the consideration, as harmful to the clearness of the main inquiry.

The practical horizontal and vertical division or office unit is naturally based on a room of comfortable area and height, and the size of this standard office room as naturally predetermines the standard structural unit, and, approximately, the size of window openings. In turn, these purely arbitrary units of structure form in an equally natural way the true basis of the artistic development of the exterior. Of course the structural spacings and openings in the first or mercantile story are required to be the largest of all; those in the second or quasi-mercantile story are of a somewhat similar nature. The spacings and openings in the attic are of no importance whatsoever (the windows have no actual value), for light may be taken from the top, and no recognition of a cellular division is necessary in the structural spacing.

Hence it follows inevitably, and in the simplest possible way, that if we follow our natural instincts without thought of books, rules, precedents, or any such educational impedimenta to a spontaneous and "sensible" result, we will in the following manner design the exterior of our tall office building—to wit:

Beginning with the first story, we give this a main entrance that attracts the eye to its location, and the remainder of the story we treat in a more or less liberal, expansive, sumptuous way—a way based exactly on the practical necessities, but expressed with a sentiment of largeness and freedom. The second story we treat in a similar way, but usually with milder pretension. Above this, throughout the indefinite number of typical office tiers, we take our cue from the individual cell, which requires a window with its separating pier, its sill and lintel, and we, without more ado, make them look all alike because they are all alike. This brings us to the attic, which, having no division into office-cells, and no special requirement for lighting, gives us the power to show by means of its broad expanse of wall, and its dominating weight and character, that which is the fact— namely, that the series of office tiers has come definitely to an end.

This may perhaps seem a bald result and a heartless, pessimistic way of stating it, but even so we certainly have advanced a most characteristic stage beyond the imagined sinister building of the speculator-engineer-builder combination. For the hand of the architect is now definitely felt in the decisive position at once taken, and the suggestion of a thoroughly sound, logical, coherent expression of the conditions is becoming apparent.

When I say the hand of the architect, I do not mean necessarily the accomplished and trained architect. I mean only a man with a strong, natural liking for buildings, and a disposition to shape them in what seems to his unaffected nature a direct and simple way. He will probably tread an innocent path from his problem to its solution, and therein he will show an enviable gift of logic. If he have some gift for form in detail, some feeling for form purely and simply as form, some love for that, his result in addition to its simple straightforward naturalness and completeness in general statement, will have something of the charm of sentiment.

However, thus far the results are only partial and tentative at best; relatively true, they are but superficial. We are doubtless right in our instinct but we must seek a fuller justification, a finer sanction, for it.

* * *

I assume now that in the study of our problem we have passed through the various stages of inquiry, as follows: 1st, the social basis of the demand for tall office buildings; 2nd, its literal material satisfaction; 3rd, the elevation of the question from considerations of literal planning, construction, and equipment, to the plane of elementary architecture as a direct outgrowth of sound, sensible building; 4th, the question again elevated from an elementary architecture to the beginnings of true architectural expression, through the addition of a certain quality and quantity of sentiment.

But our building may have all these in a considerable degree and yet be far from that adequate solution of the problem I am attempting to define. We must now heed the imperative voice of emotion.

It demands of us, what is the chief characteristic of the tall office building? And at once we answer, it is lofty. This loftiness is to the artist-nature its thrilling aspect. It is the very open organ-tone in its appeal. It must be in turn the dominant chord in his expression of it, the true excitant of his imagination. It must be tall, every inch of it tall. The force and power of altitude must be in it, the glory and pride of exaltation must be in it. It must be every inch a proud and soaring thing, rising in sheer exultation that from bottom to top it is a unit without a single dissenting line—that it is the new, the unexpected, the eloquent peroration of most bald, most sinister, most forbidding conditions.

The man who designs in this spirit and with the sense of responsibility to the generation he lives in must be no coward, no denier, no bookworm, no dilettante. He must live of his life and for his life in the fullest, most consummate sense. He must realize at once and with the grasp of inspiration that the problem of the tall office building is one of the most stupendous, one of the most magnificent opportunities that the Lord of Nature in His beneficence has ever offered to the proud spirit of man.

That this has not been perceived—indeed, has been flatly denied—is an exhibition of human perversity that must give us pause.

* * *

One more consideration. Let us now lift this question into the region of calm, philosophic observation. Let us seek a comprehensive, a final solution: let the problem indeed dissolve.

Certain critics, and very thoughtful ones, have advanced the theory that the true prototype of the tall office building is the classical column, consisting of base, shaft and capital—the moulded base of the column typical of the lower stories of our building, the plain or fluted shaft suggesting the monotonous, uninterrupted series of office-tiers, and the capital the completing power and luxuriance of the attic.

Other theorizers, assuming a mystical symbolism as a guide, quote the many trinities in nature and art, and the beauty and conclusiveness of such trinity in unity. They aver the beauty of prime numbers, the mysticism of the number three, the beauty of all things that are in three parts—to wit, the day, subdividing into morning, noon, and night; the limbs, the thorax, and the head, constituting the body. So they say, should the building be in three parts vertically, substantially as before, but for different motives

Others, of purely intellectual temperament, hold that such a design should be in the nature of a logical statement; it should have a beginning, a middle, and an ending, each clearly defined—therefore again a building, as above, in three parts vertically.

Others, seeking their examples and justification in the vegetable kingdom, urge that such a design shall above all things be organic. They quote the suitable flower with its bunch of leaves at the earth, its long graceful stem, carrying the gorgeous single flower. They point to the pine-tree, its massy roots, its lithe, uninterrupted trunk, its tuft of green high in the air. Thus, they say, should be the design of the tall office building: again in three parts vertically.

Others still, more susceptible to the power of a unit than to the grace of a trinity, say that such a design should be struck out at a blow, as though by a blacksmith or by mighty Jove, or should be thought-born, as was Minerva, full grown. They accept the notion of a triple division as permissible and welcome, but non-essential. With them it is a subdivision of their unit: the unit does not come from the alliance of the three; they accept it without murmur, provided the subdivision does not disturb the sense of singleness and repose.

All of these critics and theorists agree, however, positively, unequivocally, in this, that the tall office building should not, must not, be made a field for the display of architectural knowledge in the encyclopædic sense; that too much learning in this instance is fully as dangerous, as obnoxious, as too little learning; that miscellany is abhorrent to their sense; that the sixteen-story building must not consist of sixteen separate, distinct and unrelated buildings piled one upon the other until the top of the pile is reached.

To this latter folly I would not refer were it not the fact that nine out of every ten tall office buildings are designed in precisely this way in effect, not by the ignorant, but by the educated. It would seem indeed, as though the "trained" architect, when facing this problem, were beset at every story, or at most, every third or fourth story, by the hysterical dread lest he be in "bad form"; lest he be not bedecking his building with sufficiency of quotation from this, that, or the other "correct" building in some other land and some other time; lest he be not copious enough in the display of his wares; lest he betray, in short, a lack of resource. To loosen up the touch of this cramped and fidgety hand, to allow the nerves to calm, the brain to cool, to reflect equably, to reason naturally, seems beyond him; he lives, as it were, in a waking nightmare filled with the disjecta membra of architecture. The spectacle is not inspiriting.

As to the former and serious views held by discerning and thoughtful critics, I shall, with however much of regret, dissent from them for the purpose of this demonstration, for I regard them as secondary only, non-essential, and as touching not at all upon the vital spot, upon the quick of the entire matter, upon the true, the immovable philosophy of the architectural art.

This view let me now state, for it brings to the solution of the problem a final, comprehensive formula.

All things in nature have a shape, that is to say, a form, an outward semblance, that tells us what they are, that distinguishes them from ourselves and from each other.

Unfailingly in nature these shapes express the inner life, the native quality, of the animal, tree, bird, fish, that they present to us; they are so characteristic, so recognizable, that we say, simply, it is "natural" it should be so. Yet the moment we peer beneath this surface of things, the moment we look through the tranquil reflection of ourselves and the clouds above us, down into the clear, fluent, unfathomable depth of nature, how startling is the silence of it, how amazing the flow of life, how absorbing the mystery. Unceasingly the essence of things is taking shape in the matter of things, and this unspeakable process we call birth and growth. Awhile the spirit and the matter fade away together, and it is this that we call decadence, death. These two happenings seem jointed and interdependent, blended into one like a bubble and its iridescence, and they seem borne along upon a slowly moving air. This air is wonderful past all understanding.

Yet to the steadfast eye of one standing upon the shore of things, looking chiefly and most lovingly upon that side on which the sun shines and that we feel joyously to be life, the heart is ever gladdened by the beauty, the exquisite spontaneity, with which life seeks and takes on its forms in an accord perfectly responsive to its needs. It seems ever as though the life and the form were absolutely one and inseparable, so adequate is the sense of fulfillment.

Whether it be the sweeping eagle in his flight or the open apple-blossom, the toiling work-horse, the blithe swan, the branching oak, the winding stream at its base, the drifting clouds, over all the coursing sun, form ever follows function, and this is the law. Where function does not change form does not change. The granite rocks, the ever-brooding hills, remain for ages; the lightning lives, comes into shape, and dies in a twinkling.

It is the pervading law of all things organic, and inorganic, of all things physical and metaphysical, of all things human and all things superhuman, of all true manifestations of the head, of the heart, of the soul, that the life is recognizable in its expression, that form ever follows function. This is the law.

Shall we, then, daily violate this law in our art? Are we so decadent, so imbecile, so utterly weak of eyesight, that we cannot perceive this truth so simple, so very simple? Is it indeed a truth so transparent that we see through it but do not see it? Is it really then, a very marvelous thing, or is it rather so common-place, so everyday, so near a thing to us, that we cannot perceive that the shape, form, outward expression, design or whatever we may choose, of the tall office building should in the very nature of things follow the functions of the building, and that where the function does not change, the form is not to change?

Does this not readily, clearly, and conclusively show that the lower one or two stories will take on a special character suited to the special needs, that the tiers of typical offices, having the same unchanging function, shall continue in the same unchanging form, and that as to the attic, specific and conclusive as it is in its very nature, its function shall equally be so in force, in significance, in continuity, in conclusiveness of outward expression? From this results, naturally, spontaneously, unwittingly, a three-part division, not from any theory, symbol, or fancied logic.

And thus the design of the tall office building takes its place with all other architectural types made when architecture, as has happened once in many years, was a living art. Witness the Greek temple, the Gothic cathedral, the medieval fortress.

And thus, when native instinct and sensibility shall govern the exercise of our beloved art; when the known law, the respected law, shall be that form ever follows function; when our architects shall cease struggling and prattling handcuffed and vain-glorious in the asylum of a foreign school; when it is truly felt, cheerfully accepted, that this law opens up the airy sunshine of green fields, and gives to us a freedom that the very beauty and sumptuousness of the outworking of the law itself as exhibited in nature will deter any sane, any sensitive man from changing into license, when it becomes evident that we are merely speaking a foreign language with a noticeable American accent, whereas each and every architect in the land might, under the benign influence of this law, express in the simplest, most modest, most natural way that which it is in him to say; that he might really and would surely develop his own characteristic individuality, and that the architectural art with him would certainly become a living form of speech, a natural form of utterance, giving surcease to him and adding treasures small and great to the growing art of his land; when we know and feel that Nature is our friend, not our implacable enemy—that an afternoon in the country, an hour by the sea, a full open view of one single day, through dawn, high noon, and twilight, will suggest to us so much that is rhythmical, deep, and eternal in the vast art of architecture, something so deep, so true, that all the narrow formalities, hard-and-fast rules, and strangling bonds of the schools cannot stifle it in us—then it may be proclaimed that we are on the high-road to a natural and satisfying art, an architecture that will soon become a fine art in the true, the best sense of the word, an art that will live because it will be of the people, for the people, and by the people.

Lippincott's Magazine 57 (March 1896): 403–9.

24
May Not Architecture Again Become a Living Art?
(c. 1897)

In this previously unpublished address, Louis Sullivan called for passion in design to overcome the ubiquitous architectural mediocrity of America. During the previous few years, after designing and building a winter home for himself in Ocean Springs, Mississippi, in 1890, he had become an accomplished horticulturist specializing in roses. Just as they represented to him finely cultivated architecture, so did finely cultivated architecture represent the spontaneity of the designer's heart responding to popular feeling. But it would take passion—losing one's self in the work—to overcome the stifling mediocrity he saw around him. Beginning in the late 1890s, partly because he received fewer commissions after his break with Adler, and for personal reasons as well, Sullivan grew bitter about life in general and the architectural situation in particular, sentiments that emerge here more clearly than they had before.

I.

When I was a youngster at school, the history-book we painfully worked in told of little else but of Kings and of wars. Yet I remember, distinctly, that it regularly said of each King in turn that his "ruling passion" was this, that or the other. So often did I have to learn this phrase by rote that tho' the Kings and the wars have now faded from my ken, this stereotyped expression remains embedded and encysted like a fragment of battle, a souvenir of weary forced marches and of hours under fire in the dingy school-room. Perhaps then it may prove true that all of value remaining in the residual memories of my school-day-history-purgatory, lies in the suggestiveness of that phrase, in that it now, coming again to my mind, leads me to hope that in that illusioned and fratricidal strife that it is fashionable to call our struggle with nature, there may arise in the domain of art a man of whom it may be said, with truth, that his ruling passion is a love of Architecture.

For in our modern days, recklessness, so-called, is rather at a discount, and the gift of "plunging" is now rarely met with beyond the confines of the wheat-pit or the college gridiron.

Yet the very abandon implied in recklessness, the capacity for extravagance, consecration, immolation, martyrdom, devotion, self-forgetfulness, or whatsoever you may choose to call it, according to the direction, force and permanence of its impulsion, is it not after all an heroic quality, and do we not all adore heroes!

Is not this "ruling passion" at the last analysis a real, a great thing, however despicable at times;—is not the passion to destroy essentially as powerful, as stupendous, as awe-inspiring, as the passion to create?

Is not after all that which is admirable in these things in reality that intensity, that concentration, that oblivious singleness of purpose, to which, whether of cold or of hot blood, we give the name of *Passion?*

And is this outcry of the heart, this need of all the faculties, more noble, more admirable, more adorable in aught than in that sphere of exquisite emotion wherein dwelt Heloise and Abelard, Hero and Leander, Laura and Petrarch in their loves,—

rising so high into the tenuous regions of our human atmosphere that of them we say not, this was their "ruling passion," but we say, this is the "Grand Passion,"—because the passion of Love!

II.

And is one's art then to be a thing of seclusion and of elderly maidenly reserve, of a thin and spare refinement? Is it to find full appeasement and quiet, orderly reduplication within the proprietary bonds of a well barricaded domesticity,—always assured within the confines of a rational, regulated and sober regime, always circumspect, always penurious, suspicious, stingy, self-contemplative and respectable, always eminently, painfully correct, always of a nice, clean, well-ordered mediocrity, always satisfactory and comprehensible to the average unimaginative burgher?

Is this what I am [to] understand by the thesis? Am I to understand that the question is asked of the average by the average and for the average? Am I to answer how the one average mediocrity called Architect is to make clear to the other average mediocrity, called in the plays, 1st Citizen, 2d Citizen and 3d Citizen, that that which is dead in his heart may be made to seem alive to all the citizens under the sun,—even to the 4th and the 5th Citizen?

Could ever there have been, can there ever be a question, that any art may live at any time? He who asks it, it may be, is well advised, but he has surely little faith;—and without a faith, what are we all,—but zeros?

While the eye sees, while the ear hears, while the heart beats, can it be that so beautiful a thing as art shall have no heroic adorer, no consecrated knight, no waving gallant plume?

Alas for the times, alack-a-day for the manners, if this be so!

Poor indeed is a people having no wealth of love for beauty!

Callous of heart, truly dwarfish of mind, minus of soul, is he who does not really cherish beauty.

For love of beauty means true love of life, means true knowledge of life, means true sympathy with life in all its phases.

I who say it, most profoundly believe it,—that the acme of

life is beauty. That the flower of life,—the very perfume of that flower, is beauty!

III.

Canon Hale, in his charming "Book about Roses,"* says in the opening lines that "He who would have beautiful roses in his garden must have beautiful roses *in his heart*. He must love them well and always."

Surely the cultivation of the rose, however delicate a function, is not a more subtle one than is the eduction of an art as curious as that of architecture; and may it not as truly be said that he who would cause a beautiful architecture to grow in the garden of this world, must himself possess a nature in which are always growing beautiful impulses and a beautiful love of his art?

The simile may indeed be carried further, for storms and frosts are not unknown to the gardens, and insect pests, blights, rust, drought and worm in the bud and worm at the root cause, evermore, bitterness, anguish, disappointment, despair,—ever followed by freshly budding hope.

If it be that eternal vigilance, patience, care, are the price of a truly fine rose (and let me say few have seen a really fine rose, few know what are the possibilities resident in this gracious flower), shall it succeed that a really healthful and fine expression of the architectural art may be secured at a lesser price,—may be bought at a bargain, gained by shrewdness, as it were?

If it be a fact that few know what is a fine rose, how many, in this sense, know what it is that actually constitutes a fine architecture; how many, looking upon architecture as it appears today, can divine what it ought to be under proper and fertile cultivation?

*Sullivan was probably referring here to Samuel Reynolds Hole (1819–1904), whose *A Book About Roses: How to Grow and Show Them* (Edinburgh: W. Blackwood and Sons, 1869) was revised in 1891 for E. Arnold, Publishers, in London. The fourteenth edition appeared in 1894, shortly before Sullivan wrote this essay.

If the unfolding of the queen of flowers is as a sacramental offering, so profoundly beautiful, so unsullied as it faints half-blown into the air, is that art of which I speak, less intimate, less insignificant, less persuasive of the graciousness of all that is best, cleanest, most admirable in man and in the real, the genuine aspirations of man's inmost being?

Should anything come fresher from the soil of a richly culti-vated nature, should anything be more natural, more sponta-neous, in its unfolding plan, should anything, can anything come straighter from the life of the people, straighter from the heart, the brain, of the artist than a truly fine building?

O, joyless the times and nerveless the manners when this is not so!

Sad indeed, dim and dreary the sight, to see this dainty, this high-bred, this ethereal type of a happy possibility,—crumpled, bedraggled, soiled, starved, small, haggard, pitiable.

Of such is the contemporaneous architecture of the world to-day.

To call it an art is to blaspheme.

To imply the residence therein of character, of suggestiveness, of language, is to impute speech to a corpse.

Architecture as it exists in practice today is a social evil; a flout and an insult to all that is noble, pure and lofty in the human soul;—a degradation of that sweet gift of speech that nature gave to man.

I who have loved my art with all my soul, with all my life, feel, more and more poignantly, year by year, as the hideous shape of it comes more fully, more clearly to my sight, how deep is the shame of it, how pitiful the humiliation!

To realize then, to the full, the significance of the thesis, it must clearly be perceived, heartfully felt, that the beauteous art of architecture, as a once living presence in the heart of man, is dead and gone,—That if there is to be a new art, there must be a new birth.

I do not say that the architectural art may not, in a new form, live again,—far be this from me.

I say, indeed, that it may so live again at any time.

It awaits only the coming of a great, an intense, personal-

ity:—a man of passion:—with a great and beautiful architecture
in his heart.

Courtesy of the Louis H. Sullivan Collection, The Burnham Library, The Art
Institute, Chicago. Published with permission. Grammar, punctuation, and some
spelling slightly altered.

25
Opinions On The Use of Burned Clay
for Fire-Proof Buildings (1898)

Burnt clay, or terra-cotta, was Sullivan's preferred building
material because it could be molded and glazed in myriad
ways to accept his ornament, was much lighter than stone
but extremely durable, and was almost indestructible if
properly installed. Because it had also become such a popular fireproofing agent during the 1880s, *Brickbuilder* magazine queried several prominent Chicago architects about
its use. The magazine's ten questions and its published excerpts from Sullivan's replies about terra-cotta's fire-resis-
tant, as opposed to its decorative, possibilities are as follows:

In the last issue of THE BRICKBUILDER we published the results
of interviews with some of the leading Chicago architects in regard to the use of burnt clay for fire-proofing purposes. Reports
of further interviews are published herewith. In order to bring
again before our readers the distinct lines upon which the inqui-
ries were based, we reprint the questions to which reference is
made in the interviews. These questions cover the whole field of
our proposed inquiry, and a comparison of the replies suggested
thereby shows how firm is the belief in burnt clay as a medium
for fire-proof construction and how thoroughly this material has
been able to accomplish the desired results. These interviews, as
compared with the opinions we published some time since of
some of our leading Eastern architects, show that the use and
appreciation of terra-cotta does not materially differ in the West

from what is recognized as the best practise in the East.—ED.

The following questions were submitted to those whose names appear hereafter:

1. Do you employ burned clay in fire-proof buildings, and if so to what extent?

2. Do you prefer it to other so-called fire-proofing systems, and if so for what reasons?

3. What kind of burned-clay material do you prefer? or would you employ different kinds for different purposes?

4. Have the recent attacks on the burned clay systems of fire-proofing by promoters of other systems influenced your judgment?

5. Do you think that the makers of burned-clay fire-proofing are trying to improve and perfect their material and its method of application?

6. What do you think is the lesson to be learned from recent fires in buildings fire-proofed with burned clay?

7. Do you think it right for architects to consent to their clients always taking the lowest bid for this kind of work without regard to the differences in what the parties intend to furnish?

8. What do you think is the reason why the price and quality of burned-clay fire-proofing have been reduced during the last ten years?

9. Do you agree with the opinions given by Mr. Jenney in the July BRICKBUILDER?

10. Do you think it desirable for architects to employ fire-proofing experts to design the details of fire-proof work and supervise its erection, as is now done in the case of steel constructions?

Louis H. Sullivan, formerly of the firm of Adler & Sullivan, has had a large experience in the erection of fire-proof buildings, not only in Chicago, but in St. Louis, Buffalo, New York, and other cities. He said: "Yes, I have used burned clay largely, and in nearly all of the fire-proof buildings that I have designed. I prefer it to other so-called fire-proof materials, because it is, on the whole, better adapted to the contingencies of building construction. It is best adapted to winter building and rapid work; in fact it is unwise to employ plastic methods for large buildings, even though it is proposed to do this part of the work in sum-

mer, for contingencies might arise to compel part of it to be
done in freezing weather, when no dependence could be placed
upon the results. The use of plasters and concretes in solid bodies demands practically laboratory conditions and constant inspection, and further, it is for these reasons also that I agree with
Mr. Jenney that it is best for filling over flat arches to use as little
concrete and as much tile as possible, and, when concrete is necessary, to make it as he suggests. I prefer porous to hard tile,
but I would prefer a semi-porous tile to either, if I could get it,
because it has great strength and is less liable than hard tile to
crack when suddenly cooled by water. I wish some manufacturer
would put such a material on the market in this city. I have
heard of its having being [*sic*] used elsewhere."

In answer to the fourth question, Mr. Sullivan said emphatically "No," which requires no enlargement or explanation of his
views on that subject. In answer to question five he said: "In the
West, that is including Buffalo and Pittsburgh and points west
of those, yes; east of those points, no. The Eastern tile seems to
be the same that it was years ago, very rough and uneven, both
in form and quality. I very much dislike the Eastern system of
making a soffit tile out of an extension of the skew-back carried
under the beam on both sides. In recent work done under my
direction in New York, many of these extensions were broken
off in setting. They did not fully cover the space under the
beams, and I required the contractors to use mortar combined
with a reinforcement of metal buried within it, to supply the
deficiency. But I do not like this as well as the independent soffit
tile with an air space." Referring to Mr. Jenney's girder system
as used in the extension to the New York Life Building at Chicago, and illustrated in the July BRICKBUILDER, he said: "I like
it. It is a very simple and strong system of construction so far as
the steel is concerned, and capable of thorough fire-proofing, so
as to make flat ceilings throughout without disclosing the gir-
ders." In answer to the question, "What do you think is the
lesson to be learned from recent fires in Pittsburgh, where the
steel structure was saved though the fire-proofing was considerably damaged?" he said that the work was imperfect, but could,
with slight improvement, have been made thoroughly reliable.
"The lesson is that all fire-proofing is worthless unless thoroughly done."

In answer to question seven he said: "That is a good question that applies to everything, no matter what it is. I cannot control the commercial instincts of my clients, but try to do it."

In answer to question eight, he thought that the price and quality of burned-clay fire-proofing had been reduced during the last few years, because of the stringency of the money market and severe competition for contracts. As to whether or not he agreed with the opinions given by Mr. Jenney in the July BRICKBUILDER, he said: "In the main I do, yes." Mr. Sullivan is preparing to finish all the columns in a large store he is now designing for Chicago to a round section, and to avoid sharp angles wherever possible.*

The Brickbuilder 7 (September 1898)ı 189–90.

26
An Unaffected School of Modern Architecture: Will It Come? (1899)

Originally published in a Philadelphia T-Square Club exhibition catalogue, this was Sullivan's reply to the question set forth in the first paragraph, rephrased by him to his own liking. His answer was yes, but not now. Eventually, he believed, when architects fully immersed themselves in American culture, they would design indigenous buildings. But in 1899 most of them copied historic styles that Sullivan branded "feudal," instead of searching for ways to express the essence of democratic life.

Sir—In reply to your inquiry, "Do you as yet see any signs tending to indicate the development of an indigenous architecture in America?" I say that in my judgment there are such signs and indications, but they are not as clearly defined as I should wish to see them. The opportunities for developing an indigenous art are so abundant, so vital, so convincing, that I must confess to

*The "Mr. Jenney" referred to in these remarks is, of course, William Le Baron Jenney for whom Sullivan worked between 1873 and 1874. The "large store" is Schlesinger & Mayer (1898, 1902), now Carson, Pirie, Scott. See documents 37 and 38.

a sincere surprise that progress toward that end has not been more spontaneous and more significant.

It is not, for my mind, a thinkable proposition that from a people democratic and free, self-reliant, resourceful, possessed of their own bodies, possessed of their own souls, self-centered, deep of aspiration, there shall not some day suspire as an exhalation an architectural art germane to those gifts, responsive to that throb, eloquently voicing every form, every aspect of what is genuine in our national life.

On the other hand, it is clear to me that architecture, as now generally practiced, is feudal or monarchical; an architecture of the governed for the governing. Against this set the thought that self-government is the highest form of government; and is it not toward this that we aspire as a nation and as individuals?

Is it, therefore, reasonable to suppose that the art forms of a not free people can really express the life of a free people? Yet that is the popular supposition.

American architects as a class must become American in thought and sympathy before we can have any widespread manifestation of an indigenous art. That this will come about in due time I have not a doubt, for we certainly have an abundance of talent, and there is certainly an undercurrent of dissatisfaction with prevailing methods. Restlessness and discontent are always the heralds of great movements.

To emphasize the thought: Before we can have an indigenous architecture, the American architect must himself become indigenous. How this is to be done is very easy to explain, but rather difficult of performance; for it is equivalent to asking him to become a poet, in the sense that he must absorb into his heart and brain his own country and his own people.

The rest is difficult also, but certain as the rising of tomorrow's sun is certain; for the power of imagination and the science of expression become limitless when we open our hearts to nature and to our people as the source of inspiration. It is practically in this active, vital faculty of reciprocity that we are now paralytics.

The Artist 24 (January 1899): xxxiii–xxxiv.

27
The Modern Phase of Architecture (1899)

This paper was first read to the Chicago Architectural Club, successor to the Chicago Architectural Sketch Club, in May 1899. In June several of its members attended the founding convention in Cleveland, of the Architectural League of America, formed largely at their initiative. Composed of ninety-seven delegates from ten local societies and three American Institute of Architects chapters who were uneasy with conventional thinking and established practices, the new League looked to Sullivan as its leader and father figure even though at forty-three he was only eleven years older than the average delegate. Among those at the Cleveland gathering were Frank Lloyd Wright and H. Webster Tomlinson (Wright's partner briefly in 1901) who gave this paper a second reading. "It was the event of the convention," *Inland Architect* reported, "so thoroughly did it embody the thoughts and feelings of every draftsman present." When it was published in *Inland Architect,* and later in the *Architectural Annual,* organ of the League, the paragraph beginning "Society is, in the main, honest . . ." was omitted from the original manuscript version.*

The Cleveland meeting of the architectural clubs of the country will mark, I believe, the auspicious opening of a new era in the growth of architectural thought.

It should, in the nature of things, be of serious import to us of the present and active generation to know what the generation to follow thinks and feels.

Its thoughts may be immature, its feelings vague and formless; yet, nevertheless, in them the future life of our art is surely working out its destiny, and the sincerity of them is not to be denied.

Youth is the most ambitious, the most beautiful, but the most helpless stage of life. It has that immediate and charming idealism which leads in the end toward greatness; but it can know little of the sorrow and bitterness of the struggle for greatness.

Youth is ineffable. I have said good-bye to mine; with solicitude I welcome yours.

Perceiving, as I do, the momentous sway and drift of modern life; knowing, as I do, that the curtain has risen on a drama, the most intense and passionate in all history, I urge that you cast away as worthless the shopworn and empirical notion that an architect is an artist—whatever that funny word may mean—and accept my assurance that he is and imperatively shall be a poet and an interpreter of the national life of his time.

Do you fully realize how despicable is a man who betrays a trust?

Do you know, or can you foresee, or instinctively judge how acutely delicate will become, in your time, the element of confidence and dependence between man and man and between society and the individual?

If you realize this, you will realize at once and forever that you, by birth, and through the beneficence of the form of government under which you live—that you are called upon, not to betray, but to express the life of your own day and generation. That society will have just cause to hold you to account for your use of the liberty that it has given to you, and the confidence it has reposed in you.

You will realize in due time, as your lives develop and expand, and you become richer in experience, that a fraudulent and surreptitious use of historical documents, however suavely presented, however cleverly plagiarized, however neatly repacked, however shrewdly intrigued, will constitute and will be held to be a betrayal of trust.

You know well what I mean. You know in your own hearts that you are to be fakers or that you are to be honest men.

It is futile to quibble or to protest, or to plead ignorance or innocence, or to asseverate and urge the force of circumstances.

* Society is, in the main, honest,—for why should it not be:—and it will not ask and will not expect you to be liars. It will give you every reasonable and every legitimate backing, if you can prove to it, by your acts, that artistic pretension is not a synonym for moral irresponsibility.

If you take the pains truly to understand your country, your people, your day, your generation, the time, the place in which

you live; if you seek to understand, absorb, and sympathize with
the life around you, you will be understood and sympathetically
received in return. Have no fear as to this.

Society soon will have no use for people who have no use for
it. The clairvoyance of the age is steadily unfolding; and it will
result therefrom that the greatest poet will be he who shall grasp
and deify the commonplaces of our life—those simple, normal
feelings which the people of his day will be helpless, otherwise,
to express—and here you have the key with which, individually,
you may unlock, in time, the portal of your art.

I truly believe that your coming together will result in serious
things. You have my sympathy. I am with you in spirit; for in
you resides the only hope, the only sign of dawn that I can see,
making for a day that shall regenerate an art that should be, may
be and must be, the noblest, the most intimate, the most expressive, the most eloquent of all.

Your youth is your most precious heritage from the past. I
am with you.

The Inland Architect and News Record 33 (June 1899): 40. The complete manuscript version dated May 1899 may be found in The Louis H. Sullivan Collection, The Burnham Library, The Art Institute of Chicago, and is quoted here
with permission.

28
Remarks on the Motto, "Progress before Precedent"
(1900)

Early in 1900 *Brickbuilder* magazine invited a number of
prominent architects to comment on the Architectural
League of America's newly adopted motto, "Progress before Precedent." Although it succinctly encapsulated one of
the objectives for which he had been struggling, Sullivan
saw little value in catchy phrases, preferring action over
words.

In my judgment a maxim or shibboleth, such as "Progress before
Precedent," is in itself neither valuable nor objectionable.

The broad question involved in the advancement of our art is one that lies specifically with the rising generation, and it will answer in its own way,—theory or no theory, maxim or no maxim.

If the coming men possess in a high degree the gift of reasoning logically and unwaveringly from cause to effect, the rest, practically without qualification, will take care of itself.

The present generation does not possess this gift, nor does it trouble whether or not; hence chaos. That the younger men have it is, as far as I can observe, quite conjectural. Talk and good intentions we have, but talk and good intentions do not build beautifully rational buildings. Talk may be had for the asking and good intentions become pavements here as elsewhere; but delicate clarity of insight, sturdy singleness of purpose, and adequate mental training are notably so rare in our profession as almost to be freakish. We have muddy water in our veins.

I am an optimist, and live ever in hope; yet what I wish and what I see are by no means identical. Still, doubtless, there is a ferment working that we wot not of. I would discourage no one in the belief.

Finally, when all is said and done, the architectural art is a proposition too easy or too difficult, just as you choose to regard it. It is an art as yet without status in modern American life. Practically, it is a zero.

The Brickbuilder 9 (May 1900): 96.

29
Remarks at the Architectural League of America Convention (1900)

At a working session of the Chicago convention in June 1900, held in Sullivan's own Auditorium Building, Milwaukee architect Elmer Grey singled out "the man who, above all others, has stimulated us all by the most vital thought in architectural expression—Mr. Louis H. Sullivan." League President Albert Kelsey of Philadelphia said that Sullivan's "letter to the society at the [1899] Cleveland convention [document 27] was the corner-stone of our organization," and then introduced him to the audience. "He was greeted with continued and continued applause," *American Architect and Building News* reported, "which only stopped as he began his extemporaneous remarks." His speech "further advanced the strong hold he has upon the admiration of all draftsman," *Inland Architect* observed, "as follows":

Mr. President and Gentlemen of this Convention,—Your president is quite right in saying that I am no doubt taken by surprise. I came here as a listener and for the purpose of filling my mind with the many apt and appropriate thoughts given expression to by some of the members. I have listened with intense interest and pleasure to the remarks of Mr. Grey,* and they have impressed me as being in the highest degree thoughtful and conservative, and should have the most elevating influence upon the minds of architects. I do not know that I could add much of anything to his specific and practical suggestions. The spirit underlying this work is one concerning which for the past seven or eight years I have engaged my thoughts, all along the lines which are expressed in his paper. From the time I knew the cow in the pasture and the pine tree which stood aside of the cow, I have felt there was something in nature expressing the sentiment of identity. When at three years of age I saw a storm dashing the waves over the rocks at Cape Ann, it left an impression which at that time I could not analyze. I realize it now, but I did not realize it then, that it was the Infinite spirit working in material forms as expressed in the form of that storm. Mr. Grey has spoken of inspiration; how he realized the solemnity of it, and what it means. It occurs to me he has not dwelt upon that subject as fully as he might have done, though it must be borne in mind that not sufficient time was at his disposal to exploit to the fullest extent what he may have had in his mind. We read a

---

*In addition to praising Sullivan at this session of the convention, Elmer Grey also read a paper entitled "Indigenous and Inventive Architecture." It is this to which Sullivan refers throughout.

great deal in the books about inspiration, so much so that we have become somewhat dulled as to the intensity of its being. You can search for this inspiration, and while searching through the various forms of inspiration for the source of them, you will eventually come to the conclusion that the final source of all inspiration lies in the inscrutable secrets which pervade all nature and all mankind. In seeking for an analysis of it it may be expressed in typical words, which will lead you to investigate it as being the inmost quality of man himself. It emanates from the lowest stage of his being and advances until we arrive at the simple unchangeable quality in him which we call the soul. Man outside of himself perceives that which exists, or that which he believes to exist. He finds, if he will continue his investigation of this law of nature, that there are two laws and identical rhythms. While the scientist may think of thousands upon thousands of such laws the fundamental rhythms of nature are the rhythm of growth, relative to the upbuilding of the material world, and the rhythm of decadence, referring to the decline of life to the final place whence it came. You may search for others but you will find nothing beyond this. You will find that life and death, or growth and decadence, are progressing simultaneously in the rhythmetical [*sic*] balance. You will find that the source of this balance, the physical influence working there, the physical organism, is precisely the source of what we call the source of inspiration. What we find in nature we find precisely in the human mind. We find through all its evolution, through all its phases, small and great, these two identical rhythms of growth and decadence, and we find it precisely in the same sense that the Infinite spirit stands externally to us, so that the soul of man stands as a balance between the forces of growth and the forces of decadence. It would be a long story to carry this suggestion into the final evolution it will reach. I can not attempt it. I would merely suggest to you what will arise from this suggestion. The historical styles in themselves are absolutely without value as such and will not bear analysis. They were the expression of certain men who lived at a certain time. If these men, who lived at such times, were noble-minded and of noble spirit and heart, their work is noble. If their minds were degenerated their work is degenerated. All these qualities you will find de-

picted in the architecture of the past, running from the highest
to the lowest, from the most noble to the most degenerate. The
form in which these thoughts or feelings, or the lack of thought
or feelings, as they are disclosed, have nothing to do with the
case when fundamentally considered. As Mr. Grey has truly said,
the style is the evolution, if there be nothing other than the
expression, of its personality. If three men happened to think
and feel something alike, the work of those three men will appear something alike. The same can be said of a thousand men
acting and feeling the same way. That is practically all that can
be said relative to the consideration of the national style as applied to the individual work. What counts, what is final and of
consequence is the individual. This has always been true, is true
now and always remains true. What the individual thinks and
feels makes him either a valuable or valueless member of the age
in which he lives. If any one supposes that by study, however
reverent or serious it may be, of the spirit in which the past
expresses itself, he can make himself such valuable member, he
is wofully mistaken. It may be true that he regards those expressions with reverence because he regards all expressions of the
mind with reverence. It has been suggested by Mr. Grey, by
virtually relinquishing all the distinct forms of those styles we
might finally reach a definite expresson of our own. I see no
reason why that would not be the result. There can be nothing
else. A form which represents one state of feeling may not apply
to another state of feeling. As for instance, take the style of Fran-
cis I; it will not apply to the present age, nor conform to our
present national feeling. You have around you, it seems to me,
a national life marvelous enough to inspire anybody. Outside of
the field of nature and the spirit underlying it, I see no reason
why any one could possibly ask for a greater field and source of
inspiration than is found in America. The difficulty is he will not
be in sympathy with it. The same difficulty is experienced in
other forms of so-called American art. What does the American
painter do? He goes to Holland and paints regardless of true art
and paints what are called beautiful pictures of that country, but
what has all this to do with America? What use have we for such
a man? How does he help us? Does he express our sympathies?
Not at all. The fact that he pursues such a course, rightfully

considered, may be regarded as acts done in the lights of political economy. He is acting upon a principle that is radically wrong. It all constitutes a waste of energy. The great life of the Western plains has passed away forever. It is too late now to recall it in the interest of our national life. This representation of the life and spirit of the West has in it absolutely nothing concerning which the painter ought to be concerned. Had the painter been brought up to act in the spirit I am defending now, and had he been taught to study his own surroundings, and the peculiarities of his own people—though he may have been satisfied with what he has done—and if he had seized upon that which was vital instead of devoting his efforts to the past, he would have contributed what is far more valuable, but as it is our successors will feel more deeply than we do today what our loss has been; yet that has been the chief use of the painter in the past. Likewise let us suppose for a moment, if possible to suppose, an architect, filled with the same spirit, influenced by the want of sympathy, and under certain circumstances should build the same house in New Orleans that he builds in St. Paul, the people of New Orleans occupying such a structure would find it to be exceedingly uncomfortable. The first effort should be to adapt it to the comforts of the people with reference to the place where they live. What has style to do with it? This thought may be carried all through the discussion we have before us. What is the use of talking about books or about the style we have passed. We have before us a simple plan. Examine any ordinary building with a little care and you will find it has the expression of one idea, solely and organically unfolding itself to the smallest detail. Therefore, if I talk about books or style what will we gain by ignoring the fundamental law of development. A moment's reflection and serious thought will fill you with the correctness of the idea contended for. I know of no reason why that should not be the true idea; that architecture is the true expression of our lives. I am not opposed to books or schools in any sense of prejudice, but I am opposed to them because I believe they are essentially a waste of energy. We can do very much better elsewhere. We can get truer and more beautiful results, because when we reach the point of what nature indicates to us we are educated for life; our life becomes an unfolding of that suggestion, and that will continue indefinitely so long as man lives.

The Inland Architect and News Record 35 (June 1900): 42–43.

30
The Young Man in Architecture (1900)

The Architectural League of America's second convention was a three-day fête for Louis Sullivan. In addition to the many encomiums, he was honored as guest speaker at the annual banquet where his theme was education. He told his admirers that the workings of the human mind were comparable to those of nature, the study of which was much more valuable than the study of books or buildings. Architectural education, he maintained, should begin with observation of organic growth and development, wherein students would discover forms unfolding from an inner core into functional, beautiful, and harmonious wholes. Only after the study of nature had borne this proper method of "organized thinking" could formal education carry on without doing harm. "Mr. Sullivan sings his song into your ears," *Architecture* magazine commented, "and, as by the cadence of a lullaby, objection is disarmed and opposition stilled."

It is my premise that the Architectural League of America has its being in a sense of discontent with conditions now prevailing in the American malpractice of the architectural art; in a deep and wide sense of conviction that no aid is to be expected from the generation now representing that malpractice; and in the instinctive feeling that, through banding together, force, discretion and coherence may be given to the output of these feelings which are, in themselves, for the time being, vague and miscellaneous, however intensely they may be felt.

Did I not believe that this statement substantially represents the facts, I should be the last to take an interest in your welfare.

I would be indifferent concerning what you did or what you did not.

That you have abundant reason for discontent needs no proof; let him read who runs through the streets.

That you have cause for discontent is evident. That you should feel discontent gives one a delightfully cynical sense of shock, and a new-born desire to believe in the good, the true, the beautiful and the young.

American architecture is composed, in the hundred, of ninety parts aberration, eight parts indifference, one part poverty and one part Little Lord Fauntleroy. You can have the prescription filled at any architectural department-store, or select architectural millinery establishment.

As it is my desire to speak from the viewpoint that architecture should be practised as an art and not strictly as a commercial pursuit, and as I am assuming that you agree with me in this respect, we may now pertinently inquire wherein does this American architecture differ from the architecture of the past.

It differs in little, if in anything, provided we except the few great epochs.

Human nature has changed but little since the time man was slaughterer or the slaughtered of the great white bear.

Seldom, in the past, has man thought of aught but war, which menaced his life; religion, which menaced his soul; hunger, which threatened his stomach; or love, which concerned his progeny.

From time to time this tempestuous human sky has calmed, for a divine moment, and the glory of man has shone forth upon a fertile land. Then came again the angry elements—and the sun departed.

This, in brief, is the recurrent history of man from the beginning. You may change the values in the formula to suit the epoch, the century or the generation.

Ninety-nine years of the hundred the thoughts of nine hundred and ninety-nine people of the thousand are sordid. This always has been true. Why should we expect a change?

Of one hundred so-called thoughts that the average man thinks (and thus he has ever thought), ninety-nine are illusions, the remaining one a caprice.

From time to time in the past, these illusions have changed their focus and become realities, and the one caprice has become an overwhelming desire.

These changes were epoch-making.

And the times were called golden.

In such times came the white-winged angel of sanity.

And the great styles arose in greeting.

Then soon the clear eye dimmed.

The sense of reality was lost.

Then followed architectures, to all intents and purposes quite like American architecture of today:

Wherein the blind sought much discourse of color.

The deaf to discuss harmonics.

The dry of heart twaddled about the divinity of man.

The mentally crippled wrought fierce combats in the arena of logic.

And so it has come about that the white-winged angel has been on a far journey these six hundred years.

Now, insisting for the moment, in spite of the hierarchy, that this white-winged absence is of gentle sex, I entreat your close attention:

Let radiant and persuasive Youth lure her back again to earth!

For that she hovers in the visible blue of your firmament I can prove to you beyond a gossamer of doubt.

That she awaits with eager ear the spring-enthralling voice of adolescence, the clear sweet morning-call of a pure heart, the spontaneity and jocund fervor of a bright and winning mind, the glance of a modest and adoring eye!

That she awaits.

That she has so long awaited.

That she cannot make herself first known to you—

Alas, 'tis of her enchantment that she is invisible and dumb!

Perhaps this is enough of poesy—

Let us say, enough likewise of the prevailing cacophony; of

The howling of the vast and general horde of Bedlamites.

The purring of the select company of Ruskinites.

The gasping of the Emersonites.

The rasping of the Spencerites.

The moaning of the Tennysonites.

The whimper of the aesthetes.

The yowling of the reformers.

The yapping of strenuous livers.

The rustle of the rustlers.

The hustle of the hustlers.

The howl of the taxpayers.

And the clang of the trolley car—

All, "signs, omens and predictions" of our civilization.

We are commanded to know that there is much of mystery, much of the esoteric, in the so-called architectural styles. That there is a holiness in so-called "pure art" which the hand of the Modern may not profane.

So be it.

Let us be the Cat.

And let the pure art be the King.

We will look at him.

And we will also look at the good king's good children, the great styles.

And at his retinue of bastards, the so-called "other styles."

There is, or at least there is said to be, a certain faculty of the mind, whereby the mind or the faculty, as you choose, is on the one hand enabled to dissolve a thing into its elements, and, on the other hand, to build up these or similar elements into the same or a similar thing. This process is, I believe, called Logic— the first operation going by the name, analysis, and the second, synthesis. Some men possess the half-faculty of separating; others the half-faculty of upbuilding. When the whole faculty exists in one man, in a moderate degree, he is said to be gifted. When he has it in a high degree, he is said to be highly gifted; and when in the highest degree he is called a genius or a master mind. When a man has neither the one half-faculty nor the other half-faculty he is mentally sterile.

I fear lest the modern architect be placed in this category, by reason of his devious ways.

Let us suppose ourselves, nevertheless, moderately gifted and apply our analysis to the great styles:

Presto—dissolve!

We have as residuum, two uprights, and a horizontal connecting them.

We have two bulky masses and an arch connecting them.

Revolve your arches and masses and you have a dome.

Do the trick a few times more with a few other "styles" and you have the Elements of Architecture.

We approach in the same way a master mind—and all speedily disappears—leaving insoluble Desire.

The architectural elements, in their baldest form, the desire of the heart in its most primitive, animal form, are the foundation of architecture.

They are the dust and the breathing spirit.

All the splendor is but a gorgeous synthesis of these.

The logic of the books, is, at best, dry reading; and, moreover, it is nearly or quite dead, because it comes at second hand.

The human mind, in operation, is the original document.

Try to read it.

If you find this for the moment too difficult and obscure, try to study a plant as it grows from its tiny seed and expands toward its full fruition. Here is a process, a spectacle, a poem, or whatever you may wish to call it, not only absolutely logical in essence, because exhibiting in its highest form the unity and the quality of analysis and synthesis, but which is of vastly greater import, vital and inevitable: and it is specifically to this phenomenon that I wish to draw your earnest attention—if it be true and I sincerely hope that such is the fact, that you wish to become real architects, not the imitation brand. For I wish to show to you, or at least intimate to you, how naturally and smoothly and inevitably the human mind will operate if it be not harassed or thwarted in its normal and instinctive workings.

Some day, watch the sun as he rises, courses through the sky, and sets.

Note what your part of the earth does meanwhile.

Ponder the complex results of this simple single cause.

Some year, observe how rhythmically the seasons follow the sun. Note their unfailing, spontaneous logic; their exquisite analysis and synthesis; their vital inevitable balance.

When you have time or opportunity, spare a moment to note a wild bird, flying; a wave, breaking on the shore. Try to grasp the point that, while these things are common, they are by no means commonplace.

Note any simple thing or act whatsoever provided, only, it be natural, not artificial—the nearer undisturbed nature the better; if in the wilderness, better still, because wholly away from the perverting influence of man.

Whenever you have done these things attentively and without mental bias or preoccupation, wholly receptive in your humor, there will come to your intelligence a luminous idea of simplicity, and equally luminous idea of a resultant organic complexity, which, together, will constitute the first significant step in your architectural education, because they are the basis of rhythm.

There will gently dawn in your mind an awakening of something vital, something organic, something elemental that is urging things about you through their beautiful, characteristic rhythms, and that is holding them in most exquisite balance.

A little later you will become aware with amazement that this same impulse is working on your own minds, and that never before had you suspected it. This will be the second step in your architectural education.

Later you will perceive, with great pleasure, that there is a notable similarity, an increasing sympathy between the practical workings of your own minds and the workings of nature about you.

When this perception shall have grown into a definite clear-cut consciousness, it will constitute the closing of the first chapter and the opening of all the remaining chapters in your architectural education, for you will have arrived at the basis of organized thinking.

You will have observed doubtless, that, thus far, while endeavoring to lead you toward a sane and wholesome conception of the basis of the architectural art, I have said not a word about books, photographs or plates. I have done this advisedly, for I am convinced beyond the shadow of a doubt that never can you acquire from books, or the like, alone, even a remote conception of what constitutes the real, the living, architectural art. It has been tried for generations upon generations with one unvarying result: dreary, miserable failure.

To appreciate a book at its just value, you must first know what words signify, what men signify, and what nature signifies.

Books, taken in their totality, have one ostensible object, one just function: namely, to make a record of Man's relation to his fellow men and to Nature, and the relation of both of these to an all-pervading, Inscrutable Spirit.

To these relations, Mankind, in its prodigious effort to define its own status, has given thousands upon thousands of names.

These names are called words.

Each word has a natural history.

Each word is not the simple thing it appears, but, on the contrary, it is a highly complex organism, carrying in its heart more smiles, more tears, more victories, more downfalls, more bloody sweats, more racial agonies than you can ever dream of.

Some of these words are very old—

They still cry with the infancy of the race.

Therefore, should I begin by putting into your hands a book or its equivalent, I would, according to my philosophy, be guilty of an intellectual crime.

I would be as far from the true path as I now most heartedly [*sic*] regard most teachers of the architectural art to be.

I would be as reckless and brutal as my predecessors.

But I would not be as unconscious of it as they appear to be.

Therefore, I say with emphasis, begin by observing.

Seek to saturate your minds by direct personal contact with things that are natural—not sophisticated.

Strive to form your own judgments, at first in very small things, gradually in larger and larger things. Do not lean upon the judgment of others if it is reasonably within your power to form your own.

Thus, though you may often stumble and wander, such experiences will be valuable because personal; it is far better that they occur in youth rather than in maturer years. Gradually by virtue of this very contact with things you will acquire that sure sense of physical reality which is the necessary first step in a career of independent thinking.

But strive not, I caution you, after what is called originality. If you do you will be starting in exactly the wrong way. I wish distinctly to impress upon you that what I am advocating, and what I am in turn striving to point out to you, is the normal development of your minds. That if the mind is properly nurtured, properly trained, and left free to act with spontaneity, individuality of expression will come to you as naturally as the flower comes to the plant—for it is nature's law.

When you begin to feel the flow and stimulation of mind which are first fruits of wholesome exercise of the faculties, you may begin to read the books. Read them carefully and cautiously, not superciliously.

Bear in mind that books, generally speaking, are composed mainly of sophistries, assumptions, borrowings, stealings, inadequate presentations or positive perversions of truth.

The author, too frequently, is posing, masquerading or ambuscading. His idea is to impress you. He himself well knows how little he has to say that can in strictness be classed as truth in his possession only.

You will soon have no trouble in discerning the exception—and the exceptions, by their value, will conclusively prove the rule.

Later you may turn from the documents called books to the documents called buildings, and you will find that what I have said of books applies with equal force to buildings and to their authors. Soon you will be enabled to separate the wheat from the chaff.

Thus, one after the other, you may pass in review the documents called Music, Painting, Sculpture, Agriculture, Commerce, Manufactures, Government, etc.

You will find them, for your purposes, much alike.

You will, ere long, acquire an inkling of the fullness and the emptiness of these documents, if, as I advise, you keep closely in touch with nature.

When you know something more of the working of the human mind than you now know (and the day will not be long in coming if you follow the program I am indicating), you will not be greatly surprised, when taking a backward glance, that those in high places today seemingly believe or profess to believe that the fruit need bear no relation to the tree.

You will be no more amused than I am at the psychological irony presented by the author of a callously illogical building declaring in solemn tones that it is the product of a logical mind.

You will smile with wonderment when you recall that it is now taught, or appears now to be taught, that like does not

beget like; whereas you will know that nature has for unnumbered ages and at every instant proclaimed that like can beget
nothing but its like:

That a logical mind will beget a logical building.

That an illogical mind will beget an illogical building.

That perversity will bring forth perversity.

That the children of the mind will reveal the parent.

You will smile again when you reflect that it was held in your
youth that there was no necessary relationship between function
and form. That function was one thing, form another thing.

True, it might have seemed queer to some if a pine-tree had
taken on the form of a rattlesnake, and, standing vertically on its
tail, had brought forth pine cones; or that a rattlesnake, vice
versa, should take on the form of a pine-tree and wriggle along
the ground biting the heel of the passer-by.

Yet this suggestion is not a whit queerer than are some of the
queer things now filling the architectural view, as, for instance,
a steel frame function in a masonry form—

Imagine, for instance:

Horse-eagles.

Pumpkin-bearing frogs.

Frog-bearing pea vines.

Tarantula-potatoes.

Sparrows in the forms of whales, picking up crumbs in the
streets.

If these combinations seem incongruous and weird, I assure
you in all seriousness that they are not a whit more so than the
curiosities encountered with such frequency by the student of
what nowadays passes for architecture.

With this difference, only, that, inasmuch as the similarity is
chiefly mental, it can produce no adequate impression on those
who have felt the sensitizing effect of thought.

You will remember that it was held that a national style must
be generations in forming—and that the inference you were to
draw from this was that the individual should take no thought
for his own natural development because it would be futile so to
do—because, as it were, it would be an impertinent presumption.

I tell you exactly the contrary: Give all your thought to individual development, which it is entirely within your province and power to control; and let the nationality come in due time as a consequence of the inevitable convergence of thought.

If anyone tells you that it is impossible within a lifetime to develop and perfect a complete individuality of expression, a well-ripened and perfected personal style, tell him that you know better and that you will prove it by your lives. Tell him with little ceremony, whoever he may be, that he is grossly ignorant of first principles—that he lives in the dark.

It is claimed that the great styles of the past are the sources of inspiration for this architecture of the present. This in fact is the vehement assertion of those who "worship" them.

Would you believe it? Really, would you believe it!

So it appears that like can beget its unlike after all. That a noble style may beget, through the agency of an ignoble mind, an ignoble building.

It may be true that a blooded male may beget, through a mongrel female, a cur progeny. But the application of this truth to the above instance wherein occurs the great word Inspiration implies a brutal perversion of meaning and a pathetic depravity in those who use that word for their sinister ends.

For inspiration, as I conceive it, is the intermediary between God and man, the pure fruition of the soul at one with immaculate nature, the greeting of noble minds.

To use this word in a tricky endeavor to establish a connection legitimizing the architecture of the present as the progeny of the noblest thought in the past is, to my mind, a blasphemy, and so it should appear to yours.

In truth the American architecture of today is the offspring of an illegitimate commerce with the mongrel styles of the past.

Do not deceive yourselves for a moment as to this.

It is a harsh indictment.

But it is warranted by the facts.

Yet let us not be too severe. Let us remember and make what allowance we may for the depressing, stultifying, paralyzing influence of an unfortunate education.

After all, every American man has had to go to school. And everything that he has been taught over and above the three R's has been in essence for his mental undoing.

I cannot possibly emphasize this lamentable fact too strongly.

And the reason, alas, is so clear, so forcible, so ever present—as you will see.

We live under a form of government called Democracy. And we, the people of the United States of America, constitute the most colossal instance known in history of a people seeking to verify the fundamental truth that self-government is Nature's law for Man.

It is of the essence of Democracy that the individual man is free in his body and free in his soul.

It is a corollary therefrom, that he must govern or restrain himself, both as to bodily acts and mental acts—that, in short, he must set up a responsible government within his own individual person.

It implies that highest form of emancipation—of liberty physical, mental and spiritual, by virtue whereof man calls the gods to judgment, while he heeds the divinity of his own soul.

It is the ideal of Democracy that the individual man should stand self-centered, self-governing—an individual sovereign, an individual god.

Now who will assert, specifically, that our present system of higher architectural education is in accord with this aspiration? That the form, Education, bears any essential relation other than that of antagonism to the function Democracy?

It is our misfortune that it does not.

We as a people are too youthful. We are too new among the world forces. We are too young. We have not yet had time to discover precisely the trouble, though we feel in our hearts that something is amiss. We have been too busy.

And so comes about the incongruous spectacle of the infant Democracy taking its mental nourishment at the withered breast of Despotism.

To understand it from our point of view, examine: These are the essential points:

We are to revere authority.

We are to take everything at second hand.

We are to believe measurements are superior to thought.

We are advised not to think.

We are cautioned that by no possibility can we think as well as did our predecessors.

We are not to examine, not to test, not to prove.

We are to regard ourselves as the elect, because, forsooth, we have been instructed by the elect.

We must conform.

We are not to go behind the scenes.

We are to do as we are told and ask no foolish questions.

We are taught that there is a royal road to our art.

We are taught hero-worship—

We are not taught what the hero worshipped.

We are taught that nature is one thing, man another thing.

We are taught that God is one thing, man another thing.

Does this conform to the ideal of Democracy?

Is this a fitting overture to the world's greatest drama?

Is it not extraordinary that we survive it even in part?

Is it a wonder that our representative architecture is vapid, foolish, priggish, insolent and pessimistic?

Manifestly you cannot become truly educated in the schools.

Ergo, you must educate yourselves.

There is no other course,—no other hope.

For the schools have not changed much in my generation; they will, I fear, not change much in your generation—and soon it will be too late for you.

Strive, strive therefore, while you are young and eager, to apply to your mental development the rules of physical development.

Put yourselves in training, so to speak.

Strive to develop in your minds the agility, flexibility, precision, poise, endurance and judgment of the athlete.

Seek simple, wholesome, nourishing food for the mind.

You will be surprised and charmed with the results.

The human mind in its natural state, not drowsed and stupefied by a reactionary education, is the most marvelously active agency in all nature.

You may trust implicitly in the results of this activity if its surroundings are wholesome.

The mind will inevitably reproduce what it feeds upon.

If it feeds upon filth, it will reproduce filth.

If it feeds upon dust, it will reproduce dust.

If it feeds upon nature, it will reproduce nature.

If it feeds upon man, it will reproduce man.

If it feeds upon all of these, it will reproduce all of these.

It will reproduce infallibly whatever it is fed upon.

It is a wonderful machine—its activity cannot wholly be quenched except by death. It may be slowed down or accelerated—it cannot be stopped.

It may be abused in every conceivable way, but it will not stop, even in insanity, even in sleep.

So beware how you tamper with this marvelous mechanism, for it will record inevitably, in all its output, whatever you do to it.

The human mind is the summation of all the ages. It holds in trust the wisdom and the folly of all the past.

Beware what you do to it, for it will give you bad for your bad, good for your good—

It is a mechanism of such inconceivable delicacy and complexity.

Man through his physical infancy is most carefully nurtured.

His delicate and fragile, helpless little body is tenderly watched with all the solicitude of parental affection.

Indeed, under the law he is still a child until the age of twenty-one.

But his mind! Who cares for his mind?

After he has passed from the simple, beautiful ministrations at his mother's knee, who guards this ineffably delicate impressionable organism?

Oh, the horror of it!

Oh, ye gods, where is justice, where is mercy, where is love!

To think that the so-called science of political economy is so futile, so drugged with feudalism, that it has not noted this frightful waste, this illogical interruption of the happiness of the human family, this stark, staring incongruity in our education.

That it does not perceive, in its search for the sources of wealth, the latent richness of the human mind, its immense wealth of practical possibilities, the clearly marked indications of enormous productiveness—a productiveness sane and of vital consequence to the public welfare: so much for a science which regards man as a mechanical unit.

It is typical in a measure of the learning we have donned as a misfit garment.

You have every reason to congratulate yourselves that you are young—for you have so much the less to unlearn, and so much the greater fund of enthusiasm.

A great opportunity is yours. The occasion confronts you. The future is in your hands—will you accept the responsibility or will you evade it?

That is the only vital question I have come here to put to you.

I do not ask an answer now.

I am content with putting the question.

For it is the first time that the question ever has been put squarely to you.

I ask only that you consider this:

Do you intend, or do you not intend, do you wish or do you not wish, to become architects in whose care an unfolding Democracy may entrust the interpretation of its material wants, its psychic aspirations?

In due time doubtless you will answer in your own way.

But I warn you the time left for an answer in the right way is acutely brief.

For young as you are, you are not as young as you were yesterday—

And tomorrow?

Tomorrow!

The Inland Architect and News Record 35 (June 1900): 38–40.

31
Reality in the Architectural Art (1900)

The new Architectural League of America fueled Sullivan's hopes. Recognizing its growing influence, he felt free to speak more pointedly than ever before. In this essay, originally published in *The Chicago Tribune,* Sullivan condemned schools of architecture for discouraging progressive thinking and for ignoring modern educational methods aimed at integrating knowledge with life. Gradu-

ates of these "musty" institutions were incapable of creating indigenous architecture because they stood aloof from
the people. But in the League Sullivan detected the possibility of real reform, an avowal of the principles of inventive individualism and social involvement. Sullivan's acer-
bic, almost insulting tone here and occasionally in later
writings stemmed from his frustration with the profession's elitism and conservatism, as well as from his own
declining fortunes. With the League's apparent backing
unleashing in him a certain bravado, he decided to express
his feelings with unprecedented intemperance.

To lead the mind and to develop character so that the student
may acquire a sense of reality, physical, mental, and social, seems
to be the trend of modern educational methods, as set forth in
university, manual training school, and kindergarten. The complete union of knowledge and life is the ultimate aim.

It is an avowed belief that too many men live in a trance,
stupor or lethargy. That they lack the right sort of focus. That
life to them is, in consequence, a hazy blur, a spatter of blotches,
with noises and glimmering fogs—so far are they from the sunshine, the pure air, and the blue sky of reality. That they are men
in name only. That, on the whole, they suffer from an indefina-
ble irritation and unhappiness. That they lack the contentment
of the wild animal or the philosopher.

It is clearly recognized that educational methods, hitherto,
have been criminally false, bewildering and destructive, and an
eager desire is abroad to loosen the husk of classic, of medieval,
and of monarchical artificiality from the natural man, that he
may come into his own.

This ferment of the modern and hopeful, this perception born
of the larger liberty and saner humanity of our day, the ever
heavier penalties of ignorance have origin in the birth struggles
of a people seeking emancipation, in its most realistic and startling form—democracy.

Toward this aspiration educators, with few exceptions, are
lending strenuous and enlightened aid to youth.

Among the exceptions, notably, are the professors of architecture, brooding, like blight, over their schools. They ingest the

subtle hypodermic of I and Thou—the pharisaism of mental pride. They foster the sense of dilettantism. They extol the artificial, the unreal. They laud symbols and figments. They harken to echoes.

In so doing they assert that they teach the architectural art, whereas, in fact, not only do they obscure the reality of that art, but, quickly and surely they repress and pilfer the spontaneity and charm of youth, the sanity, the higher usefulness of the future man. This they do in systematically deadening every wholesome aspiration of head and heart; in belittling and decrying the exuberant plasticity, lively imagination, boundless curiosity, and beautiful intuition of the young.

This is done in cold blood, and in a spirit of hatred unspeakably bitter toward him who would raise a warning hand against the infallibility of tradition. Their motto: Whatever was, is right; whatever is, is wrong. And all this they do under the canting shibboleth of "conservatism."

It does not require so much keenness of observation to note that a certain amount of culture, of an uncertain kind, makes a man timid, self conscious, and distrustful alike of himself and of others. He thereupon dubs himself a conservative and adopts, as his fixed working formula, that truth lies between extremes. This is as easy as it is lazy, for it does away with the need to investigate and the capacity to judge.

For such men knowledge, to be acceptable, must bear a familiar label. It is but scant justice to say that they were of the blind led by the blind.

Nor is it more difficult to detect that, in the half-baked reformer, the tricky demogogue, the elaborate poseur, self-intoxication just fails of producing complete self-deception. The lurid gleam of a disordered imagination is not really believed to be sunlight. Hence the popular term "radical"—not a root but a fungus—parasitic of habit.

If I mistake not, it is of the essence of the most enlightened pedagogics that there exists a science of thinking—a science as far above logic as logic is above tomfoolery. Equipped with this science a man inquires not is this or that old, is it new, is it conservative or is it radical, but, is it real? Logic deals with abstractions, and, from its nature, is soon lost in the maze of futil-

ities toward which it flies. The science of thinking deals ever
with realities, whether such realities be physical, mental, moral,
or spiritual. Therefore it stands for the poise and serenity of a
highly enlightened mind. These realities are infinitely varied, yet
they center upon the individual man. They embrace his personality, and, most impressively, his relations to his fellows, to nature, and to an infinite, inscrutable spirit. They imply the brotherhood of man.

Now the teaching and the practice as an art bear today no
assignable relation to the science of thinking—that is, to reality.

Architecture, or rather that lean and grotesque simulance of
it that we are familiar with and hold in the contempt of indifference for the good and simple reason that it touches us in no
vital spot, is as unreal and bloodless as a liust.

That certain unwilling materials have been thrust into certain
specific places does not make architecture.

The singular and characteristic helplessness of the modern architect when brought face to face with the realities of time,
place, and people must, some day, give the educator pause and
must likewise some day excite the curiosity and the wonder of
the general public. For it certainly is curious enough to be worthy of comment and critical analysis that, whereas the architect,
to all intents and purposes, stands aloof from his people and his
time, American inventiveness, ingenuity, adaptability, and ver-
satility are proverbial in so many pursuits.

But current architectural practice may not be called a pursuit;
on the contrary it is a running away, an evasion of plain duty, a
dodging of the manifest issue.

This issue is not to be obscured by a mist of conventional and
shop worn phrases, for it is as plain as the daylight to any un-
biased mind that, when an architecture gives a reflection of the
true life of the people it is a natural, a real art; that, when it fails
so to reflect that life, it is artificial, unreal, and therefore not only
negatively useless but positively pernicious.

From the beginning the true, the real architectural art has
been, and it must necessarily remain, ever the same in spirit,
though constantly varying in physical forms; for, defined in its
simplest terms, it is merely an art of expressing the physical and
mental life of a people—in its buildings. Plainly, therefore, it is

a perversion of this spirit that, in America, in a most vicious and regretting form, has impeded a natural growth and expansion of the art. In short this most winsome of all arts has become, through operation of malign influences, anaemic to the verge of extinction. The most poisonous of these influences is, as I have already pointed out, the absolute falsity of architectural education.

Closeted for generations in the musty school, this art, which needs as nature the fresh air and the sunshine of green fields and limpid waters, the rejuvenance of springtime, has languished and faded in the poverty of neglect.

The remedy is self-evident—a return to natural, simple, wholesome, and sympathetic ways of thinking; a liberation of the creative impulse; an entente cordiale between architect and people—that he as an artist may interpret their true feelings in the natural language of his art, and express them with the eloquence and ardor of a poet—not, as now, to misrepresent them in the expressly cultivated cynicism of an irrelevant mental attitude. That there is need of such a change, and that the change is imminent, is keenly felt today by the younger generation of architects. The convention of the Architectural League of America held in this city early in June represented a movement in architectural thought so significant that it may easily be held the most important avowal of principles in the architectural history of the country. These principles briefly stated, stand for "the encouragement of an indigenous and inventive architecture for America," as opposed to the imported fashion plates representing the art and the lives of nations centuries ago. In other words, an art for us, by us; not an art for us, by others.

There are many indications also that the American people are beginning to understand the desirability of such an art, and, in increasing numbers of instances, they are demanding it.

American national life has now reached such development as to be unique in world history, and the individual is a unit in that life, demanding recognition.

The demand, then, is for architects of such breadth of culture and delicacy of perception, such art of expression that, from their hands may come a new phase, a new expression of the eternally youthful art of architecture that shall in turn be unique in the history of the fine arts.

It will be an art filled with optimism and humanity, in contrast with pessimism of the past.

The Interstate Architect and Builder 2 (August 11, 1900): 6–7.

32
Open Letter on Plagiarism (1900)

Manager E. C. Kelly of the year-old *Interstate Architect and Builder* in Cleveland was so impressed with the Architectural League, with Sullivan, and with "The Young Man in Architecture" (document 30) that he too published it in 1900, thereafter freely opening his pages to its author. In the December 1900 issues Kelly ran a heavily illustrated account of Sullivan's work as well as this "Open Letter," with two additional pages comparing Sullivan's drawing for a Chicago Athletic Association swimming certificate with Tenbusch & Hill's bronze door for the Cathedral of the Sacred Heart in Duluth. What Sullivan might have applauded as a design he had inspired, he instead vituperously castigated as vulgar plagiarism. *American Architect and Building News* was taken aback by Sullivan's bitterness, wondering why he had not complained earlier when architecture students at the Chicago Art Institute had "let their thoughts run in the very mould in which his have run," but it also pointed out that Sullivan had raised the very real question of the extent to which an architect had the exclusive right to his own work.

In asking you to make public an instance of plagiarism not readily to be distinguished from common thievery, I am compelled, deeply to my regret and disgust, to bring to the light a degeneracy of moral tone, a callousness of mental fibre, and a brutish incapacity to respect the rights of others, which, if persisted in, will soon complete the demoralization of the profession and ruin the beauty and the value of my art as such.

I wish to make an example of Messrs. Tenbusch & Hill, first, because the proofs are clear and incontrovertible; second, as a warning to others that harsher measures will promptly follow.

If the self-respect of a fellow practitioner will not suffice to keep him honest, let him ponder carefully the 'parallel' contained in this issue of your journal and reflect, that, when he steals my art he steals my honor—which is hardly a matter for trifling.

Aside from the question of property rights, there is involved an aspect of turpitude on the one hand, and of personal accountability on the other.

Let unprincipled vulgarisms of that sort cease.

The Interstate Architect and Builder 2 (December 8, 1900): 7.

33
Letter to the Editor on *Kindergarten Chats* (1901)

The most enduring result of Sullivan's association with *Interstate Architect* was its publication of *Kindergarten Chats* in fifty-two weekly installments from February 16, 1901, through February 8, 1902. The *Chats* was an extended dialogue between a student and the master who leads him through a kind of spiritual and psychological confrontation with nature before introducing him to social and building analysis—Sullivan's preferred method of architectural instruction. On May 11, 1901, *Interstate Architect* published a letter criticizing Chat 10, "A Roman Temple (2)," for equating bad design with criminal intent. That letter and Sullivan's reply, in the issue of May 18, are as follows:

A letter to the editor:
I have been reading with much interest and considerable edification, I trust, the series of Kindergarten Chats by Mr. Louis H. Sullivan. I do not say this to praise Mr. Sullivan nor to compliment your enterprising journal, but only to show you that the criticism which follows is not born of a spirit of general hostility to Mr. Sullivan and his ideas.

It is my opinion that Mr. Sullivan allowed his strong convictions (I admire him for his strong convictions) to lead him into error and indefensible grounds in paper No. 10 (on a Roman Temple) in your issue of April 20. In general I agree heartily with his criticism of the "Roman Temple" and would feel nothing but complacence as he toasted the perpetrator for lack of ability, but it certainly is a violation of all teachings of ethics and moral philosophy to say that a man who makes a mistake in judgment is as bad as a defaulter. Surely there can be no justice in arraigning incapacity as a crime. It may be deplorable, but it gives us no moral shock. The idiot would scarcely be hired by us to fill a responsible position, if we knew it, but if we did hire him and he betrayed his trust we could not charge him with crime.

Maybe Mr. Sullivan wants to be credited with the belief that all architects who build badly know better but build badly from "pure cussedness." Of course if this be his position, I have nothing more to say except that I hardly believe it.

A.L.F.

To the editor:

The letter of your correspondent, A.L.F., in the issue of May 11 is so reasonable in tone that I wish, in a measure, to reply. I cannot discuss with him the ethical issue he raises. I will only suggest for the benefit of himself and of those who think with him, that the Kindergarten Chats are not intended to be a series of disconnected weekly articles, but a *thesis,* gradually and organically developed. This thesis will grow and unfold in its own way, and in due time will put forth its flower. When complete it must, as must any work of art, take its chances of survival. I do not specifically object to criticism. Why should I? I propose for myself to criticize with the utmost freedom and without reserve. Why then should I deny that right for others concerning my own work? I do not, but I am writing this merely as a suggestion to your correspondent that when he shall have read up to and including the 52nd article he may find an explanation, not only of the 10th, but of all the others, and the 52nd will be explained by the other 51, and each article will be justified by its 51 companions.

When my thesis shall be completed then you may turn on all the artillery of criticism that you please. A philosophy that will not withstand rough usage is no philosophy, and by this standard, which I hereby accept in advance, my philosophy must either survive and triumph, as I think it should, and in which case there will come, by a natural process, a complete and world-wide regeneration of the architectural art or—it must go by the board. I ask no favor and give none. I ask no quarter and I give none. The time has come when a vital issue must be fought to a finish. Whether a false education is to dominate us, or whether we are to evolve from ourselves and from the conditions of democracy a true education, is that issue.

Louis H. Sullivan

The Interstate Architect and Builder 2 (May 11, 1901): 6; (May 18, 1901): 6.

Style and Social Purpose

Professional indifference to "Kindergarten Chats"—which were ambiguous and difficult even for his most determined disciples—especially among members of the Architectural League, hurt Sullivan deeply. "I shall never again make so great a sacrifice for the younger generation," he wrote Claude Bragdon. So he kept away from the League's third convention in Philadelphia in June 1901, although he did send a telegram of support (document 34). Shortly thereafter in a brief press statement (document 35), he returned to his familiar theme of style as a cultural or democratic expression of contemporary social purposes, not an imitation of historical precedent.

34
Telegram to the Architectural League of America Convention (1901)

Greetings to the convention. I regret not to be with you. I hope that your deliberations will result in a firmer stand than ever for a rational conception and working ideal of the architectural art. Push on in the good work. I am with you in spirit.

The Brickbuilder 10 (June 1901): 112.

35
Architectural Style (1901)

Architecture is an expression rather than a style and is the outcome of certain conditions in a certain civilization. If instead of
the word style is substituted the word civilization, it will be seen
how many are at fault. For instance, if instead of speaking of a
Louis Quatorze style you speak of putting a Louis XIV civilization in State Street it is easy to see how fearful of the anachro-
nism [sic]. We must seek to express our own feelings and the
form must in every case follow the function of which it is an
expression. Style is not an origin, it is an incident, and can only
be found by a faithful expression of what are our needs in a
natural manner.

The Inland Architect and News Record 38 (September 1901): 16.

36
Education (1902)

Sullivan did not attend the Architectural League of America's fourth convention in Toronto in May 1902, but he
sent this paper to be read there. Still concerned with architectural education, he argued that it should begin with the
study of democracy and nature, that it should start early in
life and be exacting, and should above all stimulate the
imagination. A generation of "real architects" so schooled,
he insisted, would be "dreamers in action." This paper concluded Sullivan's association with the League. After 1902,
his followers devoted more time to design than to debate.
As the new ideas of Frank Lloyd Wright and his midwestern contemporaries attracted more clients, keeping the
younger architects at home, the League's Chicago contin-
gent dwindled and, with that, Sullivan lost his influence.
Finding no other organization to his liking and having sev-
ered his ties with AIA to embrace the League, he became
more isolated, in the process coming to see himself as a

lonely voice crying for integrity in the architectural wilderness.

After the long night, and longer twilight, we envisage a dawn-era: an era in which the minor law of tradition shall yield to the greater law of creation, in which the spirit of repression shall fail to repress.

Man at last is become emancipated, and now is free to think, to feel, to act—free to move toward the goal of the race.

Humanitarianism slowly is dissolving the sway of utilitarianism, and an enlightened unselfishness is on its way to supersede a benighted rapacity. And all this, as a deep-down force in nature awakens to its strength, animating the growth and evolution of democracy.

Under the beneficent sway of this power, the hold of illusion and suppression is passing; the urge of reality is looming in force, extent and penetration, and the individual now is free to become a man, in the highest sense, if so he wills.

There is no estoppel to his imagination.

No limitation to the workings of his mind.

No violence to the dignity of his soul.

The tyranny alike of church and state has been curbed, and true power is now known to reside where forever it must remain—in the people.

Rapidly we are changing from an empirical to a scientific attitude of mind; from an inchoate to an organic trend of thinking. Inevitably we are moving toward the larger significances of life and the larger relations of the individual to that life as embodied in the people.

Truly we are face to face with great things.

The mind of youth should be squarely turned to these phenomena. He should be told, as he regards them, how long and bitterly the race has struggled that he may have freedom.

His mind should be prepared to cooperate in the far-reaching changes now under way, and which will appear to him in majestic simplicity, breadth and clearness when the sun of democracy shall have arisen but a little higher in the firmament of the race, illumining more steadily and deeply than now the mind and will

of the individual, the minds and wills of the millions of men—
his own mind and his own will.

He should be shown, as a panorama, as a great drama, the
broad sweep and flow of the vast life in which he is a unit, an
actor; and, that of a vital necessity, fundamental principles must
nourish the roots of his lifework and permeate its branches; just
as they must animate the work and life of the neighbor—for the
general harmony, the good of all.

He should be shown what the reality of history shows,
namely, that optimism is an abiding emotion in the heart of the
race: an emotion arising from the constant pressure of aspiring
democracy seeking its own.

He must be imbued with that pride, that sure quality of
honor which are the ethical flower of self-government and the
sense of moral responsibility. He must be distinctly taught his
responsibility to his fellow men.

He should be taught that a mind empty of ideals is indeed an
empty mind, and that there will be demanded of him, if not self-
sacrifice, at the least self-restraint, self-denial, and that the highest of ideals is the ideal of democracy.

To this end, history must be illumined for him, and the story
of his own day clarified.

To this end he must be inspired first and always with a clear,
full conception of what democracy truly means, what it has sig-
nified and now signifies for the emancipation of man; what it
costs in time, blood and sorrow, that it might emerge from the
matrix of humanity; how priceless is it as a heritage—the most
priceless of heritages; and how valiantly, how loyally, how jealously should he, as copartner in its beneficence, cherish its superb integrity. He, born into democracy, and therefore especially
apt to deem it negligible, must be taught with persistent, untiring assiduity, by constant precept, warning and eulogy, that its
existence, its perpetuation, its development, is as necessary to the
fullness of life as is the physical air he breathes.

The beauty of nature should most lovingly be shown to him,
and he be encouraged to venerate and to prize that beauty.

He should be taught that he and the race are inseparably
a part of nature and that his strength must come of her
bounty.

His mind and heart should be opened to the inspiration of nature, his eye directed to the borderland of that infinite and unknown toward which she leads the thoughtful view, that he may know how great is man and yet how fragile; so will he see life in its momentous balance.

He should be taught that the full span of one's life is but a little time in which to accomplish a worthy purpose; and yet should he be shown what men have done, what man can do.

An art of expression should begin with childhood, and the lucid use of one's mother tongue should be typical of that art.

The sense of reality should be strengthened from the beginning, yet by no means at the cost of those lofty illusions we call patriotism, veneration, love.

He should be taught that high ideals make a people strong.

That decay comes when ideals wane.

He should be taught that civilization has a higher reach than the goal of material things, that its apex lies in the mind and the heart.

He should be taught common honesty and that there is but one standard of honesty.

He should be taught to despise hypocrisy and cant.

This, in my view, is the fundamental of education, because it leads straight to manhood, because it makes for the moral and mental vigor of the race, because it leads toward a constantly expanding sense of humanity, because under its aegis a true art may flourish.

I am not of those who believe in lackadaisical methods. On the contrary, I advocate a vigorous, thorough, exact mental training which shall fit the mind to expand upon and grasp large things and yet properly to perceive in their just relation the significance of small ones—to discriminate accurately as to quantity and quality—and thus to develop individual judgment, capacity and independence.

But at the same time I am of those who believe that gentleness is a greater, surer power than force, and that sympathy is a safer power by far than is intellect. Therefore would I train the individual sympathies as carefully in all their delicate warmth and tenuity as I would develop the mind in alertness, poise and security.

Nor am I of those who despise dreamers. For the world

would be at the level of zero were it not for its dreamers—gone and of today. He who dreamed of democracy, far back in a world of absolutism, was indeed heroic, and we of today awaken to the wonder of his dream.

How deep this dreamer saw into the heart of man!

So would I nurse the dreamer of dreams, for in him nature broods while the race slumbers.

So would I teach the art of dreaming, as I would teach the science of thinking, as I would teach the value of action.

He who knows naught of dreaming can, likewise, never attain the heights of power and possibility in persuading the mind to act.

He who dreams not creates not.

For vapor must arise in the air before the rain can fall.

The greatest man of action is he who is the greatest, and a life-long, dreamer. For in him the dreamer is fortified against destruction by a far-seeing eye, a virile mind, a strong will, a robust courage.

And so has perished the kindly dreamer—on the cross or in the garret.

A democracy should not let its dreamers perish. They are its life, its guaranty against decay.

Thus would I expand the sympathies of youth.

Thus would I liberate and discipline all the constructive faculties of the mind and encourage true insight, true expression, real individuality.

Thus would I concentrate the powers of will.

Thus would I shape character.

Thus would I make good citizens.

And thus would I lay the foundations for a generation of real architects—real, because true, men, and dreamers in action.

The Inland Architect and News Record 39 (June 1902): 41–42.

Excavations and Foundations at Schlesinger & Mayer

Chicago dry goods merchants Leopold Schlesinger and Daniel Mayer hired Adler & Sullivan to modernize and expand their buildings three times between 1890 and 1892. They were also among the few clients to remain with Sullivan after the two architects parted company, commissioning him for ten different projects between 1896 and 1904 at their State, Madison, and Wabash Street commercial complex. The outcome of these projects stands today as the Carson, Pirie, Scott department store, designed in two sections: a nine-story Madison Street structure in 1898, and its twelve-story extension on State and Madison in 1902.* In the first of the following two selections Sullivan described the job's unusual circumstances, which had required unorthodox procedures in his office and at the site. In the second, originally read to the American Institute of Architects' Illinois Chapter (successor to the Illinois State Association of Architects), he revealed his discoveries about subsoil conditions he believed might affect future excavation and foundation work in Chicago. Both presentations were part of Sullivan's attempt to advertise his engineering, as opposed to his philosophical, expertise in order to boost his sagging financial fortunes.

37
Sub-structure at the New Schlesinger & Mayer Store Building, Chicago (1903)

The erection of a new department store building for the corporation of Schlesinger & Mayer, northeast corner of State and Madison streets, Chicago, for which the writer was engaged as architect, presented at the outset a problem of peculiar and unusual nature. The site, 140×180 feet, is at the very heart of Chicago's congested retail district, with street car lines and heavy team traffic on the two bounding streets. Time was the element

---

*(The five southernmost bays of today's State Street store were designed by Burnham & Company in 1906.)

of prime importance; and available working space and an efficient working method were of almost equal importance. It was desired to have the new building completed on or about October 1, 1903. Active operations could not be begun until October 6, 1902, leaving thus only substantially twelve months in which to carry out the project. Further, the business of the house must continue uninterruptedly in the premises with as little interference as possible, under all the circumstances; and, on a part of the ground, about 60×115 feet at the northeast corner of the property, stood a nine-story modern fire proof store building, built three years ago with the end in view that this building should be extended, nine stories in height, over the remainder of the property. It was determined, however, that this extension should be built twelve stories in height instead of nine, and that the existing nine-story building should subsequently be raised to a height of twelve stories to correspond.

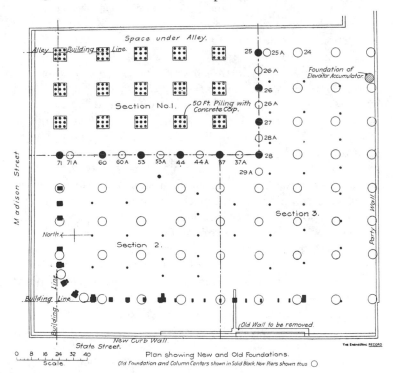

Plan showing New and Old Foundations.

Old Foundation and Column Centers shown in Solid Black, New Piers shown thus ◯

The remainder of the property was occupied by an old fashioned building, or, rather a collection of buildings erected shortly after the great fire and which, originally four stories in height, had been raised to a height of six stories. Their general construction was essentially of a flimsy nature, they had various widths, depths and floor levels; and the arrangement of columns was such that in the different sections there was no definite alignment. Further, during previous reconstructions, internal walls had been removed and many modifications made in columns, spacing, and in foundations.

The underlying soil was filled with a motley assortment of discarded foundations, discarded sewers and water pipes, and operating sewers, water pipes, underground sprinkler system pipes, etc.

Experience has shown that a modern fire proof building ten or twelve stories in height can be built and equipped complete in twelve months' time, including the demolition of such buildings as might be on the site and the installation of complete new foundations, provided that time has been taken by the forelock and working drawings made and material manufactured and stored well in advance. In this instance, no such prior allowance of time for preparatory work was possible; drawings for the building were begun about the middle of August. Furthermore, conditions determined that the building must be erected not as a whole but in two sections; which caused the limiting conditions to become so much the more strenuous. Some way, therefore, must be found to save practically three months of time, as it was out of the question that Schlesinger & Mayer should abandon an important part of their premises during the fall and holiday seasons; operation would therefore, if postponed, be thrown into severe weather, or say until after January 1. It was determined, therefore, as a radical measure, to abandon entirely the basement of the premises, promptly begin the foundation work and confine all operations to the basement. This meant logically a scheme to support the old building upon jackscrews and to sink caisson foundations. The conditions were difficult but by no means insuperable.

The general plan shows the relative locations of the new caisson foundations and the dimension stone footings, piers, columns and walls of the old building as well as the existing foundations of section 1, which consist of combinations of concrete piers and fifty-foot piling. The use of caisson foundations is not new, and shoring operations are not new; but the combination of caisson foundations and shoring operations on an extensive scale in connection with a going business is, in so far as the writer is informed, something of a novelty. It was evident that, owing to the peculiar complexity of the relations between old and new work, great loss of time would accrue if drawings must be made showing with particularity the scheme of operations in each case. The general plan of operations was, therefore, matured, and it was determined to handle each case individually, wall, column or pier by itself, and treat it as circumstances required in harmony with the general scheme. None of the operations thus carried out is of remarkable difficulty, but all of them required the extreme of painstaking care combined with all possible celerity.

The original basement was but 8 feet high, and, as caisson sinking would require head room for the sheer legs of windlass, etc., it was determined to at once excavate the soil generally to the bottom of the old foundations; meanwhile the shoring operations were put under way by prompt excavation of trenches for the cribbing and putting in place the distributing work necessary for the underpinning of piers and columns, as shown by the typical sketches. The sinking of caissons was promptly begun in section 2, section 3 being reserved as general storage and working space. Caissons in the available free space between internal columns of section 2 were begun first, and were regularly followed by those required for the support of external columns, beginning at the northwest corner of section 2 and following consecutively south and east. It was not considered expedient to sink more than five or six caissons at one time, as the operation of a greater number would require a larger gang of men than could effectively be used. Work on both shoring and the caissons was pushed night and day with three eight-hour shifts, and was suspended only between the hours of midnight of Saturday night and midnight of Sunday.

For handling and removing excavated materials and for receiving new materials, two towers of moderate dimensions were

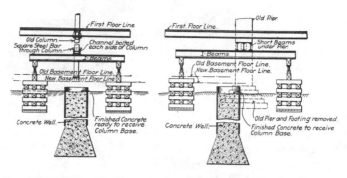

Support for Old Column while sinking
Concrete Well under for New Column.

Support for Old Masonry Pier while sinking
Concrete Well under, for New Column.

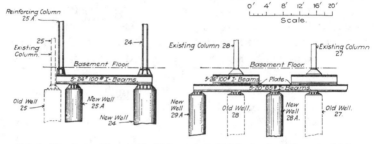

Method of Reinforcing Column in Alley Wall
to carry Three Additional Stories.

Method of Reinforcing Foundation under Existing
Columns for Three Additional Stories to Building.

Underpinning Old and Building New Substructure.

THE ENGINEERING RECORD

erected on the State street sidewalk. In one was installed a double counterbalanced wheelbarrow hoist, with platform extending over receiving wagon on the street level; in the other were installed chutes for receiving cement, sand, gravel and other materials. The excavated earth was removed at approximately the rate of 300 cubic yards per day. The full and undisturbed use of about 17,000 square feet of basement floor space, combined with an excellent system of electric lighting and the protection afforded by the existing building against all inclemencies of weather were highly favorable to the progress of the work, which, when once well inaugurated, was kept steadily under way until January 1, 1903, at which date fifty-three out of the fifty-nine caisson foundations required were in place. After due consideration it was determined to postpone the sinking of the six remaining caissons which would come under operating passenger elevators, freight elevators, package conveyor and smoke stack, until the time should come for the demolition of section 3, as their prior installation would inevitably cripple the business of the house, while their subsequent installation would in no wise interfere with the general progress of the work.

The support of certain parts of the work by means of shoring was of a nature so complicated as to be almost indescribable, and resulted in effect in a maze of beams, blocks, screws, etc. In several instances it required a full month, working day and night, to provide the necessary supports prior to the sinking of an individual well. In many instances the wells had to be sunk half way under existing foundations, or immediately under old columns and piers, or directly between existing foundations. Yet so systematically was the work undertaken and carried out that the additional cost of the installation of the sub-structure work complete, including all shoring, was within $8,000 in excess of what it would have cost had the work been carried on in an open field.

The caissons were sunk in the manner now in practice in Chicago, commencing with a circular hole dug about 6 feet below the excavated basement. This was lined with 2×6-inch tongued and grooved pine vertical lagging; a heavy iron ring being expanded near the top and bottom. The excavation was then continued in 5-foot sections, lagging inserted as before, and so on until the required depth was reached. When each well had been sunk to the proper depth for belling an auger boring was taken to make sure that the shale, which was assumed to be a satisfactory support for the foundations, extended to a further depth of at least 16 feet; the auger hole was filled with sand and the wells immediately filled with concrete dumped from wheelbarrows at the top, the upper 10 feet being packed with rammers. Concrete, in proportions of $1:3:5$, was mixed in a machine conveniently located, washed pebbles in sizes ranging from a hen's egg to a pea being used in place of broken stone. The upper foot of the concrete filling of the wells was made extra rich to serve as a suitable support for the circular cast iron bed plates. The pebble concrete has proved of superior quality, all voids being completely filled and broken samples showing a clean fracture through both pebbles and concrete.

The operation of sinking a well is very simple. It required one digger at the bottom, a bucket, rope and windlass and two men at the top; but the work was found to be laborious, owing to the actual toughness and stickiness of the clay despite the presumable softness of the plastic clay as shown by the borings. At a depth of about 50 feet below the general excavation this clay began rapidly to stiffen, and so continued until the stratum of shale was reached at a depth of about 60 feet below general level of excavation, or about 75 feet below sidewalk level. Generally speaking water was not found in the wells during sinking operations; on the contrary, it was necessary to send water to the diggers. In one instance a sudden gush of water occurred at a depth of about 40 feet, was shortly over and was quickly bailed out. The origin of this water pocket has not been traced. The shale upon which it was determined to base the concrete piers is a stratum of the glacial drift. It is exceedingly tough, almost dry, and is permeated with a very fine black gravel; it can be cut, or rather chipped, only with a mattock. To excavate it is very laborious, so that it required nearly as much time to shape the bell as to sink the shaft of the well. It was found that well sinking progressed at an average of about one well per day, or, in other words, it required about six days to sink and fill one well. This rate of progress was maintained with a fair degree of uniformity, slacking up or gaining in accordance with the delivery of material. The shorers kept suitably in advance of the diggers.

As operations progressed, a part only of the shoring was allowed to remain. Wherever possible, the piers or columns of the old buildings were reset upon the new concrete piers. Incidental to the general operations, the old curb wall, which was found to be in good condition, was underpinned to the depth required by the new basement floor; the dimension stones from old foundations being split up and used for this purpose. The south line-wall was put on drums, a small section at a time, and the new foundation inserted at a lower level; after allowing proper time for the setting of cement the wall was again underpinned and allowed to rest upon the new foundation. The handling of this wall was an extremely delicate operation owing to the fact that the rubble masonry above the old foundation was found to be of an almost unbelievably inferior quality.

The south wall of the new building is to be built within the lot lines of the property. The south row of new steel columns will therefore be cantilevered according to the method that now prevails. In order that the bells of the south line of wells shall not project into the neighboring property they were made substantially elliptical in form instead of round. All of the operations connected with the substructure work were carried out with great intelligence and care by those who had them in hand, and were brought to a conclusion without the slightest mishap of any kind.

It was found necessary, during the progress of the work, to support the existing sidewalk, not only as a measure of public safety, but to insure sufficient working space. Many difficulties were encountered in shifting and readjusting the various sewer pipes, underground pipes of the sprinkler system, water supply pipes, electric wires, cash conveyer tubes, etc., and in adjusting the shoring supports accordingly. It was found that a well could be sunk in close proximity to an old foundation, indeed partly under it, provided that foundation had been carried originally to the blue clay, without supporting such pier, column or wall by means of shoring. In such cases, however, it was not deemed advisable to sink two contiguous wells at the same time. The greater part of the old foundations rested upon a treacherous mixture of sand and clay permeated by water.

Inasmuch as it had been determined to make the new building twelve stories in height, whilst the existing section 1 is but nine stories in height, and the steel columns and the foundations of same were designed accurately for their loads, it was obvious that the steel columns for the west and south row bounding this section and their supporting concrete piers must be reinforced. This work is now under way, and will be accomplished by a system of intermediate concrete piers sunk to the same depth as the old ones and a distributing system of foundation beams. The two columns, one within the masonry of the alley wall and one within the Madison Street wall are to be reinforced by an especially designed new column with cantilever foundation-supports. The floor system of section 1 adjoining these columns is now carried upon a system of drums, screws and cribbing, reaching from blue clay to the roof beams. Column connections will be cut, columns removed, sent to the shop, cut and fitted for new lengths and replaced at a height three stories above the original position, new columns being inserted for the three lower stories.

On January 6, by careful prearrangement, the wrecking of the corner building, occupying the site of new section 2, was begun, and was completed in nine days of sixteen working hours each; operations at night being conducted by the aid of electric light. At the date of this writing, February 2, the third tier of beams for section 2 is in place. Prior to the demolition of the corner building, the usual dust and weatherproof partitions were built, housing in the adjoining parts [sic]. It is the present intention to begin wrecking section 3 about May 15. Owing to the impossibility of getting steel columns in time, it was determined to use cast iron columns of round section for section 2 of the building; a special form of connection to the floor system being devised to insure rigidity against wind strains. For section 3 it was found feasible to obtain steel columns. The metal framework of the building will therefore present a curious feature, for there will be three different types of columns in its construction, namely: Gray columns for section 1, round cast iron columns for section 2 and Z bar columns for section 3. It was considered advisable, as a matter of business policy, to proceed with the sub-structure operations as quietly as possible. The general public, therefore, had no knowledge of what was going on until the beginning of the erection of the steel work of section 2 revealed the fact that the foundation work had been completed.

Four test borings, in the basement, near the outer walls, were made to a depth of about 64 feet below the basement floor, and in general indicated a thin upper stratum of wet, sandy clay underlaid by plastic clay varying from very soft to stiff for a thickness of about 50 feet, beyond which there was a stratum 10 or 12 feet deep of dry clay with gravel and shale overlying the hardpan. At one boring the successive depths of the different strata were as follows: Concrete and cinder filling to a depth of $1\frac{1}{2}$ feet below the basement floor; wet, sandy clay to $4\frac{1}{2}$ feet; plastic clay to $26\frac{1}{2}$ feet; stiff clay to 30 feet; soft to very soft clay to $38\frac{1}{2}$ feet; stiffer to plastic clay to 53 feet; very hard, dry clay with gravel and shale to 64 feet, hardpan below. The other three borings corresponded essentially to this with different locations for the intermediate stratum of stiff clay. At another boring there was a 2-foot layer of stiff, blue clay above the plastic clay and a 1-foot layer of water bearing black sand over the hard clay 6 feet above the hardpan.

It may be noted in closing that the system of caisson foundations now coming into general use in Chicago admits of the excavation of a sub-basement at a future time. This will be presently demonstrated in Schlesinger & Mayer's building, where it had been determined to sink a sub-basement about 50×140 feet with a clear head room of 20 feet to receive boiler and machinery plant. The operation of excavating for a sub-basement is greatly simplified by the presence of the stout concrete piers which will serve as a strong and suitable support for cross bracing, should such be required. It is probable, however, that the method of operations to be followed will consist of sinking trenches to the full depth, building the retaining walls of concrete therein, and then excavating the full enclosed area; or, perhaps, to begin by excavating the full area to a reasonable and easily managed depth, and then to proceed with the trenches, retaining walls, etc., as above set forth. These matters are now under consideration.

The Engineering Record 47 (February 21, 1903): 194–96.

38
Basements and Sub-basements (1904)

I thought that the building of deep cellars was a hard proposition before I tried it. I entered upon the work with fear and trepidation, and I was astounded to find how simple it was. It is a mere matter of excavation and not an engineering feat at all, and anyone can do it. There is nothing hard about it except the digging, and that it is the hard kind of digging through stiff blue clay.

We have been used here in Chicago to believing there is a deep substratum of pulp soil and that we could put our basements down perhaps ten or fifteen feet and no deeper. I have had borings made and I find they are fallacious and that what came up does not represent the true character of the soil. At the Schlesinger & Mayer buildings the borings were unfavorable, but after the examination of them I said I was going ahead anyhow, and we started to sink our wells.

Instead of soft clay we found, after having gone about 15 feet below the sidewalk level, blue clay. This is not the kind of clay we have commonly called blue clay heretofore, but it is a stiff clay that kept getting stiffer and stiffer as we went down farther. At the depth of 50 feet this clay was so stiff the men were unable to dislodge a shovelful without dipping their shovels three or four times in water. Instead of finding water, as we had expected, we had to send water down to the men in buckets.

You may know what a task it was to excavate this clay when I tell you it took us two months to dig out a space 50×140 feet to a depth of 26 feet. I believe that there has been a complete misapprehension as to the nature of the soil under the city. We used to go down through a lot of muck and rubbish in our excavations and then at the depth of about 12 or 13 feet we would strike what was supposed to be blue clay which would be from two to four feet deep. As a matter of fact that was misleading and if we only go far enough we will find the finest kind of soil imaginable.

Now this is just what we did at the building I am speaking of. We put in 56 wells each 75 feet, and although we used the heaviest kind of shoring to hold the banks in place, as a matter of fact it was not necessary to put in any. The banks will retain themselves. At the bottom of these wells, when we came to widen them out for the bell, the clay weighed 150 pounds to the square foot. At a depth of 75 feet we came to shale that was almost chip dry and so hard the men could only chip off about two inches at a blow. I went down into a number of the wells myself and I found them all alike. I do not know just how far it is to bedrock, for although I had borings made at the bottoms of the wells the shale got so hard 12 feet down the men could not work the auger and I gave it up. I was satisfied to build on that shale for the foundations.

The real thing is that we have at last found out the exact nature of the soil under Chicago. There may be exceptions and it may be that in places the clay will be cracked, in which case water will come into the wells to a certain extent, but once you get down to the shale, which goes about 75 to 80 feet below the sidewalk level, you will have a safe foundation upon which to build. Therefore, I say, building sub-basements is a simple proposition and does not require scientific engineering, but only hard labor.

That shale is a former glacial drift. It is hard and you can moisten it and there will be no smell of clay about it. We found in it fragments of block stone, and, as I have said, it is so hard it could only be dislodged by a strong man at the rate of about two inches at a time. There is no chance for a building to settle one particle if built on caissons setting upon this shale. Pile foundations are not safe but caisson foundations are absolutely so if sunk deep enough.

[Frederick Baumann, who was present, declared that he had found in sinking wells that the soft clay extended sometimes as deep as 30 feet below the sidewalk level.] That may be so in some parts of the city, [replied Mr. Sullivan] but I venture to say that if you had continued about 40 feet you would find a stiff blue clay that I have been describing. The soil under is full of sloughs and mudholes of varying depths, but beneath it all there is good hard clay and shale foundations, non-compressible and dry.

The Economist 31 (February 20, 1904): 254.

A National Architecture

Sullivan's 1902 essay "Education" (document 36) marked the end of his relationship with the *Inland Architect,* the Chicago building magazine which had published over half of all his public papers since 1885. *Interstate Architect* in Cleveland also stopped supporting Sullivan in 1902, perhaps because its huge investment in *Kindergarten Chats* (see headnotes to documents 32, 33) produced such a meager response. But in 1905 Sullivan found a new literary outlet in *The Craftsman* magazine, founded in 1901 by Gustav Stickley (1857–1942) to promote the handmade furniture Stickley designed in his Eastwood, New York, workshop. A disciple of John Ruskin and William Morris, Stickley was a leading American proponent of the English arts and crafts movement. In Sullivan's first two pieces for *The Craftsman* he made essentially the same point: that an appropriate national architecture could be founded only upon the characteristics of the American people, certainly not on a particular historic style. His admiration for Stickley extended beyond his magazine to the Craftsman furniture style Sullivan used in his National Farmer's Bank (1906–1908) in Owatonna, Minnesota. For his part, Stickley published five pieces by Sullivan (documents 39–43) between 1905 and 1909, plus excerpts from "The Tall Office Building Artistically Considered" (document 23).

39
Reply to Mr. Frederick Stymetz Lamb on "Modern Use of the Gothic; The Possibility of a New Architectural Style" (1905)

It is too evident that Mr. Lamb* is making a special plea for Gothic *as* Gothic. In so doing he differs not a whit, in principle, from one who makes a plea for Classic as Classic. Psychologically the plea is the same in either case, in this, that it takes for granted we are to accept, as alive, objective results the subjective causes of which have gone beyond recall.

In either case the pleader persists in regarding historical architecture, not as the living thing it *was,* but as a fetish within his own mind.

---

*Frederick Stymetz Lamb, a well known New York artist, lecturer, and writer on civic and municipal aesthetics, was also a member of the Architectural League of America. The correct title of the essay in *The Craftsman* 8 (May 1905) to which Sullivan responded was "The Modern Use of the Gothic; The Possibilities of a New Architectural Style."

The flaw in our current architectural reasoning (if reasoning it may be called) lies in the fact (curious enough, to the logical mind), of a persistence in refusing to discriminate between *was* and *is;* and this,—in open view of the clear truth that nature, which surrounds us with its life,—always thus discriminates with precision. Hence with each discussion comes merely an added and ever-futile attempt to detach an art from the civilization which gave it birth.

Mr. Lamb discriminates between the plasticity of the Gothic and the fixity of the Classic, as he sees them; but he fails to balance his statement by a recognition of the tranquillity of the Classic and the restlessness of the Gothic,—both considered in their original manifestations.

He perceives that the Classic art when applied to modern American conditions loses dignity and becomes increasingly restless, even to the point of torture, as the conditions become more and more *specifically* American;—that is to say less and less Greek or Roman. And yet he affects to believe that Gothic art by the magic of a name will have a different fate!

In other words he complacently suggests that Mediaeval thought is really more American than the thought of Greece or Rome—meanwhile completely ignoring the possible suitability of twentieth century thought for our twentieth century conditions and demands. In other words, Mr. Lamb would deliberately throw over his shoulder the wonderful riches of modern thought, in order that he may have dalliance with Gothic detail.

All such special pleadings are beside the mark, and do not in the least touch upon the real problem.

This real problem is practical and immediate, and concerns the actual thinking-power of an architect, when such thinking is put to the test of simple terms.

Our real, live, American problems concern neither the Classic nor the Gothic, they concern *us* here and now.

They concern our actual, present ability to see straight, think straight, and act straight.

All this talk about Classic, Gothic, Renaissance, etc., merely indicates *inverted* thinking, and has nothing to do with *our* case. Our case is the big urge of American life as well as its many lesser urges.

When once we realize this, that instant we will have discovered a prime fact, and all historical architecture will thereupon become a secondary fact in our thought; for our thought will then have crossed the threshold of artificial thinking and entered the life-domain of natural thinking.

The primal elements of architecture are the same to-day as ever they were since the dawn of things; namely, only three— pier, lintel and arch. All other forms are secondary, tertiary, quarternary, or further derivatives of these original and elemental three.

The architectures of the Egyptian, Assyrian and Greek, based on pier and lintel, reflect, each, in its way, the nature of the three civilizations.

The Egyptian pier and lintel were results of what the Egyptian thought; the Assyrian, of what the Assyrian thought; the Greek, of what the Greek thought. There came a time when a certain section of men had other thoughts, very specific in nature, and Gothic art arose in response to Mediaeval thought.

Now in the course of time there has arisen a new people, in a new land called America. A land that but a few short centuries ago lay sleeping and dreaming, silent and alone amid the waters upon the fair round surface of the earth. This people at first few, rugged, hardy, fearless, increased marvelously in numbers. So rapidly, thoughtlessly and loosely did they organize and prosper, that disintegration (as was inevitable) kept a gaining-pace within their minds and their social structure, and, hence, corruption steadily worked an ascendency, until now, at the height of their prosperity, they have also reached appalling depths of moral degradation,—and virtue is found in hiding.

This condition of heart and mind explains the pathology of our American architecture. That architecture *is* what the American people *think*.

Corruption has gone so far, that it is time for a reaction. Not a trivial reaction from Classic to Gothic; but a fundamental reaction from irresponsibility to responsibility; from irrational to rational ideas; from confused to clear thinking. It is time for the nightmare of our feudalism to end, and for us to awaken to the reality of healthful life.

Nor need any man fear that an art of expression will fail him merely because he is honest and thinks simply. On the contrary,

such art of expression will come to him inevitably and spontaneously, just because his thoughts are clear and natural.

Nor need any man assume that this means the extinction of
intuition and imagination. On the contrary, simple thinking,
simple fearlessness of truth awakens these greatest adjuncts of
the power of reason, reveals their nature, their normal healthful
use, and the fluency and power of the great Life from which
they draw their sustenance,—and which is unitary.

To discuss architecture and ignore life is frivolous.

To discuss American architecture and its possibilities, while
ignoring the repressive force of feudalism and expansive force of
democracy, is sheer lunacy.

That the educative forces surrounding the architect have been
and are unfortunate, is but too true.

The net result has been to foster in the selfishness and egoism
of the architect, the irresponsible notion that he need not think,
and need not be a man; that the real, the spiritual interests of
his people do not concern him.

Therefore is all special pleading for Classic, Gothic, or any
other "ic" or "ance," irrelevant, immaterial, and inconsequential.

What is of consequence, is vital direct thinking stripped of all
hypocrisy, pedantry and dilettantism.

Our need is for fresh air and a general mental sanitation.

The Craftsman 8 (June 1905): 336–38.

40
Letter to the Editor on *The Craftsman* (1905)

I like the spirit you are infusing into THE CRAFTSMAN. It comes
at a critical time,—a time of ferment, a time of epoch-making
changes. I hope you have the courage to see and grasp the opportunity to draw out opinion and define an issue, believing that
you realize how noble a system of design (architectural
thinking) might be founded upon the superb underlying qualities of the American people,—a people in whom I have a profound faith, in spite of our temporary era of insanity. America

has long owed the world a new and sane philosophy, in grati-
tude for that liberty of mind which centuries of struggle have
prepared for it.

The Craftsman 8 (July 1905): 453.

41
What is Architecture?: A Study in the American People of Today (1906)

With the exception of his books—*The Autobiography of an
Idea* (1924), *A System of Architectural Ornament* (1924),
and *Democracy: A Man-Search* (1961)—this is Louis Sullivan's last major theoretical work. His final public papers
(documents 42–51, discounting the comparatively brief
document 43, which reiterated some of the themes developed here) dealt with specific subjects even though they
occasionally drifted into matters philosophical. In "What is
Architecture?" Sullivan repeated his conviction that architecture reflected social values, that nature was the best
teacher, that contemporary design was misdirected, and
that the individual was paramount. Direct and precise in
places but discursive and abstract elsewhere, it was nevertheless a reasonably accessible entrée to the sum of his
thinking at the time. One contemporary reader derived
considerable benefit from the essay, and because of it, so
did Sullivan. "What is Architecture?" helped to confirm Carl
K. Bennett, vice-president of the National Farmers' Bank
in Owatonna, Minnesota, in the opinion that he had found
the right architect. Sullivan's brilliant National Farmers'
building of 1906–1908, inaugurating his second, if notably modest career, was the first of eight new and remod-
eled banks executed in small midwestern cities and towns
by 1920. Though not approaching the scale of his earlier
commercial edifices, they were among Sullivan's most enduring contributions to America's architectural heritage.
"What is Architecture?" was originally published in the

January 1906 issue of *American Contractor* before Sullivan
revised it for *The Craftsman*.

The intellectual trend of the hour is toward simplification. The
full powers of the modern scientific mind are now directed, with
a common consent, toward searching out the few and simple
principles that are believed to underlie the complexity of Nature,
and such investigation is steadily revealing a unitary impulse underlying all men and all things.

This method of analysis reveals a curious aspect of Man,
namely: that as he thinks, so he acts; and, conversely, one may
read in his acts what he thinks—his real thoughts, be it understood, not what he avows he thinks. For all men think, all men
act. To term a man unthinking is a misuse of words; what really
is meant is that he does not think with accuracy, fitness and
power. If, then, it be true that as a man thinks so must he act in
inevitable accordance with his thought, so is it true that society,
which is but a summation of individuals, acts precisely as it
thinks. Thus are the thoughts of a people to be read in the acts
of a people, as clearly as words are read upon the printed page.

If, in like manner, we apply this method of analysis to the
complex spread of historical and contemporaneous architecture,
we perceive, clearly revealed in their simplicity, its three elementary forms, namely, the pier, the lintel and the arch. These are
the three, the only three letters, from which has expanded the
Architectural Art as a great and superb language wherewith Man
has expressed, through the generations, the changing drift of his
thoughts. Thus, throughout the past and the present, each building stands as a social act. In such act we read that which cannot
escape our analysis, for it is indelibly fixed in the building,
namely, the nature of the thoughts of the individual and the
people whose image the building is or was.

Perhaps I should not leave the three elements, pier, lintel and
arch, thus baldly set forth. It may not appear to the reader that
the truth concerning them is as clear and simple as I state it. He
may think, for example, that there was a marked difference between the Egyptian and the Greek Architectures, even though
both were based on pier and lintel only. There was a marked

difference. The difference that existed between the Egyptian and
the Greek minds. The Egyptian animated pier and lintel with his
thought—he could not do otherwise; and the Egyptian temple
took form as an Egyptian act—it could not be otherwise. So
Greek thought, clearly defined, took form in the Greek temple,
clearly defined, and the Greek temple stood clearly forth as a
Greek act. Yet both were as simply pier-and-lintel as I, in setting
one brick upon two separated other bricks, simply expose the
principles of pier and lintel.

Similarly the Roman aqueduct and the medieval cathedral
were both in the pier-and-arch form. But what a far cry from
Roman thought to medieval thought! And how clearly is that
difference in thought shown in the differences in form taken on
in each case by pier and arch, as each structure in its time stood
forth as an act of the people. How eloquently these structures
speak to us of the militant and simple power of Roman thought,
of the mystic yearning of medieval thought.

But, you may say, these structures were not acts of the people, rather, in one case the act of an emperor, in the other case
an act of the church. Very well; but what really was the emperor
but an act of the people—expressing the thought of the people;
and what was the church but similarly the thought of the people
in action? When the thought of the Roman people changed, the
vast Roman fabric disintegrated; when the thought of the medieval people changed, the vitality of the church subsided exactly
in proportion as the supporting thought of the people was withdrawn. Thus every form of government, every social institution,
every undertaking, however great, however small, every symbol
of enlightenment or degradation, each and all have sprung and
are still springing from the life of the people, and have ever
formed and are now as surely forming images of their thought.
Slowly by centuries, generations, years, days, hours, the thought
of the people has changed; so with precision have their acts re-
sponsively changed; thus thoughts and acts have flowed and are
flowing ever onward, unceasingly onward, involved within the
impelling power of Life. Throughout this stream of human life,
and thought, and activity, men have ever felt the need to build;
and from the need arose the power to build. So, as they thought,
they built; for, strange as it may seem, they could build in no
other way. As they built, they made, used and left behind them

records of their thinking. Then, as through the years new men came with changed thoughts, so arose new buildings in consonance with the change of thought—the building always the expression of the thinking. Whatever the character of the thinking, just so was the character of the building. Pier, lintel and arch changed in form, purpose and expression, following, with the fidelity of Life, Man's changing thoughts as he moved in the flow of his destiny—as he was moved ever onward by a drift unseen and unknown—and which is now flowing and is still unseen and unknown.

This flow of building we call Historical Architecture. At no time and in no instance has it been other than an index of the flow of the thought of the people—an emanation from the inmost life of the people.

Perhaps you think this is not so; perhaps you think the feudal lord built the fortified castle. So he did, ostensibly. But where did his need and power so to build come from? From his retainers. And whence came the power of his retainers? From the people. As the people thought, so they acted. And thus the power of the feudal lord rested upon the thought, the belief of the people; upon their need and upon their power. Thus all power rests upon the consent of the people, that is, upon their thought. The instant their thought begins to change, that instant the power, resting upon it and sanctioned by it, begins its waning. Thus the decay of the old and the formation of the new are synchronous effects of one cause. That single cause is: Thought. Thus we perceive that the simplest aspect of all human activity is change.

To analyze the influences that cause thought to change would take me, now, too far afield. Suffice it to say that thought, once having undergone change, does not again become the same—however great the lapse in time. Thus is there ever new birth, never rebirth.

It may now become clear to my reader that we ought, in viewing historic Architecture, to cease to regard it under the artificial classification of styles, as is now the accepted way, and to consider (as is more natural and more logical) each building of the past and the present as a product and index of the civilization of the time, also, as the product and index of the thought of the people of the time and place. In this way we shall develop

in our minds a much broader, clearer panorama of the actual
living flow of Architecture through the ages; and grasp the clear,
simple, accurate notion, that Architecture always has been, and
still is, a simple impulse of which the manifestation in varied
form is continuously changing.

I should add, perhaps, that, in speaking of the people, I do
not use the word in the unhappy sense of the lower classes, so-
called. I mean all the people; and I look upon all the people as
constituting a social organism.

I am quite aware that these are views not generally held
among architects. Indeed you will not find a thesis of this kind
set forth in books or taught in schools. For the prevailing view
concerning Architecture is strangely artificial and fruitless, as indeed are the current American ideas concerning almost any
phase of the welfare of all the people. That is to say; in our
democratic land, ideas, thoughts, are weirdly, indeed destruc-
tively, undemocratic—an aspect of our current civilization
which, later, I shall consider.

I therefore ask my reader, for the time being at least, to repose sufficient confidence in my statements, that he may lay
aside his existing notions concerning Architecture, which are of
necessity traditional, and, as such, acquired habits of thinking,
unanalyzed by him; and thus lay his mind open to receive and
consider the simple and more natural views which make up my
paper, to the end that he may perceive how far astray we are
from an Architecture natural, truthful and wholesome, such as
should characterize a truly democratic people. I ask this because
the welfare of democracy is my chief concern in life; and because
I have always regarded Architecture, and still so regard it, as
merely one of the activities of a people, and, as such, necessarily
in harmony with all the others. For as a people thinks concerning Architecture, so it thinks concerning everything else; and as
it thinks concerning any other thing, so it thinks concerning Architecture; for the thought of a people, however complicated it
may appear, is all of-a-piece, and represents the balance of hereditary and environment at the time.

I trust, further, that a long disquisition is not necessary in
order to show that the attempt at imitation, by us of this day,
of the by-gone forms of building, is a procedure unworthy of a

free people; and that the dictum of schools, that Architecture is finished and done, is a suggestion humiliating to every active brain, and, therefore, in fact, a puerility and a falsehood when weighed in the scales of truly democratic thought. Such dictum gives the lie, in arrogant fashion, to healthful human experience. It says, in a word: The American people are not fit for democracy. Perhaps they are not. If so, we shall see how and why. We shall see if this alleged unfitness is really normal and natural, or if it is a feudal condition imposed upon the people by a traditional system of inverted thinking. We shall see if those whom we have entrusted with leadership in our matters educational have or have not misled us. We shall see, in a larger sense, if we, as a people, not only have betrayed each other, but have failed in that trust which the world-spirit of democracy placed in our hands, as we, a new people, emerged to fill a new and spacious land.

All of this we shall presently read in our current Architecture, and we shall test the accuracy of that reading by a brief analysis of the thought and activities of the American people as they are expressed in other ways. For, be sure, what we shall find in our Architecture, we shall as surely find elsewhere and everywhere.

If it is assumed that the art of reading is confined to the printed page, we cannot go far. But if we broaden and quicken our sense of reading until it appears to us, in its more vital aspect, as a science, an art of interpretation, we shall go very far indeed. In truth, there will be no ending of our journey; for the broad field of nature, of human thought and endeavor, will open to us a book of life, wherein the greatest and the smallest, the most steadfast and the most fleeting, will appear in their true value. Then will our minds have escaped slavery to WORDS and be at liberty, in the open air of reality, freely and fully to deal with THINGS.

Indeed, most of us have, in less or greater measure, this gift of reading things. We come into it naturally; but, curiously enough, many are ashamed because it does not bear the sanction of authority, because it does not bear the official stamp of that much misunderstood word scholarship, a stamp, by the way, which gives currency to most of the notions antagonistic to the development of our common thinking powers. It is this same

scholastic fetichism, too, that has caused an illogical gap between
the theoretical and the practical. In right thinking such gap cannot exist. A true method of education, therefore, should consist
in a careful and complete development of our common and natural powers of thinking, which, in reality, are vastly greater, infinitely more susceptible to development than is generally assumed. Indeed, the contumacy in which we habitually underrate
the latent powers of the average human mind is greatly to our
discredit. It constitutes, in fact, a superstition. A superstition
whose origin is readily traceable to the scholasticism of past centuries, and to the tenacious notion of social caste. It is definitely
the opposite of the modern and enlightened view now steadily
gaining ground, that the true spirit of democratic education consists in searching out, liberating and developing the splendid but
obscured powers of the average man, and particularly those of
his children.

It is disquieting to note that the system of education on
which we lavish funds with such generous, even prodigal, hand,
falls short of fulfilling its true democratic function; and that particularly in the so-called higher branches its tendency appears
daily more reactionary, more feudal.

It is not an agreeable reflection that so many of our university
graduates lack the trained ability to see clearly, and to think simply, concisely, constructively; that there is perhaps more showing of cynicism than good faith, seemingly more distrust of men
than confidence in them, and, withal, no consummate ability to
interpret things.

In contrast, we have the active-minded but "uneducated"
man, he who has so large a share in our activities. He reads well
those things that he believes concern him closely. His mind is
active, practical, superficial; and, whether he deals with small
things or large, its quality is nearly the same in all cases. His
thoughts almost always are concerned with the immediate. His
powers of reflection are undeveloped, and thus he ignores those
simple, vital things which grow up beside him, and with which,
as a destiny, he will some day have to reckon, and will then find
himself unprepared. The constructive thinking power of such
men, the imaginative reach, the incisive intuition, the forceful
will, sometimes amaze us. But when we examine closely we find

that all this is but a brilliant superstructure, that the hidden foundation is weak because the foundation-thought was not sought to be placed broad, deep and secure in the humanities. Thus we have at the poles of our thinking two classes of men, each of which believes it is dealing with realities, but both in fact dealing with phantoms; for between them they have studied everything but the real thoughts and the real hearts of the people. They have not sufficiently reckoned with the true and only source both of social stability and of social change. If, in time, such divergence of thought, as it grows in acuteness, shall lead to painful readjustments, such will be but the result, natural and inexorable, of a fatal misunderstanding, the outgrowth of that fatal defect in our system of thinking which is leading us away from our fellows.

If I say that these aspects of our thought are readable in our current Architecture, I am not saying too much, for acts point surely to the parent thoughts, and in everything that men do they leave an indelible imprint of their minds. If this suggestion be followed out, it will become surprisingly clear how each and every building reveals itself naked to the eye; how its every aspect, to the smallest detail, to the lightest move of the hand, reveals the workings of the mind of a man who made it, and who is responsible to us for it. Everything is there for us to read, to interpret; and this we may do at our leisure. The building has not means of locomotion, it cannot hide itself, it cannot get away. There it is, and there it will stay—telling more truths about him who made it, who thought it, than he in his fatuity imagines; revealing his mind and his heart exactly for what they are worth, not a whit more, not a whit less; telling, plainly, the lies he thinks; telling with almost cruel truthfulness of his bad faith, his feeble, wabbly mind, his impudence, his selfish egoism, his mental irresponsibility, his apathy, his disdain for real things. Is it cruelty to analyze thus clearly? Is it vivisection thus to pursue, step by step, to uncover nerve after nerve, dispassionately to probe and test and weigh act after act, thought after thought, to follow every twist and turn of the mind that made the building, sifting and judging it until at last the building says to us: "I am no more a real building than the thing that made me is a real man!"

If so, then it must, correspondingly, be a pleasure and a genuine beneficence to recognize and note, in some other building, the honest effort of an honest man, the kindly willingness and frankness of a sincere mind to give expression to simple, direct, natural thinking, to produce a building as real as the man who made it.

And is it not, as naturally, helpful to recognize and note in still another building a mind perhaps not too well trained, perhaps not very sure of itself, but still courageously seeking a way; the building showing where the mind stumbles and tries again, showing just where the thought is not immanent, not clear, not self-centered?

Is it not the part of wisdom to cheer, to encourage such a mind, rather than to dishearten it with ridicule? To say to it: Learn that the mind works best when allowed to work naturally; learn to do what your problem suggests when you have reduced it to its simplest terms; you will thus find all problems, however complex, taking on a simplicity you had not dreamed of; accept this simplicity, boldly, and with confidence, do not lose your nerve and run away from it, or you are lost, for you are here at the point men so heedlessly call genius—as though it were necessarily rare; for you are here at the point no living brain can surpass in essence, the point all truly great minds seek—the point of vital simplicity—the point of view which so illuminates the mind that the art of expression becomes spontaneous, powerful and unerring, and achievement a certainty; so, if you would seek and express the best that is in yourself, you must search out the best that is in your people; for they are your problem, and you are indissolubly a part of them; it is for you to affirm that which they really wish to affirm, namely, the best that is in them, and they as truly wish you to express the best that is in yourself; if the people seem to have but little faith it is because they have been tricked so long; they are weary of dishonesty, much more weary than you know, and in their hearts they seek honest and fearless men, men simple and clear of mind, loyal to their own manhood and to the people. The American people are now in a stupor; be on hand at the awakening. The lion is now in the net, or the larva in the cocoon—take the simile you prefer.

But to simplify the mind is, in fact, not so easy. Everything is against you. You are surrounded by a mist of tradition which you, alone, must dispel. The schools will not help you, for they too, are in a mist. So, you must develop your mind as best you can. The only safe method is to take nothing for granted, but to analyze, test and examine all things, for yourself, and determine their true values; to sift the wheat from the chaff, and to reduce all thoughts, all activities, to the simple test of honesty. You will be surprised, perhaps, to see how matters that you once deemed solid, fall apart; and, how things that you once deemed inconsequential, take on a new and momentous significance. But in time your mind will clarify and strengthen, and you will have moved into that domain of intellectual power wherein thought discriminates, with justice and clarity, between those things which make for the health, and those which make for the illness of a people. When you have done this, your mind will have reached its balance; you will have something to say, and you will say it with candor.

In the light of the preceding statements, the current mannerisms of architectural criticism must often seem trivial. For of what avail is it to say that this is too small, that too large, this too thick, that too thin, or to quote this, that or the other precedent, when the real question may be: Is not the entire design a mean evasion, a parasitic growth? Why magnify this, that or the other little thing, if the entire scheme of thinking, that the building stands for, is false, and puts a mask upon the people, who want true buildings, but do not know how to get them so long as architects betray them with architectural phrases?

Why have we not more of vital architectural criticism? Is it because our professional critics lack penetration? Because they lack courage? Is it because they, who should be free, are not free? Is it because they, who should know, do not know? Do they not see, or will they not? Do they know such buildings to be lies, and refrain from saying so? Or are they, too, inert of mind? Are their minds, too, benumbed with culture, and their hearts, thus, made faint?

How is a people to know what, for them, a real and fitting Architecture may mean, if it is not first made clear to them that the current and accepted Architecture with which their minds are rapidly being distorted—is false to them! To whom are we to look if not to our trusted critics? And if these fail us, what then?

But—the cynic may observe—what if they do fail us! They write merely in the fashion. For everybody else betrays everybody else. We are all false; and why should a false people expect other than a false Architecture? A people always gets what it deserves, neither more or less. It's up to the people, anyway. If they want a real Architecture, let them become real, themselves. If they do not wish to be betrayed, let them quit betraying. If they really wish loyalty, let them be loyal. If they really wish thinkers, let them so think. If they really do not wish humbug Architecture, let them cease being humbugs themselves. There is so much of truth in this discouraging view, that I shall later clarify it.

For the moment, however, it is significant in passing to note, concerning our architectural periodicals. They float along, aimlessly enough, drifting in the tide of heedless commercialism—their pages filled with views of buildings, buildings, like "words, words, words." Buildings in this "style," that and the other; false always, except now and then and here and there in spots, where the "style" has been dropped in spots, and where, in consequence, the real building appears in spots; or where the architect, under "compulsion," has had to let the "style" go—and do something sensible; or, rarely, where the architect, of his own free will, has chosen to be clean, and has expressed himself with feeling and simple, direct eloquence. The publishers may well say: Make the Architecture and we will publish it; we are but mirrors of the times. If our pages are filled with pretentious trash, it is because architects make it. We publish what our critics write, such as it is, and what architects write, such as it is. We give our readers, who are mostly architects, what they give us. If they want better, they will let us know. We are willing.

And a word concerning "Handbooks on Architecture." All that need be said of them is that they are the blind leading the blind.

Concerning more ambitious works: while they contain certain, or rather uncertain, attempts at philosophy, such discussion is left in the air as a vapor; it is not condensed into terms of vital, present use.

Thus, it happens that the would-be searcher after architectural reality finds no air, no comfort. He is led into a jungle within whose depths his guides are lost, and he is left without compass and without a star. And why is this so? The answer is at hand: Because it has long and tacitly been assumed, by our would-be mentors, that the Architectural Art is a closed book, that the word FINIS was written centuries ago, and that all, obviously, that is left for us moderns is the humble privilege to select, copy and adapt. Because it has not been assumed that ALL buildings have arisen, have stood, and stand as physical symbols of the psychic state of the people. Because no distinction has been made between WAS and IS. And—what is most dispiriting—this lunacy continues its erratic parade in plain open view of the towering fact that modern science, with devoted patience of research, has evolved, is perfecting and has placed freely at our service the most comprehensive, accurate and high-powered system of organic reasoning that the world has known. These methods and powers, the breadth and fertility of this supreme search for the all-life-process, this most fruitful function of democracy, is, by those connected with the Architectural Art and its teaching, today regarded vacantly. Strangely they undervalue that which for us all, in all truth, in the serenity of human hope, heralds a sunrise for the race. Truly, procreant modern thought, clothed in all its radiance of good will, is a poet, a teacher and a prophet not known in the land of these.

Confronting this ignoble apathy of those we have trusted, let us assume, if it be but in fancy, a normal student of Nature and of Man. Let us assume a virile critic, human and humane, sensitive to all, and aware of this modern daybreak. He will have been a life-seeker of realities. His compass pointing ever to the central fact that all is life; his drinkwater, the knowledge that act and thought are fatefully the same; his nourishing food, the conviction that pure democracy is the deepest-down, the most persistent, while the most obscured desire within the consciousness of man—so equipped, he will have traversed the high seas and the lands, from poles to equator, all latitudes and longitudes of the prolific world of repressed but aspiring humanity. He will hold history, as a staff, in his hand. He will weigh the Modern Man in a just balance, wherein he will set against that man his accountability to all the people. He, as dispassionately, will weigh the people, collectively, against their manifest responsibility and accountability to the child and to the man.

Let us suppose him, now, in his wandering, to have come into Our Land. That he views our Architecture, weighs it, evaluates it; then, turning in thought, looks out upon us, as a people, analyzes us, weighs us, takes our measure, appraises us; that he then places People and Architecture in the great balance of History, and thoughtfully weighs, carefully appraises; then places the people, with all their activities, in the new balance of Democracy, again to weigh, again to appraise; and then puts us with our self-called Common Sense into the serene balance of Nature; and, at the last, weighs Us and Our All, in the fateful balance of All-Encompassing Life—and makes the last appraisement! What, think you, will be his revaluing of our valuations of things, of thoughts, of men? What, in the sifting, would prove wheat, what, in the weighing, would have substance, what in this refiner's fire would be the dross? After his reflections, what will he say? What will he say, after weighing us against our broad, fertile land, with its many waters, its superb and stimulating air, its sumptuous and placid beauty? How will he define us when he shall have searched our minds and hearts? For we cannot hide! What will he say when he shall come to hold us in a close accounting of our stewardship of the talent, Liberty, the treasure that the world has paid so dear in sorrow to transmit to us?

What he might say, would prove a new and most dramatic story.

But surely he might, in part, speak thus:

As you are, so are your buildings; and, as are your buildings, so are you. You and your Architecture are the same. Each is the faithful portrait of the other. To read the one is to read the other. To interpret the one is to interpret the other. Arising from both, as a miasma: What falsity! What betrayal of the present and the past! Arising from both, as the most thrilling, the more heart-piercing of refrains, as the murmur of a crowd, I hear the cry: "What is the use?" that cry begun in frivolity, passing into cynicism, and, now, deepening into pessimism. That cry which in all time and in all peoples became the cry of death or of revolution, when from frivolity it had merged through pessimism—into an utterance of despair! Your buildings, good, bad and indifferent, arise as warning hands in the faces of all—for they are what you are. Take heed! Did you think Architecture a thing of books—of the past? No! Never! IT WAS, ALWAYS, OF ITS PRESENT AND ITS PEOPLE! IT, NOW, IS OF THE PRESENT, AND OF YOU! This Architecture is ashamed to be natural, but is not ashamed to lie; so, you, as a people, are ashamed to be natural but are not ashamed to lie. This Architecture is ashamed to be honest, but it is not ashamed to steal; so, then, by the unanswerable logic of Life, you are ashamed to be honest but are not ashamed to steal. This Architecture is filled with hypocrisy and cant. So, likewise, are you, but you say you are not. This Architecture is neurasthenic; so have you burned the candle at both ends. Is then this Democracy? This Architecture shows, ah, so plainly, the decline of Democracy, and a rank new growth of Feudalism—sure sign of a people in peril! This Architecture has no serenity—sure symbol of a people out of balance. This Architecture reveals no lucid guiding principle— nor have you yet evolved a lucid guiding principle, sorely though you now need it! This Architecture shows no love of Nature—you despise Nature. In it is no joy of living—you know not what the fullness of life signifies—you are unhappy, fevered and perturbed. In these buildings the Dollar is vulgarly exalted—and the Dollar you place above Man. You adore it twenty-four hours each day: it is your God! These buildings show lack of great thinkers, real men, among your architects; and, as a people, you are poor in great thinkers, real men—though you now, in your extremity, are in dire need of great thinkers, real men. These buildings show no love of country, no affection for the people. So have you no affection for each other, but secretly will ruin each and any, so much do you love gold, so wantonly will you betray not only your neighbor but yourselves and your own children, for it!

Yet, here and there, a building bespeaks integrity—so have you that much of integrity. All is not false—so are you not wholly false. What leaven is found in your buildings—such leaven is found in you. Weight for weight, measure for measure, sign for sign—as are your buildings, so are you!

A colossal energy is in your buildings, but not true power—so is found in you a frenzied energy, but not the true power of equipoise. Is this an indictment? Not unless you yourselves are an indictment of yourselves. There stand the buildings, they have their unchanging physiognomy. Look! See! Thus, this is a reading, an interpretation.

Here and there are buildings, modest, truthful and sincere: products of a genuine feeling existing in you. They are not truly ashamed where you are not ashamed; they are natural where you are natural; they are democratic where you are democratic. Side by side they stand against the false and feudal—all intermixed. So are your thoughts and acts intermixed, democratic and feudal, in a strange and sinister drift.

Your buildings show no philosophy. So have you no philosophy. You pretend a philosophy of common sense. Weighed in the balance of your acts, your common sense is light as folly: a patent-medicine folly, an adulterated-food folly, a dyspeptic folly, the folly of filth and smoke in your cities, and innumerable every-day follies quite the reverse of that common sense which you assume to mean clear-cut and sturdy thinking in the affairs of daily life. You boast a philosophy of Success. It has long been your daily harangue. But, weighed in the balance of Democracy, your successes are but too clearly, in the main, feudal. They are pessimisms, not optimisms. You did not think to count the cost; but you are beginning now to catch a corner of its masked visage. The sight of the true full cost will stagger you—when the mask is fully drawn aside, and it stands clearly revealed! You would not foresee a crisis, BUT CRISIS FORESAW YOU, AND NOW IS UPON YOU.

You tacitly assumed philosophy to be an empty word, not a vital need; you did not inquire; and in so blindfolding your minds, you have walked straight to the edge of an abyss.

For a Sound Philosophy is the Saving Grace of a Democratic People! It means, very simply, a balanced system of thinking, concerning the vital relations of a people. It is intensely practical. Nothing can be more so. For it saves waste. It looks far behind and far ahead. It forestalls Crisis. It nurtures, economizes and directs the vitality of a people. It has for its sole and abiding objective, their equilibrium, hence their happiness.

Thus, foibles and follies have usurped in your minds the vacant seat of Wisdom. Thus, has your Dollar betrayed you, as it must. And thus, has NOT been given to the World that which was and still remains your highest office, and your noblest privilege to give, in return for that Liberty which was once yours, and which the world gave to you: A sane and pure accounting of Democracy; a philosophy founded upon Man—thereby setting forth, in clear and human terms, the integrity, the responsibility and the accountability of the individual—in short, a new, a real Philosophy of the People.

It is not yet too late.

Let such philosophy be the spiritual first-fruit of your fair and far-flung land. For you must now think quickly, and with a penetration, concentration, simplicity, accuracy and nerve, the necessity of which you have hitherto belittled and denied. Your one splendid power and reserve lies in your resourceful intelligence when forced by your distress into a crisis. Your Architecture hints at this in its many-sided practicalities. Your history in this land has proved it. Use this power at once!

Again, this Architecture, in the large sense, is barren of poetry; yet, strangely enough it faintly contains in its physiognomy a latent suggestion, which bespeaks dramatic, lyric, eloquent and appealing possiblities. In fine, it expresses obscurely the most human qualities you as a people possess, and which, such is your awkward mental bashfulness, you are ashamed to acknowledge, much less to proclaim. One longs to wash from this dirty face its overlay of timidity and abasement; to strip from its form the rags of neglect and contumely, and to see if indeed there be not beneath its forlorn and pitiful aspect, the real face and form of unsuspected Cinderella.

I surmise—or is it a hope born of visible possibilities? A sense of not negligible probabilities? For, truly, what in all the world is more sweet, in the last analysis, however fickle and at times childishly cruel, than is the American heart!

On this foundation, deeper and stronger than you suspect, I would, if I were you, build a new superstructure, really truer to yourselves, and more enduring, than that which now is crumbling upon its weak support of over-smartness and fundamental untruth.

Fortunate, indeed, are you, that your corruption has been so crude; for you can still survive the surgery of its eradication.

It is on this sound heart, and that still better part of it as yet unmatured and unrevealed to your own consciousness, that I would build anew and aright.

For he who knows even a genuinely little of Mankind knows this truth: The heart is greater than the head. For, in the heart, is Desire; and, from it, comes forth Courage and Magnanimity.

To be sure, you had assumed that poetry meant verses; and that reading such was an unworthy weakness for men of brains and hard-headed business. You have held to a fiction, patterned upon your farcical common sense, that sentiment has no place in affairs. Again you did not inquire; you assumed, took for granted—as is your heedless way. You have not looked into your own hearts. You have looked only at the vacancy of convention from which realities have long since departed. Only the husks remain there, like the shells of beetles upon the bark of a living tree.

You have not thought deeply enough to know that the heart in you is the woman in man. You have derided your femininity, where you have suspected it; whereas, you should have known its power, cherished and utilized it, for it is the hidden wellspring of Intuition and Imagination. What can the brain accomplish without these two! They are the man's two inner eyes; without them, he is stone blind. For the mind sends forth their powers both together. One carries the light, the other searches; and between them they find treasures. These they bring to the brain, which first elaborates them, then says to the will, "Do"— and Action follows.

Poetically considered, as far as the huge, disordered resultant mass of your Architecture is concerned, Intuition and Imagination have not gone forth to illuminate and search the hearts of the people. Thus are its works stone blind. If such works be called masculine, this term will prove but a misuse of neuter. For they are empty of procreant powers. They do not inspire the thoughtful mind, but much do they depress it; they are choked with inarticulate cries which evoke pathos in the hearer.

Consider, now, that poetry is not verse—although some verse may be poetic. Consider, now, poetry as apart from words and as resident in things, in thoughts, in acts. For if you persist in regarding print or language as the only readable or hearable things—you must, indeed, remain dull interpreters of the voices of Nature, and of the acts and thoughts of the men of the present and the past, in their varied, but fundamentally alike activities. No; poetry, rightly considered, stands for the highest form of intellectual scope and activity. Indeed, it were truer to say psychic activity, if it be known what realities lie behind the mask of that word.

And, be it said in passing, most words are masks. Habit has accustomed you to this company of masks, beautiful some of them, repellent others, but you seldom draw aside a word-mask to see, for yourselves, the countenance of reality which it may both reveal and conceal. For, as I have said, you do not inquire, you are prone to take things for granted. You have seen masks since childhood, and have assumed and still assume them to be real, because, since childhood, you have been told they were, and are, real, by those to whose selfish interest it was, and is, that you cherish the illusion. Latterly, however, you have sufficiently awakened to draw aside the mask-word "Respectability."

You dearly love the mask-word, "Brains," which means physical action; and sniff at the word "Intellect," which stands for clear, powerfully constructive reflection. Therefore, as this is your thought, naturally enough, you are the victims of your impulsive acts, and of your apathy toward far-reaching, inevitable, yes, inexorable, consequences.

It is vitally with realities that poetry deals. But you say it does not; so that settles the matter as far as you are concerned —at least you think it does—in reality it settles you—it keeps you self-bound.

You say that poetry deals only with metaphor and figures of speech. What is your daily talk but metaphor and figures of speech! Every word, genuinely used, is a picture; whether used in conversation or in literary production. Mental life, indeed physical life, is almost entirely a matter of eyesight.

Now poetry, properly understood, means the most highly efficient form of mental eyesight. That is to say, it is that power

of seeing and doing which reveals to Man's inner self the fullness
and the subtle power of Life.

Poetry, as a living thing, therefore, stands for the most telling
quality that man can impart to his thoughts and his acts. Judged
by this test, your buildings are dreary, empty places.

Further, these buildings reveal no genuine art of expression—
and neither have you as a people genuinely expressed yourselves.
You have sniffed at this, too; for you are very cynical, and very
pert, and very cocksure. The leer is not long absent from your
eyes. You have said in substance: "What do we want of an art
of expression? We cannot sell it!" Perhaps not. But you can and
have sold yourselves.

You have assumed that an art of expression is a fiction, something apart from yourselves; as you have assumed almost all
things, of genuinely preservative value, to be fictions, apart from
yourselves—things negligible, to be put on or off like a coat.

Therefore look at your body of laws—complicated, grotesque
and inefficient, spiked with "jokers," as guns are spiked. Look at
your Constitution. Does that now really express the sound life
in you, or is there a "joker" in that, too, that is surely strangling
you? Look at your business. What is it become but a war of
extermination among cannibals? Does it express Democracy?
Are you, as a People, now really a Democracy? Do you still possess the power of self-government of a people, by a people, for
a people? Or is it now perished, as your Abraham Lincoln, on
the field of Gettysburg, hoped it might not, and as hoped a
weary and heartsick people at the close of an awful struggle to
preserve Democracy in its integrity, to preserve that fundamental
art of expression whereby a people may, unhampered, give voice
and form to the aspiration of their lives, their hopes, as they
press onward toward the enjoyment of their birthright, the
birthright of every man—the right to happiness!

Do you realize with what caustic accuracy this stupor is
shown in your buildings? They, too, stand for the spiked laws
of an art of expression. For what is there to express but the true
life of a people? What is there, in a Democracy, but All the
People? By what right does any man say: "I am! I own! I am
therefore a law unto myself!" How quickly among you has
I LEAD! become—I POSSESS! I BETRAY! How glibly have you

acquiesced! With what awful folly have you assumed selfish ego-
tism to be the basis of Democracy!

How significant is it, that, now, a few rough hands are shak-
ing you, a few sharp shrill voices calling: "Awake before it is too
late!"

"But," I hear you say, testily, "we are too young to consider
these accomplishments. We have been so busy with our material
development that we have not found the time to consider them."

Know then, that, to begin with, they are not accomplishments but necessaries. And, to end with, you are old enough,
and have found the time to succeed in nearly making a fine art
of—Betrayal, and a science of —Graft!

Know, that you are as old as the race. That each man among
you has in him the accumulated power of the race, ready at hand
for use, in the right way, when he shall conclude it better to
think straight and hence act straight, rather than, as now, to act
crooked and pretend to be straight.

Know, that the test, plain, simple HONESTY (and you all
know, every man of you knows, exactly what that means), is
always at your hand.

Know, that as all complex manifestations have a simple basis
of origin, so the vast complexity of your national unrest, ill
health, inability to think clearly and accurately concerning simple
things, really vital things, is easily and swiftly traceable to the
single, actual, active cause—Dishonesty; and that this points
with unescapable logic and in just measure to each INDIVIDUAL
MAN!

The Remedy: INDIVIDUAL HONESTY.

A conclusion as logical and as just!

"But," you may say, "how absurdly simple."

Doubtless it is absurd, if you think it is, and will so remain,
as far as you are concerned, just so long as you think it is—and
no longer. But just so long will your social pains and aches and
unrest continue; and these you do not consider absurd.

When Newton saw the apple fall, he saw what you might
likewise call an absurdly simple thing. Yet with this simple thing
he connected up the Universe.

Moreover, this simple thing, Honesty, stands in the Universe
of Human Thought and Action, as its very Center of Gravity,

and is our human mask-word behind which abides all the power of Nature's Integrity, the profoundest FACT which modern thinking has persuaded Life to reveal.

What folly, then, for Man to buck against the stupendous FLOW of LIFE; instead of voluntarily and gladly placing himself in harmony with it, and thus transferring to himself Nature's own creative energy and equipoise.

"But," you say, "All this is above our heads."

No it is not! IT IS CLOSE BESIDE YOUR HAND! And therein lies its power.

Again you say: "How can honesty be enforced?"

It cannot be enforced.

"Then how will the remedy go into effect?"

It cannot GO into effect. It can only COME into effect.

"Then how can it come?"

Ask Nature.

"And what will Nature say?"

Nature is always saying: "I center at each man, woman and child. I knock at the door of each heart, and I wait. I wait in patience—ready to enter with my gifts."

"And is that all that Nature says?"

That is all.

"Then how are we to receive Nature?"

By opening wide the door of your minds! For your greatest crime against yourselves is that you have locked the door in Her face, and have thrown away the key! Now you say: "There is no key!"

"Then how shall we make a new key?"

First: Care scrupulously for your individual and collective physical health. Beware of those who are undermining it; they are your deadliest danger. Beware of yourselves if you are undermining it, for you are then your own deadliest enemy. Thus will you achieve the first vital preliminary—a quiet, strong and resilient nervous system. Thus will your five senses become accurate interpreters of your physical surroundings; and thus, quite naturally, will the brain resume, in you, its normal power to act and react.

Second: Begin at once the establishment of a truly democratic system of education. The basis of this must be CHARACTER; and the mind must be so trained in the sense of reality that it may reach the fullness of its power to weigh all things, and to realize that the origin and sustenance of its power comes from without, and is Nature's bounteous, unstinted gift to all men.

Such system of education will result in equilibrium of body, mind and heart. It will therefore develop real men and women—as is Nature's desire.

It will produce social equilibrium in every aspect of human affairs. It will so clearly reveal the follies that have cursed you, that you will abandon them forever. For you will then recognize and gladly accept the simple, central truth that the individual grows in power only as he grows in integrity, and that the unfailing source of that integrity lies in the eternal integrity of Nature and of that Infinite Serenity of which Nature is but a symbol.

Thus will you make of Democracy a religion—the only one the world will have developed—befitting freemen—free in the integrity of their bodies, free in the integrity of their thought.

So doing, all aspects of your activities will change, because your thoughts will have changed. All of your activities will then take on organic and balanced coherence, because all of your thoughts will have a common center of gravity in the integrity of individual Man.

And, as the oak-tree is ever true to the acorn from which it sprang, and propagates true acorns in its turn, so will you then give true expression and form to the seed of Democracy that was planted in your soil, and so spread in turn the seeds of true Democracy.

Thus, as your thoughts change, will your civilization change. And thus, as Democracy takes living and integral shape within your thought, will the Feudalism, now tainting you, disappear. For its present power rests wholly upon your acquiescent and supporting thought. Its strength lies wholly in you, not in itself. So, inevitably, as the sustaining power of your thought is withdrawn, this Feudalism will crumble and vanish!

So have you no need of Force, for force is a crude and inefficient instrument. THOUGHT is the fine and powerful instrument. Therefore, HAVE THOUGHT FOR THE INTEGRITY OF YOUR OWN THOUGHT. For all social power, for good, or for ill, rests upon the thought of the People. THIS IS THE SINGLE LESSON

IN THE HISTORY OF MANKIND THAT IS REALLY WORTH THE WHILE.

Naturally, then, as your thoughts thus change, your growing Architecture will change. Its falsity will depart; its reality will gradually appear. For the integrity of your thought, as a People, will then have penetrated the minds of your architects.

THEN, TOO, AS YOUR BASIC THOUGHT CHANGES WILL EMERGE A PHILOSOPHY, A POETRY, AND AN ART OF EXPRESSION IN ALL THINGS: FOR YOU WILL HAVE LEARNED THAT A CHARACTERISTIC PHILOSOPHY, POETRY AND ART OF EXPRESSION ARE VITAL TO THE HEALTHFUL GROWTH AND DEVELOPMENT OF A DEMOCRATIC PEOPLE.

As a People you have enormous latent, unused power.

Awaken it.

Use it.

Use it for the common good.

Begin now!

For it is as true today as when one of your wise men said it:—"THE WAY TO RESUME IS TO RESUME!"

The Craftsman 10 (May 1906): 145–49; (June 1906): 352–58; (July 1906): 507–13.

42
Letter to the Editor on Gutzon Borglum (1908)

Sculptor Gutzon Borglum (1867–1941) was as critical of America's art as Sullivan was of its architecture. Because *The Craftsman*'s editor Gustav Stickley thought that Sullivan exemplified the very spirit Borglum found lacking in America, he invited the architect to comment on the sculptor's thesis.

You have called my attention to Mr. Gutzon Borglum's strictures on American art in the October issue and request a word from me.

That is easy, and I need be but brief. Mr. Borglum is ninety-nine per cent right all the way through.

Let us boil things down to basic principles:—art consists in *doing things right*. Science consists in *inquiring how to do things right*. Poetry consists in vision; that is, in *seeing things right*. Thought consists actively of *attention* and *reflection*.

Very well. Apply this trite test to our American architecture and what is the abrupt and net conclusion, judged by the *works*? This, namely, that *we neither do things right, inquire how to do things right, see things right, nor attend, nor reflect*.

Therefore, our American architecture, judged by its works—*always by its works*—is devoid of art, science, poetry and thought.

Therefore, it is phantom, not real.

This I hold is incontrovertibly true and can be proved in detail to the last dot on the last i.

I have been preaching this for twenty-five years. Therefore why prolong the discussion now, further than to say that what I have stated as true concerning our American architecture may with the same emphasis and the same exactitude be proved true of every phase of our American civilization.

Mr. Borglum and I therefore arrive at substantially the same conclusion, he in his way, I in my way.

The Craftsman 15 (December 1908): 338.

43
Is Our Art a Betrayal Rather than an Expression of American Life? (1909)

In his last contribution to *The Craftsman* Sullivan's answer was yes, America's art was a betrayal of American life. More than forty years before, he had derived the German idealist notion of "suppressed functions" from John William Draper's *History of the Intellectual Development of Europe* (1876). Sullivan adapted this notion to mean that feudalism—which he equated with authoritarianism—had suppressed human creativity by restricting freedom. Democracy, on the other hand, was a liberating system encouraging individual expression as a means of seeking uni-

versal truths. Unfortunately, America still clung to feudalism, Sullivan believed, especially in its architecture. To the
man whose credo was "form follows function," nothing
was worse than the inability to express in architectural
forms the social functions characterizing American life.

It is futile to seek an understanding of architectural conditions
in America without a prior survey of social conditions. For, little
as we Americans believe it, social conditions are basic—all else
superficial thereto. If, therefore, I were asked to name the one
salient, deeply characteristic social condition, which with us underlies everything else as an active factor in determining all other
manifestations, I should without the slightest hesitation say *betrayal*. It is so clear that no one can avoid seeing it who does not
take express pains to shut his eyes.

That the first and chief desire, drift, fashion, custom, willingness, or whatever you may choose to call it, of the American
people, lies in this curiously passionate aptitude for betrayal is, I
am aware, a startling statement; but it is nevertheless as star-
tlingly true.

This, therefore, being my thesis, I purpose to develop it
briefly but with care, with the end clearly in view and near at
hand of showing that a non-betraying architecture can no more
be expected of a betraying people than figs can be expected of
the proverbial thistle; and that a genuine architecture—that is,
an architecture which does not betray but really expresses—can
begin to appear only when the American people shall begin to
right themselves in their fundamental social position, and
seek not to betray each other but to *express* each other. This
should seem an elementary and axiomatic statement. But it is
not accepted as such by us—for we good and simple Americans have a horror of simplicity and efficiency, just as we
practical and sensible Americans, as we like to term ourselves,
are the most visionary and impractical of any people on
earth.

The proof that we are impractical and super-sentimental lies
in the fact which at once confronts us, that we have no social
scheme, view, theory or method that is practical, clear and efficient. We are, in fact, mere grown children, and unruly children
at that. A really practical and sensible people would seek to un-

derstand itself and the conditions essential to its social health and functioning; we do not.

The truth is we are not American in our thought, but Mediæval European. And our civilization is not democratic, as we fondly suppose, but utterly feudal through and through. We have not glimpsed the simple nature of Democracy and there is no hint of such glimpse even in university, college, public school, church, text books or the public press. For the fundamental of Democracy is that *man shall not betray*. This is a truth of such simplicity and force that it has never occurred to us that it could be real. It is perhaps, therefore, asking too much of us as a people that we develop a sensible and beautifully expressive architecture, germane to ourselves; while we have not even as yet developed a science and art of living.

IT IS a remarkable fact that eighty millions of people, living together as one political aggregation, are without a philosophy—that is, without a real reason for living. The spectacle is startling enough, to be sure; and yet it does not startle us, for we do not see it. We are so busy, foolishly betraying each other, that we see nothing real—not even the betrayal and the folly of it, and our thoughts are so saturated and deeply dyed with old-world feudalism that we do not even see the feudalism and what it means, what its tragedy is in everyday fact. No, we do not see and we do not listen. Now, a people which neither sees nor listens is not practical, and cannot, therefore, be expected to produce a practical and fitting architecture, which architecture must of necessity be based on seeing and listening.

The reason we do not see is simple; *we do not look*. The whole vast spectacle of ourselves is right before our eyes; but we do not look at it. Hence, of course, we do not look at our architecture. The absence of clear vision amongst us is astounding. It follows thus that we are the victims of mountebanks and demagogues of every grade, shade and kind, architectural and otherwise, and everywise. Because we will not be effectively simple, we pay the price of complication and inefficiency, and we do not perceive either the real nature of the complication or the real nature of the price—*because we do not look!*

Were we to look, we would see how extraordinary and how

tragic is our betrayal of each other, and to what friction and consequent unhappiness it leads. We would see that the prime evil lies not so much in the betrayal itself as in the basic fact that such betrayal prevents the expression of a people by and for itself; and that social health can come only with expression; that suppression of function always means disease; and disease, in practice, is simply another name for inefficiency.

Now, social inefficiency is in itself a convincing symptom of betrayal; and, *per contra*, efficiency is the requirement for health. And if it be asked, efficiency in what? the answer is clear; efficiency in social expression: that is to say, in the expression of our real lives, our real beliefs, aspirations and hopes as a people; in other words, the real art of living, the true contact with nature and with man, and the true response to such contact.

Between ourselves and nature and our fellow man we now allow curious fogs, phantasms and abstractions to intervene. On account of these our contact is not clear and our responses are unkind. That is, we are not our real selves, because we suppress ourselves in favor of fantastic traditions which are not ourselves.

A really modern architecture can, of course, come only from a really modern people. And this we are not.

A truly modern people could not betray—would not think of such thing as entertainable.

And this, therefore, is the indictment: that we betray our true selves; that we are not modern.

This, of course, will shock your good American who thinks he is as modern as the clock, and who will be aghast to hear that he has no clear notion of things social.

The Craftsman 15 (January 1909): 402–4.

44
Artistic Brick (c. 1910)

This essay appeared shortly after Sullivan had begun to experiment—on two banks, two residences, and other small buildings—with "tapestry brick," a gamut of variously tinted units that, carefully arranged, suggested the rich texture of mosaics or antique rugs. Here he explained how recent developments in something as elemental as brick-making could enhance the character and even the plan of a building. His warning about manipulating new materials and processes in "a literal mechanical way" to express only the "facts" of structure should serve to caution those who classify him as a father of modernism or a prophet of some particular movement. Sullivan's buildings were certainly about structure, but more important to him were their emotional, cultural, and intellectual associations. "The brick itself," he wrote, "is but the visible symbol of a train of social activities."

There are many instances in modern building construction where the use of a clean-cut mechanically perfect pressed brick is desirable. Particularly so perhaps for large office buildings and structures where exact surfaces and lines are desired. As the modern mechanically pressed brick with its many colors and shades is a development of the old red brick, so is the rough-faced brick an outgrowth of the "Paver."

The paver served to call attention to the artistic advantages of a brick not strictly uniform in color and shape. This created the desire and made possible the change from the old single or "shirt front" buildings, to the full four-front or all-around structures of simple but excellent materials.

The growth in the use of terra cotta kept pace with the new practice and the new demand; and improvements in manufacture and coloring quickly followed. New glazes and slips were produced, and the use of terra cotta and brick took on new life and new meanings.

With these facilities at the hand of the architect, he began to feel more sensible of the true nature of a building as an organism or whole: an individual or fully-expressed structure, rather than a mere slice showing one character for the front and another for the sides. And with this sensibility began to come the vision that the exterior of the building is, in essence, the expression, the full expression of the plan.

Hence this new style brick, if we may call it so, has led to a new development, namely, that in which all the functions of a given building are allowed to find their expression in natural and appropriate forms — each form and the total shape evidencing, instead of hiding, the working conditions of the building as exhibited in its plan.

This is nature's continuously operative law, whereby every single thing takes up its individual form in materials, and is recognizable as such. This law is not only comprehensive, but universal. It applies to the crystal as well as to the plant, each seeking and finding its form by virtue of its working plan, or purpose or utility; or, if you choose to say so, by virtue of its desire to live and to express itself.

This desire to live and to express itself is also just as characteristic of the plan of the building, for such plan is but the expression of a desire for something useful, something that will functionate or work freely. The building plan therefore clamors for expression and freedom, not indeed in any one particular way or mannerism, but in a way that will satisfy its desires, and thus, in the so doing, express them unmistakably. This is, in essence, the natural basis of the anatomy and physiology of architectural planning and design. It is simple, perhaps too simple. For few have had the vision to see it entire and the will to grasp it entire. Thus, as all large things turn upon small, so a significant and promising architectural movement has hinged upon the advent of a new kind of brick. Yet this new kind of brick was but the herald of better things. Manufacturers by grinding the clay or shale coarser, and by the use of cutting wires, produced on its face a new and most interesting texture, a texture with a nap-like effect, suggesting somewhat an Anatolian rug; a texture giving innumerable highlights and shadows, and a moss-like softness of appearance. Thus the rough brick became really a fine brick and brought with it new suggestions of use and beauty.

A feature, however, that was positively fascinating lay in the fact that these bricks, as they came from the kiln showed a veritable gamut of colors. Not merely a scale of shadings or graduations of intensity all related to a single average color, as in the "pavers," but a series of distinct colors, having each its own graduations and blendings. These colors are soft in tone and very attractive, modified in intensity as they are in each brick and in mass by the nap of the brick surface. They were at first, and, in many cases are now, the accidental effect of the position in the kiln and the kind of fuel used.

In these later days the subject has been made a matter of technical research, and specific treatment of the clays (burning in individual kilns, muffling the kilns, and fuel variations) have produced an added series of colors and shades, some of remarkable individuality and character.

Progress in the manufacture of terra cotta kept pace in tone and texture with the new color series in brick.

As might be expected, these recent bricks, depending, as they do, for their full effectiveness upon color and texture, are handicapped when laid with a flush mortar joint of whatever color or width. They are at their best when laid with a raked-out joint leaving the individual brick to play its part as a unit therein, and the mass free to express its color and texture in a broad way.

Inasmuch as the color scale varies from the softest pinks through delicate reds, yellows, (varying the intensity) through the light browns, dark browns, purples and steel blacks — each of these colors with its own graduations and blendings — the possibilities of chromatic treatment are at once evident. When laid up promiscuously, especially if the surface is large, and care is taken to avoid patches of any one color, the general tone suggests that of a very old oriental rug and the differing color values of the individual bricks, however sharply these may seem to contrast at close view, are taken up and harmonized in the prevailing general tone. Composed of many colors, this general tone is, in a sense, neutral and is rich and impressive. It lends itself admirably to association with other materials susceptible to color selection or treatment, such as stone, terra cotta, wood, glass and the metals, and admits in these, because of its broad, supporting neutrality, a great variation in range of treatment.

Thus arises before the mind of the architect the possibility, indeed the certainty of a feasible color scheme for the entire building, which it is within the power to vary from a substantial

monotone to the higher development of polychromatic treatment. He may segregate his bricks into separate color mosaics,
he may graduate or blend them in any desired way, he may use
them with mosaic effect, he may vary his forms to any rational
extent, and finally he may effect combinations with other materials of any desired degree of richness or plainness of color and
surface, in such wise as to secure an effect of totality or singleness of purpose.

To be sure a building may have its functions of plan and purpose expressed in a literal mechanical way that tends to repel,
just as music may be written strictly according to rule and yet be
unmusical. This certainly is up to the architect. For if the head
and its intellectual activities be not suffused by that complexity
of emotions and sentiments we call the heart, no building can
be beautiful, whatever means in the way of materials may be at
hand.

In this sense architecture is truly a social function and form,
and it is the feeling of humanity that makes a structure a beautiful creation. In its absence the building can be at the best but
a statement of facts and at the worst a mis-statement of facts.

But this does not change the fact that the invention and perfection of a brick, new in texture and color, has opened up a
new and wide field for the architect.

The brick itself is but the visible symbol of a train of social
activities, an expression of industrial thought and energy.

It used to be said that it took two to make a building, the
owner and the architect, and that each was necessarily the psychological counterpart of the other. It takes more than two. The
intelligent brick manufacturer is today a most essential factor in
modern building construction. The two may initiate, but it takes
many men working their various ways and contributing technical support. Such is the development of modern society — new
requirements, new forms to give them expression, and each re-
acting upon each and all.

We never know how important anything may become, no
matter how small and seemingly insignificant its initial appearance.

So small a thing as a brick has wrought a significant modifi-
cation in the architectural art, and this has reacted upon the sen-

sibilities of the social body, through the subtle influence of its mere presence.

Foreword to *Suggestions in Artistic Brick* (St. Louis: Hydraulic-Press Brick Co., c. 1910).

45
Lighting the People's Savings Bank, Cedar Rapids, Iowa: An Example of American Twentieth Century Ideas of Architecture and Illumination (1912)

In this illuminating essay Sullivan commented on "democratic" architecture (in the case of banking), on the efficiency of his design, and on how it exemplified his universal formula, "Form follows Function." Using Frank Lloyd Wright's terminology, he explained that the structure was conceived "from within, outward"—"from the inside out," Wright would have said— its exterior form being a logical consequence of its interior utilitarian requirements. The People's Savings Bank was the second in his series of small, midwestern financial institutions, but was quite different in appearance from the first, in Owatonna, Minnesota, demonstrating Sullivan's contention that every architectural problem held within itself its own unique solution.

Probably no phase of the science and art of illumination, briefly called "illuminating engineering," has been so much discussed as its relation to the science and art of building, briefly called "architecture." The fact that a building can fulfill no purpose, either utilitarian or artistic, without the use of light sufficiently indicates the importance of the correlation of the two sciences. A complete discussion of an architectural work therefore necessitates an examination of the methods of supplying both natural and artificial light, and, conversely, the study of the lighting of a building demands a general analysis of its architectural motives and details.

We have on previous occasions lamented the fact that America has thus far produced little that is new, original and expressive of twentieth century conditions as they exist in this country, and has not only been contented with, but actually insisted on endless repetitions of the motives and structural ideas developed in other countries and in other ages that have little in common with the present. It is therefore highly gratifying to note any worthy exception to this rule. The building discussed in this instance is such as exception. It is remarkable not for its size or cost, but as the result of what we believe is the only logical procedure in architecture, and this logic could not be more tersely or clearly set forth than in Mr. Sullivan's own words.

The same general principles will also apply to illuminating engineering. We particularly commend the description of this building and the views expressed to all who are seeking to unite the results of modern science with the highest esthetic ideals in the art of building.—THE EDITOR.

GENERAL DESCRIPTION EXTERIOR

The exterior treatment is of brick, with terra cotta trimmings. The brick used are Indiana shale wire cut, with a nap surface. The brick come from the kiln in about fourteen colors or shades. They are laid up promiscuously with ⅜-in. joints raked out ⅜ in. deep. The general effect is that of an antique Oriental rug. The terra cotta is given an average tone to match the brick and also a corresponding roughness of texture.

All frames and sash are painted white. The windows in the clearstory are filled with leaded opalescent glass of a superior quality. The lower windows are of polished plate.

The keynote of the design is found in the clearstory, which surmounts the public space below. It is cornered by four vent stacks, one of which contains the smoke pipe. The lower part houses the working departments, etc. The scheme of the design is to produce by the use of simple lines and plain surfaces a quiet, dignified effect, which will show to the best advantage the natural beauty of the material employed.

The exterior is thus a logical outcome of the plan, the building being designed from within, outward, the prime governing considerations being utilitarian—that is, an effort was made to secure a banking layout specially adapted to its class of business, and which should be, as nearly as possible, an automatically working machine.

INTERIOR

The high point of interest is the interior. It was designed, with all its adjuncts, strictly as a banking room. Its plan may be called "democratic," in that the prospect is open and the offices are in plain view and easily approached. This may be called the modern "human" element of the plan, as it tends to promote a feeling of ease, confidence and friendship between officers, employees and customers. The comfort of patrons is further cared for by rest rooms, etc., for men and women.

All parts are well supplied with daylight.

The general treatment of the interior is very rich, a well devised color scheme being maintained throughout. The general effect is attractive and inviting, all repellant aspects of mystery, reserve, dullness and frigidity (so characteristic of the older banks) being carefully eliminated, and the social fact brought into prominence that banking is a function of society and not a secluded mystery apart from the people.

The materials used are of the best quality. The floor is of green and white encaustic tiles, 1 in. square. The marble of the counters is statuary veined Italian. All grill work is of copperplate, with verde antique finish. The woodwork is all of selected oak, stained to a walnut shell tone. All leaded glass is opalescent and is made part of the color scheme. The columns are of cast iron, richly decorated in many colors. The fixtures in tellers' quarters are all specially designed by the architect. Wire partitions and overhead work are not used.

The system of electric lighting is indirect for the main public hall and direct for the balance. The bowls of the indirects are treated in many colors; the remaining fixtures are mostly verde antique.

The color scheme reaches its climax in the four mural paintings on the lower walls of the clear story. Only one of these is formal. It represents the relation of banking to labor. (Most of the bank's clients are of the working class.) It is painted in high color on a gold background. The three remaining paintings deal with agricultural scenes characteristic of Iowa, and symbolize not only the source of the wealth of the state, but the bank's dealings with the farmer.

The entire scheme, therefore, is a complete inversion of the traditional notion of what a bank should be, and as complete a statement of what this particular bank, with its special needs, ought to be and is.

Starting with a thoroughgoing search into and analysis of these special needs, and with unwavering logic following the *demands* of these special needs to a complete conclusion, has resulted in this case (as it might in the case of any other bank) in a highly specialized, unique and individual building.

The philosophy ever present throughout the plan and design of this structure is expressed in the formula, form follows function. This law is universal. It applies not only to things organic and inorganic, but to every phase of human thought and activity. And inasmuch as men create in the image of their thoughts the validity of their creations is subject to the acid test of this law. Supplemental to the above is the following—namely, *every problem contains and suggests its own solution*— which means that one is to seek and find the solution within the problem itself, under the general law above given. All our problems are modern and of ourselves; therefore all our solutions must be of our day and of ourselves—by and for ourselves.

The Illuminating Engineer 6 (February 1912): 631–35.

46
Tribute to Solon S. Beman (1915)

Solon S. Beman (1853–1914) was the architect for George Pullman's Building (1883) in Chicago, for the "model town" (1880–1884) on its outskirts to house the Pullman Palace Car Company, and for many other substantial structures across the Middle West. When presenting Beman's portrait to the Illinois Chapter of the American Institute of Architects on June 8, 1915, Sullivan used the Beman-Pullman association to comment on clients as spokesmen for the people's desires.

Mr. Chairman, Members of the Illinois Chapter of the American Institute of Architects, and Guests:—
I esteem it a high privilege to be called upon to speak in memory of my life-long friend, Solon Spencer Beman. I think of him as friend first, and as architect second, because throughout the past our relations have been so much in accord and so full of affections. I esteem it an honor to be selected by Mr. Beman's family to present this portrait in their behalf.

I have to think far back to recall my first recollection of Mr. Beman. He was born, I understand, in 1853 in Brooklyn. He came to Chicago at the age of 26 or 27 at the request of Mr. George Pullman to plan the new city of Pullman. Mr. Pullman was one of the live wires of his day and one of the moving forces of this city. Mr. Pullman saw in Mr. Beman a man who was the possessor of unusual intelligence and courage, a man who could carry out ideas successfully to a completion. It was a huge undertaking for so young a man and I think few of us realize what a task he had been called upon to undertake. He was well chosen and he performed well. I doubt if any architect in the country at that time could produce work superior to that of Mr. Beman, when you consider the nature of the work. Mr. Beman was always a true and loyal friend of Mr. Pullman,—it was solid friendship, as well as mutual.

This was the beginning of Mr. Beman's work. It was followed on a smaller scale at Ivorydale. His first important office building was the Pullman Building. In fact, Mr. Beman had always been a leading spirit in solving new problems which came his way and he always showed his superior intelligence and the same clearness of mind.

Mr. Beman appeals to me peculiarly in connection with the town of Pullman, because years ago when I was a youngster and played around the banks of the Calumet Lake I belonged to a Boat Club down there and the mystery of Calumet Lake was to find a way out of it and not get drowned in the mud.

Mr. Beman always worked on untiring, faithful in all his

works and always worked quietly. You know his various buildings in this and other cities. He was always in advance of his
time, always very willing and always in accord with spirited
movements of the day.

To me his leading characteristic was his great enthusiasm conjoined with an extraordinary perseverance. Whenever and whatever he was doing, that was the one important thing that he had
done in all his life. And yet I never knew him to be satisfied with
anything he had accomplished.

He was always complaining to me about it and always trying
to improve his work and accomplish something better.

Mr. Beman's association with Mr. Pullman to me is typical,
for I always agree that it takes two to make a building. An architect alone cannot make a building. An architect is generally
the instrument whereby a building is made, and, from the surface of things he appears to be the creator of it. That is only,
however, the surface of things, — beneath that surface comes
the impulse for the creation of things, and that impulse comes
through the client. The client is interested in the character of the
building. It is the client's thought that goes into the building, it
is the client's thought that leads to the selection of the architect
and it is this impulse and selection that brings men together and
produces the result.

The thoughts of the people are constantly changing and in
this way the character of the buildings will change. The people
will demand that their buildings be improved upon and these
improvements will continue forever. The architecture of a city
represents the thoughts of the people of that city, and it is up to
the architects to keep in line with all these movements and to
respond to such changes.

This is bound to make various transit periods that we are
passing through continually. This style and that style so long
standing will gradually pass away and in place of them will come
new and modern ideas that will appeal to the people because
they are of the thought of the people. That time may be some
distance ahead of us, yet I do not think it is very very far in
coming, because I think we have observed the changes that are
being made from day to day and they prove that the American
people are of a singularly aspiring life and full of democratic
inspiration.

Mr. Beman contributed in a large measure toward this movement and this we fully realize. There are many struggles yet to go through and we must come into a fair consciousness of what we have before us. So, on an occasion of this sort we all know what we owe to Mr. Beman.

It gives me profound pleasure to make this tribute to his memory and to present this portrait to your Institute to join your collection of portraits which some day will be invaluable.

Manuscript courtesy of the Louis H. Sullivan Collection, The Burnham Library, The Art Institute, Chicago, Published with permission.

47
Development of Construction (1916)

At a meeting of the American Institute of Architects, Illinois Chapter, in June 1916, Louis Sullivan eulogized his longtime partner, Dankmar Adler, who had died in 1900. Reviewing several major buildings on which they had collaborated between 1879 and 1893, he paid particular attention to Adler's acoustical, mechanical, and structural innovations. Given in one reading under the present title, it was a lengthy enough tribute to be published in two parts, the second called "Development of Building, II" by the magazine's editor. The speech amounted to a retrospective on the significance of Adler's firm in the evolution of Chicago building. But it also suggests that Sullivan, who was virtually without work in 1916, was reminding his listeners, and perhaps himself too, of just how important *he* once had been.

To recall Dankmar's contributions to his profession, I will make a little sketch of the growth of architecture since 1878 and up to the present time, from what was practically an inarticulate form of building to the present highly scientific equipment. I believe it will be interesting especially to the younger members of the profession who did not live through those days. Our first serious joint undertaking was the Borden block at the northwest corner of Dearborn and Randolph streets. To understand just what that meant in construction at that time we must know a little of what the prevailing practice was prior to that. Ordinary buildings at that time were three or four stories high. Wall thicknesses had some traditional dimensions. I don't know how they were arrived at, but one man had made in 1873 a very important contribution to building construction. This related to foundations, and that man was Frederick Baumann. His work on pier foundations practically revolutionized the entire system by abolishing the continuous foundation wall constructed as if the same load was to be sustained throughout. That was a highly important contribution. Perhaps few of you understand that Frederick Baumann invented that system. Along about that time the average commercial building was built with an indefinite thickness of walls. If it was a three-story building, it would be about three feet; if it was going to be four stories, it would be about four feet, and if it happened to be five stories it was still more. As to the posts inside, they were very poor. Few cast iron posts were used and when cast iron posts were used they were about 12×12 for the first and 10×10 for the second, and so on up, and you would assume that about 2×2 would be all right for a twenty-foot span. The front of the building was a stone ashlar, four inches thick, a long slab backed up with brick. The top almost invariably was a galvanized iron cornice that was of the cheapest construction, little or no attention being paid to the wall supports.

New Devices After the Fire

Immediately after the great fire, buildings had to be rushed up in a way to meet the general poverty, and the full effects of the panic of 1873 were reached about the time that Mr. Adler and I came together, and from that time on conditions began to improve, and they were beginning to recover from its effect. Prior to that time one or two attempts had been made at what was called fireproof buildings in Chicago. One of them was the old First National Bank, in which non-combustible material was used in making a so-called fireproof building before the Chicago fire. Then long afterward, about 1879, began the improvement in the plan of building foundations as demonstrated in the Borden block. The building actually had solid stone piers on isolated foundations, which was a great innovation. At that time no one went up to exceed eight or ten feet. That was Mr. Adler's own contribution in planning a great improvement. Another innovation of that day was the carrying of plate glass entirely through a building, and another was finishing entirely in hardwood. That meant a great deal more than we of today understand. The result was that the building was rented six weeks before it was finished and it did us much good professionally. About 1879 we completed the Central Music Hall, which was a wonderful success in all respects so far as its acoustic properties were concerned. About the time the Borden block was completed, Mr. Borden had the old Foley billiard hall turned over into the Grand Opera House, spending about $60,000. I then discovered what Mr Adler knew about acoustics. I did not know anything about them and I did not believe that anybody else did. That is the popular impression today, that nobody really knows anything about them. I found out the extent of Mr. Adler's knowledge in connection with that building. It was not a matter of mathematics, nor a matter of science. There is a feeling, perception, instinct, and that Mr. Adler had. Mr. Adler had a grasp of the subject of acoustics which he could not have gained from study, for it was not in books. He must have gotten it by feeling. I absorbed that very quickly and there has not been much occasion to learn it since, because the subject was covered. The Grand Opera House was immediately a great success. It was quite a luxurious theater for that day and quite a wonder in architecture. You must remember that in those days the telephone was practically unknown; electric lights were practically unknown; the typewriter did not exist; blue printing was not known, and even the hektograph process was not known. All reproductions in an architect's office had to be made by tracing, and after those tracings had been on the job for a while they were not very pretty nor very useful.

About the same time we built a house that John Borden is living in near Thirty-ninth street. It was a solidly built, well equipped house, standing there now, and the owner is still living there at the age of 94.

The Modern Chicago

That time may be said to be the beginning of a new era of building in Chicago. It is difficult for us to understand, especially the
young members, the comparatively crude conditions and the
limitations of those days, the manner in which foundations were
laid, when the water-balanced elevators for raising were of the
horizontal type of hydraulic elevator. They were the beginning.
Then, buildings were not fireproof. They were plaster and wood
lath, but there was an attempt made at fireproofing. Plate glass
at that time was imported from Belgium and France. It was not
manufactured in this country. There was not in this country
what is now known as a steel structure. Iron was very high in
price. Then came the fireproof structures. Peter B. Wight at the
time was in the business of furnishing fireproof building material. The building now belonging to Martin A. Ryerson and occupied by A. H. Revell & Co. was the first building in which
commercial fireproofing was begun on iron columns, iron gir-
ders, wooden joists, but those columns were surrounded with
fireproofing material supplied by Mr. Wight. The ceilings and
floors were deadened. It showed the efficiency of that age in
fireproofing. The fireproofing in that building only amounted to
something like $60,000 to $75,000. That was a thoroughly built
and solid structure and it was a marked improvement on anything existing at that time. Then came a series of buildings for
Mr. Ryerson, six in an interval between 1881 and 1884.

Meanwhile, I was developing a little technical knowledge myself. Then came some other theaters, a great many alterations
and a great many of those old buildings had to be held up and
put into shape. There first came the alteration of the old Mc-
Vicker's Theater, I think, in 1885. There was spent about
$35,000. At that time, I believe, was made the first decorative
use of the electric lamp. It was a little innovation of my own,
that of placing the lamps in a decoration instead of clustering
them in fixtures, but even then the installation of an electric
lighting system was primitive to the last degree. The wires were
bedded in plaster. The lighting conduit was not known. The
dynamos were run by little primitive engines. The boilers were

of the tubular type. The original wires were torn out when McVicker's was rebuilt. Mr. Adler wanted to have some offices put in when the theater was rebuilt. He had the notion that some offices might be carried over that theater, and, as far as I know, that is the first time that thing was done. Two stories of offices were carried by trusses over the theater. The fire came in a day, in the midst of a very cold winter, and the question was how it could be reconstructed during that time. Mr. Adler got up a very clever scheme of building a housing of wood under which work could proceed, and that was adopted and carried out successfully. Mr. McVicker thought he would like a ventilating system. We put one in for him. He seemed to take a great interest in ventilating at that time. We put in a system that cost $6,000. Mr. McVicker thought it would cost him about $1,000. This simply gives you an idea of the primitive days out of which we have grown and the extraordinary progress represented by this great development that has taken place since 1880—only 36 years—with the series of commercial buildings which have been steadily improving.

Then there was a movement started by N. K. Fairbank for the building of a great opera house in this city, and we made some sketches, but somehow the thing did not pull through. It lagged along. No one took a special interest in it, that is, interest enough to put up the money. In 1885, Ferdinand W. Peck got the idea of getting a great operatic festival here and he came to us because of Mr. Adler's reputation in handling structures of that sort. In the meanwhile, we had handled several political conventions, of which Mr. Adler had taken personal charge and which were very successful. Mr. Peck had the opinion that Mr. Adler was the only man who could handle that, and it was to be done, in a considerable measure, as an experiment. We took the old Exposition Building and fixed it up with an addition, according to a plan by Mr. Adler, so that 6,200 people on the floor were accommodated for the season, which was two weeks and was highly successful in every respect. That demonstrated the possibility of seating a large audience and having them all see and hear. It was from that opera festival hall that sprang Ferd Peck's idea of the great Auditorium in this city, and he kept at it until we made the preliminary sketches shortly afterward for the present Auditorium Building.

Foundations for the Auditorium Building

Up to that period there had not been very much technical improvement merely in building materials. I do not remember the exact year in which we began the construction of the Auditorium Building. I think it was in 1886 we made the first studies. At first I did not know what on earth we were going to do with all that ground. Inside of a week I did not know how we were going to get a building in there, a great big hall to seat 4,250 people, and a hotel and an office building. Then the plan was to build a structure to cost about $1,500,000. It had a brick exterior with some stone trimmings, with a very fine foundation, with a stage well, but technical improvements began to grow with a great deal of rapidity at that time. Also, the board of directors of the Auditorium were constantly enlarging their own ideas and amplifying them. The foundations were based, on estimates made by General William Sooy-Smith, an expert in that line, on the wall, with tanks loaded with water, taking accurate levels of the sinkages that took place, and he recommended that the loads be 4,250 on the foundation to the foot. The accepted maximum up to that time had been 3,000 pounds to the square foot and the usual maximum settlement was two inches, so that if a building was set up as built two inches higher than it was intended to be that would bring the building down to normal. On that recommendation Mr. Adler put in foundations that were still of the old type, the lower course being 12×12 timbers that were carried throughout, with rubble on top of that. I think it was a fortunate thing the building took so long to build. We were practically working on drawings that were uncertain because conditions were changing so rapidly and we had to consider the greatest load that had ever been figured upon in our profession. The estimated cost of the building, $1,500,000, suddenly jumped to about $3,000,000 and then changed to $3,500,000 in four short years.

No Steel Used in the Auditorium Building

At that time you must understand and bear in mind the fact that there was not a pound of steel in the Auditorium Building; it is every bit iron. The material required taxed the capacity of the Carnegie works at Pittsburgh, and then overtaxed their capacity so that we were delayed for months and months. They would wire us that work had been shipped when it had not been rolled, and the Carnegie Company staggered under the contract for the iron work for the Auditorium Building. That is only 26 years ago. There is not a steel column in it, nor is there any kind but cast iron.

The great problem was to handle the tower. All the foundation under the Auditorium is a single footing, 67 × 100 bed. Under that condition the job was something stupendous. I do not suppose there had ever been work done like it in any of the great projects, with the added difficulty of the elements entering into the construction of that foundation. The tower rises 95 feet above the main building. According to the laws of settlement, the settlement would progress uniformly as the building continued to rise. When the main building had reached its terminal of ten stories, the tower would still have 95 feet to go. What would you do about it? If the foundation were made under the tower for it to settle with the rest of the building, the foundation would be too small when the tower was completed. Mr. Adler invented a very ingenious notion of a load for the tower. The basement and lower stories of the tower were loaded with pig iron gradually as the main building went up and then at the time the main building had reached the tenth story, the full loading would be on the foundation of the tower, but that, 95 feet above the main building, was put on that foundation with pig iron. The next problem was how to get out of the order of things. He did that by simply reversing the process; as the tower continued to rise above the main building he began taking off a corresponding weight of pig iron until when the tower reached its limit there was no pig iron left. That was a regular Columbus egg stunt.

Problem of the Tower

The building of the tower, however, was a comparatively simple thing compared with what Mr. Adler had to do when it came to the heating and ventilating propositions. Heating in those days was the most primary affair. The electric lighting system was primitive and all the wires had to be pulled out afterwards. There was still no such thing as a conduit; the wires were all bedded in plaster. Generators were the preferred engines. The building had ten or twenty engines scattered around with ten or twenty boilers all over the premises.

Then came the great question never before tackled in this city, how to get the stage down below the water level and keep it dry. That was a strenuous problem. Then came the increasing load on the building itself for which nothing could be done. The brick exterior was changed to stone. The floors throughout the building, in the main part, were changed from wood to mosaic. Mosaic work, as far as I know, was unknown until about that time when an Englishman was the first to introduce it, and almost contemporaneously with its introduction it was used in the Auditorium. There are 9,832,716 little pieces of mosaic used in that building.

Heart-Breaking Problems

The problems that Mr. Adler had to meet in that building were simply heart-breaking. In those days there were very few consulting engineers, and the few there were were employed mostly by the railroads, the iron companies and mines. There was one man who gave some attention to sanitary and heating matters, but that was about all the professional advice Mr. Adler could call to his aid. He practically had to dig it out for himself and it was a tremendous proposition. The ventilating problem was not so difficult in the Auditorium.

The Monadnock building, for which plans had been drawn, was held for a year or two to see whether the Auditorium tower would go down or not. If it did that would settle the question and they would not build it, but if it did not go down to China, then they would go ahead with the building. Attention has been called to some settlements in the Auditorium, but you must consider the fact that there was an added load of over one-third in changing the exterior from brick to stone, and other changes also increased the load. Over the front entrance was placed a banquet hall, meaning an additional 600 tons, so you have some idea of the reasons for the settlement of the Auditorium Building. In dealing with this fundamental question of load, Mr. Adler had to work out many difficult problems himself. The Auditorium, perhaps, may be considered the last of the old style buildings. In that way it is a monument, in that sense, a pathetic monument to think it had been so soon superseded. The hotel at that time was considered the most magnificent in the country, and they had one bath for every ten rooms.

Along about that year Mr. Adler anticipated skeleton construction in the suspension of the organ chamber over a passageway for teams. That was essentially a beginning of the skeleton construction, for that was steel construction. The organ chamber was simply a building over the walls.

CARRYING THE STAGE TO AN UNPRECEDENTED DEPTH

Then there was the great problem of handling the stage, involving the stage mechanism and the carrying of the stage to such an unprecedented depth. Mr. Adler was helped out in his problem, however, by a young English hydraulic engineer who came here during Mr. Adler's struggles, with an English invention that was called the "Shone Ejector," which you could place anywhere at the bottom of the well, so that you became for the first time independent of the depth to which our sewers were laid. Prior to that we had to keep our house trap above the sewer level, because drainage worked by gravitation. But by the utilization of this Shone ejector you could go as much below the sewer as you pleased and eject all your sewage. This ejector was worked by compressed air and you could blow to any height into the sewer. Mr. Adler saw the advantage to that and the entire basement floor was lowered two feet. That proposition covered the most trying period of Mr. Adler's life. It is very difficult to understand it today, but if you can only grasp the idea of what that Auditorium Building was and what it became very soon after it was completed, you will see the signal position that it occupied in the history of Chicago architecture; that it was a tremendous advance and was soon superseded.

Very soon after the great theater was opened, on December 10, 1890—there had been merely a tentative use of structural steel—the engineers of the steel companies were beginning to see that it would be a big thing for their companies if they could interest architects in the use of steel structurally for columns as well as frames. Just how the steel frame, the skeleton frame, originated, nobody knows, but my attention was first called to it by an architect named Buffington who had a scheme for building tall buildings before such a thing was ever done. He wanted to make a frame of railroad rails tied together in some mysterious manner. He was not an engineer himself but he had this idea. He never carried it out. The first practical use of that method made here was at the instance of Mr. Wight, who had been urging the use of railroad iron in foundations and he finally persuaded builders to use it under the walls of the Monadnock. That was the first great step, and how amazingly and suddenly it blossomed out in all its aspects, the steel frame, which was tried at the instance of the companies which were beginning to make steel. They had introduced the Bessemer process. I can remember when the only mills in Chicago were the North Chicago Rolling Mills out on the north branch at Clybourne Avenue, a miserable little thing, another at South Chicago and another one called the Union Iron Works at Halsted and Twenty-second Streets.

WILLIAM E. HALE AND OWEN P. ALDIS

The men who are responsible for the modern office building were William E. Hale and Owen Aldis. Along about that time the World's Fair was in sight. Preparations began to be made for it. When the steel frame construction came in, it came in suddenly and came to stay. The possibilities of its use were too manifest. At that time we had a great undertaking on hand, the building of what was then the Annex and subsequently became the Congress Hotel. There we had to handle a great power plant which in its day was a wonder, and we learned that they actually made dynamos over in Germany and that those great dynamos were operated by direct connected engines. We learned from the Allis-Chalmers Company that it was possible to build high duty pumps, and we learned that it was possible to stack boilers up in the air instead of on the ground. That problem was handled by Mr. Adler individually and it cost about $250,000. Then came a very sudden development, an extensive development at that time with which all of you are familiar, the development of the steel frame.

There had been no progress yet in foundations, and it occurred to me when we had the Schiller Theater to build that we would have some disastrous settlement with the old style of footings, and thought It would be a good idea to put in foundations that would not settle. I suggested to Mr. Adler that we put in piles and he agreed with me. So we went ahead and put in 770 piles under the Schiller Theater Building, and it is my belief that that was the first time piles were used in a downtown building.

The Stock Exchange Building

In 1893 we handled for the Peck estate the Stock Exchange Building. The general foundation and system of piling was determined upon there, but it became necessary to take particular care with the foundation adjoining the wall of the Herald Building, so as to avoid any possible disturbance to the printing presses. General Sooy-Smith was called into consultation and he advocated the sinking of caissons next to the wall, and he stated that he would not undertake to do the work but advised it. Mr. Adler immediately agreed and they were installed. These were the first caisson foundations ever put in in Chicago and they proved an immediate success. Since then it has become almost a fundamental proposition that to insure permanency of a building you can only do it through stability of foundations and since that time the use of caisson foundations has become thoroughly successful.

This practically gives you a sketch of building operations in Chicago up to date and to our present stage of development, with which all are familiar. Now manufacturers have awakened. They were almost in their infancy forty years ago. Almost everything had to be manufactured abroad. Our first sanitary plumbing fixtures came from England but now we manufacture almost everything.

The Economist 55 (June 24, 1916): 1252; 56 (July 1, 1916): 39–40.

48
Remarks at the American Institute of Architects Convention (1922)

The drawings of which Sullivan spoke in the following paragraphs were commissioned by the Art Institute of Chicago's Burnham Library in January 1922 and were completed in June 1923. With two short essays and accompanying notes they were published the next year by the Press of the American Institute of Architects as *A System of Architectural Ornament, According with a Philosophy of Man's Powers*. There were nineteen plates in all, seven of which showed how Sullivan derived his ornamental patterns from geometrical developments of simple organic forms. He had finished the first twelve drawings, then on exhibit at The Art Institute, by convention time in June 1922. During that month the *Journal of the American Institute of Architects* ran the opening chapter of his memoirs, *The Autobiography of an Idea,* which the Press also published as a book in 1924. Having made his peace with AIA, Sullivan attended its fifty-fifth convention to speak about the one project and to drum up interest in the other. These were the last two major works of his career.

THE PRESIDENT. You will remember the vogue, which obtained in Chicago, of Mr. Louis Sullivan's style of ornament which he developed, and which made a great impression upon Chicago and the country. He has been drawing a series of plates illustrating the philosophy of ornament as devised and perfected by him.

Some twelve or more are now under glass on exhibition at the Art Institute. Mr. Sullivan's work made so great an impression in his time, that I am sure any of you who have time will desire to see his work in the Burnham Library in the Art Institute. Would Mr. Sullivan like to say a word in regard to this matter?

MR. SULLIVAN. I came here not to speak but to listen. I wished especially to see how matters of education were progressing. Incidentally I reported to the President that these drawings would be on exhibition.

Along about January the Burnham Library, an architectural library, thought it would be well if I would put on record a number of drawings to illustrate the philosophy and lines of designs which I devised at the expense of some forty years of experience. At the time it seemed preposterous that such a work could be done, it was very laborious and I did not want to undertake it. There are thirty plates in all, twelve of which have been completed. There is some probability that when these plates are completed for the Library, they may be reproduced in book form. That matter has not been seriously thought of yet. It will probably take four months to complete the remaining plates.

Proceedings of the Fifty-fifth Annual Convention of the American Institute of Architects (New York: American Institute of Architects Press, 1922), 63. Reprinted with the permission of the American Institute of Architects Information Center, Washington, D.C.

49
The Chicago Tribune Competition (1923)

Sullivan thought that Raymond Hood and John Mead Howells's winning Gothic Revival entry to the *Chicago Tribune's* 1922 competition for new headquarters represented "dying ideas." Eliel Saarinen's second place "master-edifice," on the other hand, was a "priceless pearl." Sullivan described it, in fact, in much the same language he had used twenty-seven years before to explain his own skyscrapers in "The Tall Office Building Artistically Considered" (document 23). Saarinen's scheme was "soaring," he wrote, and "lofty," and it achieved its purpose better than any American-designed building ever had. He was shocked—pleasantly so, perhaps—that a "foreigner" could express a characteristically American phenomenon so much more intelligently than native-born architects. If the *Tribune's* rejection of Saarinen reinforced Sullivan's belief that something was terribly wrong with American culture, he had at least found an architect to admire.

Some seventy years ago, a philosopher, in the course of his studies of the Ego, separated men into two classes, distinct, yet reciprocally related, to wit: Masters of Ideas, and those governed by ideas. It was upon ideas as powers for good or ill that he laid the heavy hand; upon ideas as a living force obedient to the mastery of vision, springing forth from imagination's depths, from the inexhaustible reservoir of instinct.

Ego, considered solely as free spirit, stands out visibly as Master of Ideas. Ego, examined as a spirit benumbed through lack of action, hence inert and unfree, becomes dim of vision and renounces its will. It thus becomes the slave of imposed ideas whose validity it assumes it has not the strength to test, even were the idea of testing to arise. Hence, in timidity, it evokes the negative idea of Authority as a welcome substitute for its declining volition.

Masters of ideas are masters of courage; the free will of adventure is in them. They stride where others creep. The pride of action is in them. They explore, they test, they seek realities to meet them face to face—knowing well that realities and illusions exist commingled within and without, but also knowing well that Ego is its own. Hence they walk erect and fearless in the open, with that certitude which vision brings—while slaves are slaves by choice. They seek shelter in the *shadows* of ideas.

Ever such were the great free spirits of the past, and such are those of our own day.

Masters of ideas of the past and now, frequently have sought and seek dominion, and have reached it because the idea of dominion coincides precisely with the idea of submission. Other masters of ideas then and now, mostly those of immense compassion, have been and still are crucified by those so long in the dark that the idea of spiritual freedom is abhorrent.

A consciousness is now growing and widely spreading in our modern world of thought, among masters of truly great ideas, that unless we become free spirits casting off the cruel, and awakening to the constructive power of beneficence, we shall vanish in decay and self destruction.

The simple world idea, now in process of becoming, in the hearts of men, is the idea of freedom from the domination of feudal ideas. Is there a power that can stop this becoming? There is not.

The eyelids of the world are slowly, surely lifting. The vision of the world of men is slowly, surely clearing. A world-idea is sprouting from its seed in the rich soil of world-sorrow. Beneath the surface of things as they are, everywhere it is germinating, unconsciously with the many, consciously with the few.

The old idea that man must ever remain the victim of Fate, will fade as fear fades. The new idea that man may shape his destiny will appear in its place, in a dissolving scene of the world-drama, as Democracy arises through the humus of the age-long feudal idea. For Democracy would remain, as now it is, a senseless word, a vacant shell, a futile sentimentalism, a mere fetish, did it not carry in its heart the loftiest of optimistic aspirations, wholly warranted, spite of all appearance to the contrary, and grasp the mastery of ideas wholly beneficent in power to create a world of joy devoid of fear.

The world is growing more compact every day, and every day the day is shortening, while the fleeting hour becomes thereby so much the fuller. The cold rigidity of frontiers is melting away, unnoted by the blind—every day the world becomes increasingly mobile, every day there is a silent interchange, every day communication is more fleet, and humanity, in response, more fluent. Slowly day by day, with enormous and gathering momentum, the hearts of the world draw together. The process is silent and gentle as the dewfall. There are those who see this; there are those who do not. There are those who see in the lightnings and the raging storms of the feudal idea, reaching now the climacteric of its supreme mania for dominion, the symbol of self-destruction of a race gone wholly mad. But that is not so. The masters of the feudal idea alone have gone mad with hate; the multitudes are sound. They have lost a pathetic faith in the feudal concept of self-preservation which has wooed and betrayed them. They are moving somnambulistically now, upwards towards a faith that is new and real, a constructive idea, common to all, because springing from the hearts of all, of which all shall be masters, and about which shall form for the first time beneath the sun, a sane hope and faith in Life, a faith in Man—an idea which shall banish fear and exalt courage to its seat of power.

This idea will become the luminous, the central idea of all mankind because it is the offspring of that which is deepest down in all. It is and will continue as long as life lasts in the race, the shining symbol of man's resurrection from the dead past, of man's faith in himself and his power to create anew.

There are those who will decry this hope as they view in despair a world writhing in the depths of pessimism, of mendacity and intrigue. Yet are they those who are without faith in mankind, without faith in themselves. For this is the modern affirmation: Man is not born in sin, but in glory.

All of this has sharply to do with the Tribune Competition, for in that showing was brought into clearest light the deadline that lies between a Master of Ideas and one governed by ideas. There they came, squarely face to face: the second prize and the first. All the others may be grouped aside, for what is involved here is not a series of distinctions in composition or in detail, but the leading forth into the light of day of the profoundest aspiration that animates the hearts of men. This aspiration has remained inarticulate too long; its utterance at large has been choked by varied emotions of fear; the splendor of its singleness of purpose has been obscured by the host of shadows generated in bewilderment of thought, in a world that has lost its bearings and submits in distress to the government of dying ideas.

In its preliminary advertising, The Tribune broadcasted the inspiring idea of a new and great adventure, in which pride, magnanimity and its honor were to be inseparably unified and voiced in "the most beautiful office building in the world," to be created for it by any man sufficiently imaginative and solid in competence in whatever spot on the surface of the earth such a man might dwell.

Specifically, on the third page of its formal and official program, these statements are made:

"To erect the most beautiful and distinctive office building in the world is the desire of The Tribune, and in order to obtain the design for such an edifice, this competition has been instituted."

These words are high-minded; they stir imagination.

At the beginning of the paragraph immediately succeeding are found these words:

"The competition will be of international scope, qualified architects of established reputation in all parts of the world being eligible."

These words are magnanimous; they stir not only the world of architectural activity, but as well that of enlightened laity. Never perhaps, in our day, has such interest in architecture been aroused.

Not yet content in its eagerness, and purposing to make assurance of good faith and loyalty to an ideal triply sure, there is to be found on page 13, the final page of the program, the following statement:

"It cannot be reiterated too emphatically that the primary objective of The Chicago Tribune in instituting this Competition is to secure the design for a structure distinctive and imposing— the most beautiful office building in the world."

The intensive use of the word PRIMARY gives to the full clause the imposing promise of a token, of a covenant with the Earth. With that one word, PRIMARY, The Tribune set its bow in the cloud.

The craving for beauty, thus set forth by The Tribune, is imbued with romance; with that high Romance which is the essence, the vital impulse, that inheres in all the great works of man in all places and all times, that vibrates in his loftiest thoughts, his heroic deeds, his otherwise inexplicable sacrifices, and which forms the halo of his great compassions, and of the tragedy within the depths of his sorrows. So deeply seated, so persistent, so perennial in the heart of humanity is this ineffable presence, that, suppressed in us, we decay and die. For man is not born to trouble, as the sparks fly upward; he is born to hope and to achieve.

If a critique of architecture, or any other art, or any activity whatsoever, is to be valid, it must be based upon a reasoned process. It must enter with intelligence into the object or subject at hand, there to seek what signifies, and yet maintain such detachment as to render judgment unconstrained and free. A true critique is not satisfied with the surface of things, it must penetrate that surface to search the animus, the thought; it must go deeply to the roots, it must go to origins, it must seek the elemental, the primitive; it must go to the depths and gauge the status of the work thereby. A true critique must likewise derive of the humanities. It is not its function to deal with cold truths but with living truths.

Viewed in this light, the second and the first prize stand before us side by side. One glance of the trained eye, and instant judgment comes; that judgment which flashes from inner experience, in recognition of a masterpiece. The verdict of the Jury of Award is at once reversed, and the second prize is placed first, where it belongs by virtue of its beautifully controlled and virile power. The first prize is demoted to the level of those works evolved of dying ideas, even as it sends forth a frantic cry to escape from the common bondage of those governed by ideas. The apposition is intensely dramatic to the sensitive mind. Yet it is in this very apposition that we find a key wherewith to unlock and swing open wide a door, and reveal to all the vast and unused power resident in the great architectural art when inspired into motion by a Master of Ideas. The Finnish master-edifice is not a lonely cry in the wilderness, it is a voice, resonant and rich, ringing amidst the wealth and joy of life. In utterance sublime and melodious, it prophesies a time to come, and not so far away, when the wretched and the yearning, the sordid, and the fierce, shall escape the bondage and the mania of fixed ideas.

It is wretched psychology to assume that man is by nature selfish. The clear eye of sympathy sees beyond a doubt that this is not so; that on the contrary, man by nature is a giver; and it is precisely this one discerns in this beauteous edifice; the native quality of manhood giving freely of inherent wealth of power, with hands that overflow, as to say: There is more and more and more in me to give, as also is there in yourselves—if but ye knew—ye of little faith.

Qualifying as it does in every technical regard, and conforming to the mandatory items of the official program of instructions, it goes freely in advance, and, with the steel frame as a thesis, displays a high science of design such as the world up to this day had neither known nor surmised. In its single solidarity of concentrated intention, there is revealed a logic of a new order, the logic of living things; and this inexorable logic of life is most graciously accepted and set forth in fluency of form. Rising from the earth in suspiration as of the earth and as of the universal genius of man, it ascends and ascends in beauty lofty and serene to the full height limit of the Chicago building ordinance, until its lovely crest seems at one with the sky.

This is not all; there remain, for some, two surprises; first, that a Finlander who, in his prior experience, had not occasion to design a soaring office building, should, as one to the manner born, have grasped the intricate problem of the lofty steel-framed structure, the significance of its origins, and held the solution unwaveringly in mind, in such wise as no American architect has as yet shown the required depth of thought and steadfastness of purpose to achieve.

Philosophy has been defined by a modern philosopher as the science of substantial grounds. It is the notable absence of substantial grounds, in the ambitious works of our American architects, that so largely invalidates such works, and groups them as ephemera. But the design of the Finlander, Master of Ideas, is *based* upon substantial grounds, and therefore it lives within the domain of the enduring.

Second surprise: That a "foreigner" should possess the insight required to penetrate to the depths of the sound, strong, kindly and aspiring idealism which lies at the core of the American people: one day to make them truly great sons of Earth; and that he should possess the poet's power to interpret and to proclaim in deep sympathy and understanding, incarnate in an edifice rising from Earth in response to this faith, an inspiring symbol to endure.

Why did the men behind The Tribune throw this priceless pearl away?

Would that one might say words of similar nature, if less fervent, for the unfortunate first prize; but it is the business of this review to make a searching psychological analysis and summary of the two designs, as *types,* in order that the heavy of eye may see revealed the architectural art as a vast beneficent power, lying now in continental sleep, ready, ever ready, to be awakened by Masters of Ideas, who shall affirm its reality in eloquence of form.

Then shall we become articulate as a people; for to reveal one art is to reveal all arts, all aspirations, all hopes; and the substantial ground of it all shall arise from out our timid faith in man—a faith patient and long suffering under the superstitious tyranny of insane ideas. But once let the beckoning finger of the Free Spirit be seen in the open, and a voice heard that saith: Arise; come unto me, for I am Life—then will that timorous faith come forth inquiringly, and in the glow of the Free Spirit grow strong. The Ego of our Land shall thus find its own; for Man shall find Man. Why, therefore, deal in trivialities? Why inquire, with spectacles on nose, why this or that dewdad should be thus or so?

Confronted by the limpid eye of analysis, the first prize trembles and falls, self-confessed, crumbling to the ground. Visibly it is not architecture in the sense herein expounded. Its formula is literary: words, words, words. It is an imaginary structure—not imaginative. Starting with false premise, it was doomed to false conclusion, and it is clear enough, moreover, that the conclusion was the real premise, the mental process in reverse of appearance. The predetermination of a huge mass of imaginary masonry at the top very naturally required the appearance of huge imaginary masonry piers reaching up from the ground to give imaginary support. Such weird process of reasoning is curious. It savors of the nursery where children bet imaginary millions. Is it possible that its author in his heart of hearts, or his head of heads, really believed that bathos and power are synonyms? It looks that way. It also looks like the output of a mind untrained in the mastery of ideas, in the long discipline of realities and the test of substantial grounds. It looks also like the wandering of a mind unaccustomed to distinguish between architecture and scene painting. This design, this imaginary building, this simulacrum, is so helpless, so defenseless when brought face to face with mastery of ideas and validity of grounds, that it is cruel to go on, for analysis is now becoming vivisection, unless we recognize the palpable effect of self-hypnotism. This is not to say that the individual who made the first-prize design did not *believe* he had a great idea. Certainly he believed it, otherwise he would not have taken himself so seriously. Such seriousness prevented him from seeing the humor of it, from seeing something funny and confiding. If the monster on top with its great long legs reaching far below to the ground could be gently pried loose, the real building would reveal itself as a rather amiable and delicate affair with a certain grace of fancy. And even so, it could be but as a foundling at the doorstep of the Finn—for it seems they breed *strong* men in Finland.

So much, for the present, concerning the second and the first prize.

Our attention now shall concentrate upon The Tribune. By "The Tribune" is here meant, not alone printed white paper, but incisively the men behind its screen, who stand for ownership and control. These men made a solemn promise to the world. Why did they renege? Individually and jointly they made a triple promise—as set forth above—as members of the Jury of Award. A design setting forth the most beautiful conception of a lofty office building that has been evolved by the fertile mind of man, was presented squarely to them at the last moment. Were they frightened? Why did they welch? Did it come upon them as a ghost, an apparition—a revelation most unwelcome at a time when everything seemed nicely settled? Was this vision as trebly disconcerting as the remembered triple-promise, arising now also as a confronting ghost—the two ghosts standing side by side—likewise the two designs, in material form, standing side by side?

For no choice can exist without motive. Men are both revealed and betrayed by their acts. For men's acts show forth their inmost thoughts—no matter what their speech may be. Man can create solely in the image of this thought; for thoughts are living things—words may dissemble. In men's acts alone is the reality of their thought to be sought and found—there is no hiding place secure against the tracking searcher. In the same sense the two competing drawings are acts. Each clearly reveals the thought of its responsible author. Each sets forth in the materials of a drawing, presented as a symbol of an edifice to be, the power or the frailty of the thought within.

No manipulation of words or felicity of phrasing can screen from view the act of the Jury of Award, or the dominating will of one or more of its personnel. The final choice is most obviously an act of dominion—of brutal will. For, to cast aside, with the sop of a money prize, the surpassing work of a "foreigner" of high distinction and thorough discipline in executed works, was an act of savagery in private, regardless of how neatly, how sweetly, thereafter, the man may have been shown the door, as a parting and an honored guest, as one whose presence in the house had indeed triply honored his host.

Thus vanished from sight The Tribune's bow in the cloud.

Its act has deprived the world of a shining mark, denied it a monument to beauty, to faith, to courage and to hope. Deprived an expectant world of that Romance for which it hungers, and had hoped to receive. "It cannot be reiterated too emphatically that the primary objective of The Chicago Tribune in instituting this Competition is to secure the design for a structure distinctive and imposing—the most beautiful office building in the world."

The Architectural Record 53 (February 1923): 151–57. Reprinted with permission.

The Imperial Hotel

Eliel Saarinen was not the only architect Sullivan admired. Another was Frank Lloyd Wright, his employee from 1888 until their angry separation in 1893. Their reconciliation began with Wright's tribute to his "master" at the 1900 Architectural League of America convention; it accelerated during World War I when he helped to support Sullivan morally and materially. In the first of the two essays below, his last public papers, Sullivan diagnosed the Imperial Hotel (1913–1922) as Wright's interpretation of Japanese culture based on universal humanistic principles, discussing its particulars at great length and, for him, with unusual specificity. In the second essay he explained why Wright's spiritual and structural foresight, enabling the hotel to weather the April 1922 earthquake, revealed its architect as "a seer and a prophet, a craftsman, a masterbuilder." The Imperial was "so great that it places Frank head and shoulders above all American architects," Sullivan wrote elsewhere, "in a class with Eliel Saarinen." By comparing the Imperial Hotel to his own Auditorium Building and acknowledging his long relationship with Wright for the first time in print, Sullivan in effect designated him the heir apparent, the carrier of the architectural flame into the next generation. That Louis Sullivan should pass the torch to Frank Lloyd Wright in the last words he wrote for publication was particularly fitting and poignant.

50
Concerning the Imperial Hotel, Tokyo, Japan (1923)

On the vast stage of the world drama, two ideas, both of them immense in power, confront each other in spectacular appeal to the fears and the courage of mankind.

And it is precisely this condition that gives animus and validity to what is to follow in contemplation of the Imperial Hotel, of Tokyo, Japan, as a high act of courage—an utterance of man's free spirit, a personal message to every soul that falters, and to every heart that hopes.

It is becoming clear that a new thought is arising in the world which is destined to displace the old thought.

The new thought partakes of the nature of that freedom of which men long have dreamed. It is now breaking through the crust of the old thought which thus far in history has dominated the world of men and which embodies the idea of dominion and of submissive acquiescence.

The old idea, or fetish, is dying because it no longer satisfies the expansion of thought and feeling of which the impressive revelations of modern science are a primary factor; and especially because it is no longer at one with those instincts we call human; it does not recognize the heart as a motive power.

Yet is the old idea tenaciously fixed in the minds of a majority of those engaged in commerce, the industries, the law, the courts of justice, and especially among parasites of all kinds and degrees.

The old idea reaches from top to bottom of the social strata, and also from bottom to top. It is an age-old fixed idea, based upon a concept of self preservation, which once may have had an outward semblance of validity even though its stability of superstructure rested upon a foundation of human slavery, ignorance and suppression.

While in modern times bodily slavery as such has been done away with in theory, the old idea has persisted, curiously transformed into a slavery of the mind, which also ranges through all the social strata, even as men appear to be bodily free.

This new slavery of mind is manifest in a strange, ever-present disturbing fear, anxiety, and incertitude, which permeates society and which leads the individual to cling for safety to the old ideas, superstitions, and taboos, in order that he may conform and not appear too obvious as an individual, a target; that he may, above all, escape the fashionable epithets, "crank," "visionary," "dreamer," "freak." Hence comes about a new economic slavery causing the man, high or low, to fear for his job, and live in a nightmare so terrifying that he dare not say one word that might be construed as disturbing. Such minds in their nature are asleep to the significance of great world movements in thought.

But the idea of freedom is also old; older indeed than the slave-idea. For it is of the nature of any organism that it wishes to be free to grow and expand. This instinctive desire for freedom has been held in check and dominated by the intellectual idea of fear, resulting in unnumbered inhibitions and suppressions, which have led to an obscuration in the minds of men of the two ideas of slavery and freedom.

But the idea of freedom *also* is beginning to permeate the thoughts of men, with a new urge, *also* through all the strata of society, and is massively defining, taking form, and becoming energized, through an ever-growing knowledge and ever-increasing understanding of the true nature, the true status of man not as creature but creator; an enlarging view of man's inherent powers and a growing consciousness that his slavery has been self-imposed.

It was in this sense that I have had occasion recently to comment upon the splendid interpretation of the spirit of the American people manifest in the design submitted in the competition for the *Tribune* Building in Chicago—by a Finlander—Eliel Saarinen.

It is in this sense that we are now about to contemplate the new Imperial Hotel in Tokyo, Japan.

This great work is the masterpiece of Frank Lloyd Wright, a great free spirit, whose fame as a master of ideas is an accomplished world-wide fact.

Through prior visits he had discerned, and added to the wealth of his own rich nature, the spirit, as evidenced in forms, of the ideals of Old Japan, which still persist, in slumber, among its living people, needing but the awakening touch.

It is a high faculty of what we call genius to penetrate and temporarily to reside within the genius of another people foreign to our own local ways. And it is this quality of vision, this receptivity, this openness of mind, that especially signalizes the free spirit—the mind free from provincialism and the fear of life.

Next in order to the power of vision comes the power to interpret in thought; and, next to this, the power to express the thought, the state of feeling, in concrete terms.

In this structure is not to be found a single form distinctly Japanese; nor that of any other country; yet in its own individual form, its mass, and subsidiaries, its evolution of plan and development of thesis; in its sedulous care for niceties of administration, and for the human sense of joy, it has expressed, in inspiring form as an epic poem, addressed to the Japanese people, their inmost thought. It is characterized by the quality, *Shibui,* a Japanese word signifying the reward of earnest contemplation.

In studying the concrete expression, the embodiment of idea in solid form, the magnitude of this structure should always be borne in mind. It is 300 × 500 feet on the ground, the area thus equaling 150,000 square feet, or nearly two and one-half times the area covered by the great Auditorium Building in Chicago. The structure is three stories high in the main, with special masses equivalent in height to seven stories.

In a sense it is a huge association of structures, a gathering of the clans, so to speak; it is a seeming aggregate of buildings shielding beauteous gardens, sequestered among them. Yet there hovers over all, and as an atmosphere everywhere, a sense of primal power in singleness of purpose; a convincing quiet that bespeaks a master hand, guiding and governing.

Upon further analysis, aided by reference to the floor plans, it is disclosed that the structure is not a group, but a single mass; spontaneously subdividing into subsidiary forms in groups or single, as the main function itself flows into varied phases, each seeking expression in appropriate correlated forms, each and all bearing evidence of one controlling mind, of one hand moulding materials like a master craftsman.

It is this coming to grips with realities that infiltrates the mind of the observer, until he feels the reward of earnest contemplation in the sense that what at first he had regarded as a material structure is sending forth to him an emanation of beauty, the presence of a living thing, a wondrous contribution to the architecture of the world, an exposition of the virile thought of modern man.

So much for the ever-growing fascination of external forms, which appear as eloquent expressions of a something that must reside within them and justify them, upon logical grounds, as forms developed from functions of utility.

In considerations both of analysis and synthesis, one must regard the plan as the mainspring of the works; and this plan in turn as but the organization of the primal purposes of utility, manifold in their nature, of service to be rendered.

Now, in examining the plans at the various floor levels, one discovers that the big idea of service divides into two specialized forms: the first constituting as a complex group a hotel complete in all details for the comfort and entertainment of the traveling public, or residentials; the second, more formal and sumptuous part, is discernible as a group embodiment of the necessity for a clearing-house not only for the social obligations incurred by Japanese official life in its contacts with representatives of other lands, but also for the great social functions now inevitable in the high life of the Capital.

Consequent upon the relation of these two groups there exists a most felicitous system of interpenetrations, and communications, with a circulatory system, all worked out in a manner signifying not only mental grasp but creative imagination, based on the human being as a unit and a motive.

The dispositions throughout the entire building are so dexterously interwoven that the structure as a whole becomes a humanized fabric, in any part of which one feels the all-pervading sense of continuity, and of intimate relationships near and far. In this especial sense the structure, carrying the thought, is unique among hotel buildings throughout the world. Japan is to be felicitated that its superior judgment in the selection of an architect of masterly qualifications, of such nature as to welcome new problems of time and place, has been justified. The longer the contemplation of this work is continued, the more intense becomes the conviction that this Master of Ideas has not only performed a service of distinction, but, far and above this, has presented to the people of Japan, as a free-will offering, a great gift which shall endure for all generations to come as a world exemplar, most beautiful and inspiring, of which Japan may well be proud among the nations as treasuring it in sole possession.

In further study of the plans, in their aspect of economics, one should carefully note the differences of levels, shown thereon but more clearly set forth in the longitudinal section. These differences of level are, in one aspect, a part of the charm of the work considered from the human point of view, and, technically, as a skillful method of deployment. They favor also the interpenetrations and the easy accessibility of the larger units and, thus, the compactness of arrangement and economy of space. A notable feature in this regard is the location of a single great kitchen, centrally placed in such wise as to serve the cabaret directly, the main restaurant directly, the private dining rooms by stairways and capacious electric service elevators, and likewise the banquet hall and ballroom above.

Beneath the banquet hall is a theatre seating 1,000, and at the level of the main floor of the theatre the entire structure is traversed and in a manner bisected by a grand promenade twenty feet in width and 300 feet in length. This promenade brings the two long wings of guest rooms in touch with the central group and acts as a foyer from which are entered the theatre, four groups of private dining rooms, and opposite the theatre a large parlor, the projecting balcony of which overlooks the restaurant. The floor of the promenade is sixteen feet above sidewalk level. Beneath the promenade at the north end is situated the formal social entrance with attendant service rooms and hallway leading to passenger elevators. Spaciously around the intersection point of the axis of the promenade with the central axis of the grand-plan are grouped stairways, passenger elevators, service elevators, service stairs, and other utilities. Within this group the service element is logically vertical. Elsewhere the circulation is mainly in the horizontal sense, as there are but three tiers of guest rooms.

The two great wings, each 500 feet in length, contain the guest rooms, 285 in number, to be hereinafter described. These two huge parallel masses act as guardians of the inner courts, the gardens, and the more open structural effects, protecting them against the heavy prevailing winds and insuring a large measure of quiet, a sense of retirement and relief from a busy and noisy world without.

There remains to be considered an introductory group, placed within the open space bounded by the main guest wings and the formal social group, and lying symmetrically along the main axis of the grand-plan. It is connected to the wings by means of open bridges over terraces, leading to elevators and stairways. This group constitutes the welcoming feature of a grandiose and most hospitable plan—a plan based upon a rare sense of human nature, everywhere discernible throughout the structure.

At the western, or initial, beginning of the grand-plan, the parallel wings throw out minor wings of an enfolding character. Between these two wings lies a large formal pool, on each side of which are the driveways for automobiles. For jinrikishas separate entrances and runs are provided through the main wings. The entrance feature of the central group stands well back from the pool. One ascends a few steps and enters a spacious vestibule, from which lead up and down special stairways. A broad flight carries one to the main lobby from which one may enter the lounges, and side wings, or directly ahead, the main restaurant. At higher levels the group contains tea rooms, library, roof garden; and below, the executive offices, the bazaar, and the swimming pool. Beautiful form combinations and vistas make the interior treatment highly interesting and inviting. The level of the restaurant floor is seven feet above the sidewalk grade and nine feet below the grand promenade. The latter is reached from it by means of stairways, upper-level terraces or by elevators.

It cannot too often be reiterated that the terrace idea is the key to the development of the plan in its entirety and that this idea, seized upon by the constructive creative imagination, and carried into logical and beautiful extension, reveals the secret of the serenity and joy of this edifice. Nowhere is the sense of size oppressive, for the eye finds interest everywhere. Thus the structure may truly be called epic, as one views its large simplicity of utterance and richness of well ordered detail. Peculiarly entrancing in this latter regard is the treatment of the lava within and without the structure. Everywhere its surface is wrought in in tricate pattern. Constantly varying in expression in accord with location, and so beautifully conceived and cut as to appear *of* it, integral with it, not applied. The effect is of a continuous, velvety shimmer of lava surface.

Among functional details are to be noted the system of external night-lighting, organically incorporated in large perforated units within the masonry at carefully considered strategic points; the terraced bridges which seem to float; the sumptuous treatment of the entrance to the social group; the recognition of the terminals of elevator shafts and of dumbwaiters. These latter utilitarian things are not hidden or denied, they are *affirmed,* as they should be, and add to the fullness and fidelity of expression. Indeed, it seems to be but little understood that fidelity to the finer truths inhering in material things is of the essence of romance. And this is a romantic edifice, heroic, dramatic and lyric in expression of function and of form.

A notable selection of local materials has been adopted for the external effects: hand-made brick and hewn lava are chiefly used with a most interesting interspersion of copper for the cornices and delicately worked copper roofs. All flat roofs are of concrete and are treated as gardens.

The color effect is quiet, yet piquant. The bricks are buff, the lava greenish yellow with deep brown spots, the copper turquoise. Minor color effects are secured in various materials, while to all of these effects appertains the added charm of gardens, and distributed shrubs and flowers—all of which are daily cared for; and potted and vased effects are renewed as occasion requires and the changing seasons suggest.

The general construction of the building is definitely based upon the reinforced-concrete-slab idea, carried out by the architect theoretically and practically to its limits, in a manner so novel, so logical, so convincing, as to be of the highest technical interest to those familiar with the general slab idea. The specific application here has to do directly with a flexible resistance to earthquakes, developing shocks, undulations, oscillations, and twists, in action.

The entire structure rests upon a layer of spongy soil, beneath which is found mud of undetermined depth. Short concrete piles are inserted in the upper layer, where required and as numerous as required, capped by reinforced concrete slabs which receive their direct loads at calculated points. The entire structure thus rests upon a flexible foundation which is free to yield to the mutations of earthquake disturbance and come back to place again.

By a system of distribution of steel rods everywhere the masonry superstructure is knitted thoroughly together in such wise as to render it yielding but resilient, hence secure against fracture or distortion. The slabs are as tenaciously yet flexibly adjusted to the vertical supports, and, where occasion requires, the slab system merges from the concept of lintel into that of cantilever. There is here so general a use of this latter method, on account of its adaptability to projecting horizontal slabs otherwise unsupported and the resulting ease of creating unobstructed areas, that it may perhaps be described as in essence a reinforced-cantilever-slab-system.

In the construction of all outer walls wooden forms were dispensed with; the outer layer of specially notched bricks, and the inside layer of hollow bricks, serving as such. In the cavity between, rods, vertical and horizontal, were placed, and then the concrete filler, the wall thus becoming a solid mass of varied materials, into which the floor slabs are so solidly tied as to take on the character of cantilevers, as conditions of disturbance might demand.

Thus we have a structure almost literally *hand made*—the use of machinery having proved relatively inefficient—a structure so solidly built of materials inseparably united as to possess all the virtues of a monolith, and yet so completely threaded through with steel fibres as to add the virtues of elasticity and resilience.

The policy of administration of actual construction work was based upon the traditional habits of the Japanese skilled laborer and craftsman. These active and tireless little men are so deft and nimble that results were most thorough, even though at first they required instruction in the use of materials with which they were not familiar.

This structure, designed theoretically and worked out practically to withstand distortion or fracture by earthquake, was put to the test while nearing completion in April, 1922, in broad daylight, during the heaviest temblor in point of severity Japan has known in fifty years. Wide destruction was wrought in the city of Tokyo. The shock was terrific. The Imperial was violently jolted. It visibly trembled, swayed and rocked in the upheaval, and at its ending quietly steadied to position, free of distortion, rents or damage of any kind.

So much for a system of construction altogether novel in conception and execution, carried out by a strong, persistent mind, as imaginative in its insight into fundamental principles of engineering as in its profound insight into the romance of breathing life and beauty, humanity and spirit, into forms and materials otherwise helplessly inert.

It is thus that the master mind works, to bring forth, out of the fabric of a dream, a fabric of enduring reality.

As to the interior, a noteworthy feature is the use of lava and brick in the grand promenade, the theatre, the restaurant and the banquet hall. It was a happy thought to penetrate the interior with materials of the exterior, thus giving a sense of enduring construction.

The equipment is thorough and complete; electric heating, light and motive power, the usual telephone service, and a system of mechanical ventilation constantly in use and so arranged as to deliver cooler air in summer.

All furniture, rugs and hangings of the public rooms are of special design, simple, strong and rich, partaking of the character and specifically related to the forms of the structure in a fine play of polychrome.

The guest room arrangement of the wings has been worked out to conserve space, concentrate conveniences and preserve a quiet effect. The rooms are not large, but are arranged and furnished to become sitting rooms; the beds are in evidence more as couches than as beds. The typical small room is 15 by 18, with a 6 by 10 bathroom deducted. The typical large room is 15 by 22, bathroom similarly deducted. Average ceiling height 9 feet 4 inches. The electric heating and indirect lighting are combined in a standard attached to twin tables in the center of each room. These tables have a small writing table and a small tea table beneath them which may be removed to any part of the room, and, when not in use, may be returned to their places as part of the central group. The electric heat is thus at the center of the room. The wardrobe is a built-in feature of each bedroom, and is designed to accommodate a steamer trunk, a wardrobe trunk and two suit cases. It has ample hanging space for clothes, and the drawers of the old-fashioned dresser have been worked into this feature. There is storage space above it for purchases. A feature of this wardrobe is a guest-box accessible from the corridor or the bedroom at the will of the guest. This guest-box also contains the telephone. A full length mirror is placed against the side wall, and a small dressing table placed beside it. The central group of tables and this dressing table, together with an overstuffed easy chair or two, a light, wooden chair or two, and a hassock, are all the furniture of the room, except the couch-beds. It will be seen in this arrangement that great simplicity has been arrived at. An individual color scheme characterizes each room. A specially designed rug to correspond is upon the floor. The furniture covering, bed covers and window hangings are of the same stuff and color, and correspond in each case with the color note of the room. The color scheme ranges through the whole gamut of color from quiet grays to bright rose and old blue or gold. The effect of the whole is quiet and complete. Everywhere there is ample light. Privacy is insured by the omission of the transom and the device of the guest-box. Cross-ventilation is secured in every room and bathroom by means of forced draught acting through ducts and a series of square ventilators set in the corridor partition above the picture rail. These are easily adjusted for summer or winter use. The corridor ceilings are all dropped beneath the concrete slabs to make continuous ducts, to which are connected the vertical vent shafts between every pair of rooms. These vertical shafts extend from basement to attic space and contain pipes and wiring, which are accessible and free of the construction everywhere.

The bathroom is an adjunct of the bedroom; in every case treated as a part of it. It is lined with ivory colored mosaic tiles, all external and internal corners curved. The bathtub is a sunken pool in the floor of the room, formed, with curved corners, of the same mosaic tile as the floor and walls. The room has a vaulted ceiling, and screened windows in the outer wall. The whole is drained and impervious to water in every part. The floor is electrically heated from below

The main corridors of the guest wings are six feet wide, exposing the brick-faced concrete piers that support the floor, giving to the whole the effect of a cloistered promenade. The corridors are artificially lighted through perforated metal screens set into the ceiling. The corridor floors are cork-tiled. The threshold has everywhere been eliminated. Where plaster has been used the walls are treated with ground pearl shell splashed on to a heavy coat of paint in the Japanese manner. All the windows in the building are screened, shaded and curtained. The wood, where used in the trimming, is throughout of Hokkaido oak, waxed. Outside each large room is a tiled balcony or terrace reached by low windows opening upon it. Baggage rooms, in each wing, for the storage of guests' luggage, easily accessible at any time, are located next to the elevators on the general level.

Thus an attempt has been made by this writer to set forth as clearly as may be the nature of a great work of architectural art founded in this particular case upon the utilities associated with human needs, in its aspects of hotel life and administration; or, in another sense, the forms that have been caused by a luminous thought to arise in sublimated expression of these needs in visible forms of beauty.

The true meaning of the word PRACTICAL is completely elucidated in this structure. For "practical" signifies explicit and implicit human needs. Such needs run a wide gamut of desire, ranging from the immediately physical and material, gradually upward in series through the desires of emotional, intellectual and spiritual satisfactions.

Thus we can understand how important is the play of imagination; for imagination is distinct from intellect. It lies deeper in life, and uses intellect as a critical executive instrument wherewith to carry its visions of reality into reality itself, while determining its quality of procedure, at every stage. Otherwise intellect would dominate imagination, and pervert its ends.

Thus what we call art and what we call science are indissoluble within a masterful imagination. But imagination must be free to act in true accord with need and with desire as fundamental human traits; and intellect must be disciplined by the will to act in accord with imagination's fine desires. But for this initiative, and to this end, man's spirit must be free: unimpeded by irrelevant inhibitions. The vision of the free spirit ever seeks to clarify, to amplify what we call the commonplace. It sees within the so-called commonplace the elements of sublimity. Thus the architect who combines in his being the powers of vision, of imagination, of intellect, of sympathy with human need and the power to interpret them in a language vernacular and true—is he who shall create poems in stone, consonant with the finer clearing thought of our day, and the days of our expectancy.

In this regard the Imperial Hotel stands unique as the high water mark thus far attained by any modern architect. Superbly beautiful it stands—a noble prophecy.

The Architectural Record 53 (April 1923): 332–52. Reprinted with permission.

51
Reflections on the Tokyo Disaster (1924)

In the course of my article in the February, 1923, RECORD concerning the Chicago "Tribune" Competition and its baseness, I took occasion to utilize the saying of a philosopher that men are self-divided into two classes: *Masters of ideas and those dominated by ideas.* And my comment on the Imperial Hotel in Tokyo, in the April, 1923, RECORD I prefaced by saying: "On the vast stage of the world drama, two ideas, both of them immense in power, confront each other in spectacular appeal to the fears and the courage of mankind."

The casual reader, as a rule, is not accustomed to those generalizations which go under the—to him—somewhat repellent name of philosophy, and in so far as philosophy has dealt and deals solely with abstractions and nonentities, he is right in his disdain—which I share. Such philosophies as have gone by the names Platonic, Neo-Platonic, and German Transcendentalism, have done their huge share to fill the world with sorrow, for they and their kind are the intellectual basis of tyranny. And this same casual reader is as casually apt to be unaware that day by day he lives under the tyranny of abstract dehumanized ideas; that he is under the dominion of ideas he had no share in making, ideas so diaphanous and all-pervading that they are as the air he breathes. His disdain of philosophy therefore is but disdain of a *word*. Of the saturnine content of that word he is as unsuspecting as a kitten. If he is a university man, an aspirant in philosophy, he has been taught to revere that word and its content; and in innocence he reveres them both—and so another kitten, not in the least comprehending the utter heartlessness of it all; not in the least perceiving in the world about him the corruption and dislocation that have followed in its train.

To be sure there are readers and readers. One reads industriously, and learns nothing—he is credulous. Another reads industriously and learns nothing—he is cynical. Another reads even more industriously and widely and learns nothing—he is pessimistic. But of all three, and their varieties, the credulous one is in the most pitiful plight. He may read the philosophies of abstraction and find them ennobling, he may believe himself to be lifted up and to have entered the highest attainable domain of pure thought—the realm of the ideal, the perfect, the absolute, in which the intellect reigns supreme—regarding itself in its own supernatural mirror, its gaze fatefully turned away from man and from his world. And of such belief in the unreal is the basis for all credulity—especially in evidence in the wool-gathering highbrow. Yet there is another class of reader—he who regards not authority, eminence, nor prestige, as finalities, but who seeks that which nourishes and enlarges his comprehension of life, and who, therefore, as by instinct of self-preservation, rejects that which sterilizes life—that is to say the abstract. To him therefore Life becomes an ever broadening, deepening, subliminating and impressive flow, within which, he finds himself moving—his own life unfolding, and with the passing years thus arises, within, a deep religious and moral sympathy with the vast spectacle of immediate life, enfolding mankind, which he envisages as participant and spectator. In sympathy there arises within a new pity allied to a new faith in man.

With spontaneous gesture the newly-arising philosophy, with the voice of which I speak, sweeps aside the spooks and phantasms which have tyrannized the credulous and made slaves of high and low, even in our own day of so-called enlightenment, and with mind thus cleared for action and merging with the flow of life, seeks therein a comprehension of mankind, in order to arrive at an outline of conservation, which, in its directness of purpose, may supersede the abominable wastage of humanity due to the prevailing confusion of ideas.

In one aspect the eye views an incredibly frantic industry, with no objective but to *sell*, and in another aspect—an inexorable reaction of the first—a steady decline in thought beyond the immediate frenzy, a terrifying inability to foresee the consequences of a thought or an act; or worse, a wanton and brutal disregard.

And while it is a fact that the thoughts here above set down arise immediately out of contemplation of the helplessness, the shabbiness, the ruthless debauchery of commercialized American architecture—which means death—the same thought reaches out over the world and crossing the wide waters arrives at Japan with its city of Tokyo, in which has been staged, as but yesterday, a startling tragedy of ideas, wherein the abstract has crumbled in universal ruin, while one *living* thought and living thing survives. This is what is involved in the significance of the statement that on the vast stage of the world-drama two ideas, both of them immense in power, confront each other in spectacular appeal to the fears and the courage of mankind.

The emergence, unharmed, of the Imperial Hotel, from the heartrending horrors of the Tokyo disaster, takes on, at once, momentous importance in the world of modern thought, as a triumph of the living and the real over the credulous, the fantastic, and the insane.

It emerges moreover before our gaze as an imposing upreared monument to the power of common sense; to that consummate common sense which perceives, comprehends, and grasps the so-called commonplace, the real, as distinct from the abstract; to that common sense which founds its logic upon the power inhering in nature's processes, when interpreted in terms of action, as affecting results; soundly scientific in foreseeing results; and which towards this end employs an accurate imagination. For it requires unusual imagination to see stone as stone, brick as brick, wood as wood, steel as steel, the earth as the earth and human beings as human beings.

We may call this power Inspiration if we please, and if we think the word sounds pleasanter than Philosophy. But it is well to bear in mind that Inspiration is philosophy in its highest estate, and that true philosophy is systemized common sense in its finest human reach.

In planning the erection of a structure in a terrain habitually given to earthquake it would seem to be natural to regard earthquake—otherwise seismic disturbance—as a fundamental. For earthquakes are not imaginary or abstract or illusory; they are real—and at times calamitous. It would seem, therefore, to be but the part of common sense *not to invite destruction*. Yet such is the pervading American credulity, such its inability to think straight; such its impulsive acceptance of "go-gettism" and "pep" and "progress" and "enterprise" as substitutes for reflection and sound thought, and social responsibility, that it succeeded by sales-methods in imposing upon the Japanese, structures so childish, so absurd, so uncomprehending, as verily to invite destruction. When came the fateful hour they danced their dance of death. To be sure the Japanese themselves were credulous enough to take the bait of boosted land values, and multiplied areas; and in their cupidity were induced to hold the bag. When the time came they found the bag filled not with purring kittens, but with terrifying wildcats.

Prior to the American invasion, there had been an English invasion; and prior to the English, a German invasion, both invasions carrying with them the sophisticated credulity of European culture. Both of these alien cultures erected solid masonry buildings upon earthquake land. When the time came, these structures groaned, and buried their dead.

Now, further, Japanese society being heaviest at the top, it would seem but in keeping that its indigenous structures, designed in the native idiom, built on narrow and tortuous lanes, should also be topheavy. When the time came the flying heavy roof tiles did their share in the general slaughter, and as well the flimsy bridges and the flimsiness in general. Thus ruined Tokyo became the prey of conflagration. Thus death arose out of the temblor and spread forth its arms over Tokyo doomed by a false premise.

It may seem quite easy to draw conclusions after the fact. If you really think so, try your hand on the European war. Or, make a diagnosis of contemporary American architecture. Or attempt an analysis of the American mind, tracing its activities back to their common source. These are, all of them, matters after the fact.

We are now to deal with the reverse aspect of the problem. That is to say, with the primary assumption of earthquake and disaster, and how to forefend. Some five years prior to the now historic temblor a young man of fifty was called to Tokyo to consult as architect regarding the planning and construction of a great hotel to be called the "Imperial." This man, a poet, who had reduced thinking to simples, began his solution with the fixed fact of earthquakes as a basis and made an emotional study of their nature and movements. The second move was the resolve never to relax his grip on the basic fact of earthquake as a menace, and to devise a system of construction such as should absorb and dispose of the powerful shocks, waves and violent tremors, and yet maintain its integrity as a fabricated structure. It may be remarked in passing, that the quality and power of emotion dramatizes the power of thought; that the poet is he whose thought, thus enriched, imparts telling power to the simple and the obvious, bringing them into the field of vivid consciousness.

It is precisely this power of the poet to bring earthquake vividly into consciousness and hold it there, that distinguishes him, in this instance, from the uninspired engineer. The latter is an extremely useful person, wherever and whenever his formulas, his slide-rule, his tables and his precedents—to which he is a slave—apply. Within the limits of routine he may successfully vary his processes in application; and there his social value ends. The same, in substance, may be said of the uninspired practicing architect, except that the latter, in addition, is invertebrate. Wherever he thinks with reasonable clearness, he approaches the engineer; but he is not a Yea-Sayer—he prefers to trim. Yet the great creative engineer—and there have been such—by virtue of clear eyesight, material realization, and the power to dream, is again the poet if he fail not in the human sense of beauty, even though he may not think so, and out of prudence may not say so. Yet he is essentially of the Yea-Sayers—and the Yea-Sayers are the great modern poets.

For many years I have contemplated man in his folly, and in his marvelous powers. But I never expected to live to read about a man who had attained to the dainty quintessence of asininity, by driving huge timber piles through sixty feet of Tokyo mud, to reach the solid underlying hard pan, and to set upon this system of piling, tightly bound to it, a high, extra-rigid, steel frame to serve as the supporting skeleton of a habitable building. Or was it not asininity at all but merely betting on a long chance? In any event the long chance became suddenly a short one. *The invitation to disaster* was instantaneously accepted. And if the asininity was real, it merged into the degenerate in its disregard of the human being. It was an even bet that the quake might obligingly come at night while the tall buildings were empty and asleep. Their shattered remains now tell a weird story, many chapters long, for the quake came at noon.

The architect of the Imperial Hotel, whose name by the way is Frank Lloyd Wright, a fact I should in all honor have mentioned earlier, had I not been so engrossed in an attempt to clothe in words the basic idea of my thesis—the most dangerous and destructive of all ideas—the idea of Credulity; this architect I say, whom I have known since his eighteenth year, and the workings of whose fine mind I believe I fairly follow, is possessed of a rare sense of the human, and an equally rare sense of Mother Earth, coupled with an apprehension of the material, so delicate as to border on the mystic, and yet remain coordinate with those facts we call real life. Such mind, sufficiently enriched by inner experiences as to become mellow in power, and reinforced by a strong tenacious will, is precisely the primary type of mind that resolves a problem into its simples, and out of these simples projects in thought a masterful solution, and in the process of transmuting thought into actual material fact, displays a virtuosity in the manipulation of the simples of technique.

I admit it is difficult for a mind academically trained and hence in large measure deprived of its freedom and its natural susceptibility, to grasp an idea so foreign to its heritage of tradition as is, necessarily so, the idea of *simples*. I go further and assert that such idea may be repugnant to such minds—may even alarm such minds—it is too disturbing in its ominous suggestion that thoughts may be living things—Now!—Here! The intrusion of Life upon such minds may indeed be disheartening. And the same statements may apply with equal force to the mind technically trained exclusively—the world of life shut out; and as well to the business mind, with its airy system of phantasies, its curious rules of the game, its pontifical utterances of the higher wisdom of mendacity, and its one, solid, credulous faith in the abstract notion, deeply cherished, that human life is and must ever be a battle, a struggle for existence, and thus believing render itself "the unfit" to analyze its own symptoms which predicate periodical collapse of the structure it has reared upon the soil of an earthquake thought. And yet, in contrast, the open mind which may have won its freedom through valor, going forth into the world of men and thoughts and things, discerns basic simples everywhere and in all things. To such mind the confusion of the world is no mystery.

It is no part of my business here, nor of my intent, to go into the technical refinements, the subtleties of reaction, and the plastic sense of balance and free movement that enter into the structural theory and actuality of the Imperial Hotel. Mr. Wright may do this if he so sees fit. The vast, sumptuous building, in all its aspects: structural, utilitarian, and aesthetic, was the embodiment, and is now the revelation, of a single thought tenaciously held by a seer and a prophet, a craftsman, a masterbuilder.

This most significant architectural monument that the modern world can show, stands today uninjured because it was thought-built, so to stand. It was not and is not an imposition upon the Japanese, but a free will contribution to the finest elements of their culture. The fame of the building and its author is now world-wide; and we will let it go at that.

Meanwhile, I declare as my real business and my true intent herein, to be that of one of enquiring mind who seeks in this disaster the realities behind its terrifying mask.

The Architectural Record 55 (February 1924): 113–17. Reprinted with permission.

BIBLIOGRAPHY

BIOGRAPHIES

Willard Connely. *Louis Sullivan: The Shaping of American Architecture.* New York: Horizon Press, 1960.

Mervyn D. Kaufman. *Father of Skyscrapers: A Biography of Louis Sullivan.* Boston: Little, Brown, 1969.

Hugh Morrison. *Louis Sullivan: Prophet of Modern Architecture.* New York: W. W. Norton & Co., 1936.

Robert Twombly. *Louis Sullivan: His Life and Work.* New York: The Viking Press, 1986.

Frank Lloyd Wright. *Genius and the Mobocracy.* New York: Duell, Sloan, and Pearce, 1949.

INTERPRETATIONS

David S. Andrew. *Louis Sullivan and the Polemics of Modern Architecture: The Present Against the Past.* Urbana: University of Illinois Press, 1985.

Hugh Dalziel Duncan. *Culture and Democracy: The Struggle for Form in Society and Architecture in Chicago and the Middle West During the Life and Times of Louis H. Sullivan.* Totowa, NJ: Bedminster Press, 1965.

Narciso G. Menocal. *Architecture as Nature: The Transcendentalist Idea of Louis Sullivan.* Madison: University of Wisconsin Press, 1981.

Sherman Paul. *Louis Sullivan: An Architect in American Thought.* Englewood Cliffs, NJ: Prentice-Hall, 1962.

ORNAMENT

Office of Cultural Arts and University Museums. *Louis H. Sullivan: Architectural Ornament Collection, Southern Illlinois University at Edwardsville.* Edwardsville: Southern Illinois University, 1981.

Paul E. Sprague, ed. *The Drawings of Louis Henry Sullivan: A Catalogue of the Frank Lloyd Wright Collection at the Avery Architectural Library.* Princeton, NJ: Princeton University Press, 1979.
Wim de Witt, ed. *Louis Sullivan: The Function of Ornament.* New York: W. W. Norton & Co., 1986.

INDIVIDUAL BUILDINGS

Larry Millett. *The Curve of the Arch: The Story of Louis Sullivan's Owatonna Bank.* St. Paul: Minnesota Historical Society Press, 1985.
Daniel H. Perlman. *The Auditorium Building: Its History and Architectural Significance.* Chicago: Roosevelt University, 1976.
John D. Randall. *The Art of Office Building: Sullivan's Wainwright and the St. Louis Real Estate Boom.* Springfield, IL: John D. Randall, 1972.
John Vinci. *The Art Institute of Chicago: The Stock Exchange Trading Room.* Chicago: The Art Institute, 1977.

IN ADDITION

Albert Bush-Brown. *Louis Sullivan.* Masters of World Architecture Series. New York: George Braziller, 1960.
Leonard K. Eaton. *American Architecture Comes of Age: European Reaction to H. H. Richardson and Louis Sullivan.* Cambridge: The MIT Press, 1972.
John Szarkowski. *The Idea of Louis Sullivan.* Minneapolis: University of Minnesota Press, 1956.

INDEX